T0248351

Debunking the
Yule Log Myth

Debunking the Yule Log Myth

The Disturbing History of a Plantation Legend

Robert E. May

ROWMAN & LITTLEFIELD
Lanham • Boulder • New York • London

Published by Rowman & Littlefield
An imprint of The Rowman & Littlefield Publishing Group, Inc.
4501 Forbes Boulevard, Suite 200, Lanham, Maryland 20706
www.rowman.com

86-90 Paul Street, London EC2A 4NE

Distributed by NATIONAL BOOK NETWORK

British Library Cataloguing in Publication Information Available

Library of Congress Cataloging-in-Publication Data Available

ISBN: 979-8-8818-0178-6 (cloth: alk. paper)
ISBN: 979-8-8818-0179-3 (ebook)

♾™ The paper used in this publication meets the minimum requirements of American National Standard for Information Sciences—Permanence of Paper for Printed Library Materials, ANSI/NISO Z39.48-1992

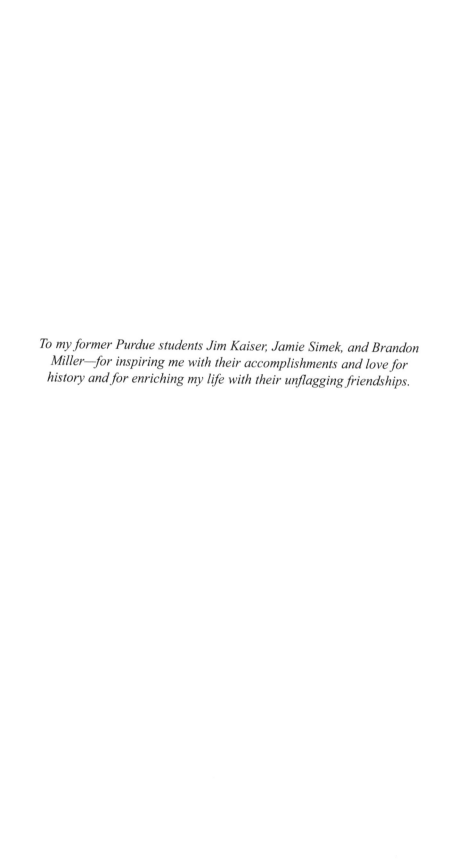

To my former Purdue students Jim Kaiser, Jamie Simek, and Brandon Miller—for inspiring me with their accomplishments and love for history and for enriching my life with their unflagging friendships.

Contents

List of Illustrations

Introduction

The Biggest Sweet Gum We Could Find

During Christmas, enslaved people in the American South took a week or more of vacation time depending on how long a grossly oversized "Yule log" burned at the back of their master's fireplace. Or so a widely believed bit of American folklore claims. So long as this log lasted, slaves escaped heavy labor and their master's whip and enjoyed the freedom to go and do what they wished as well as party and gorge themselves on food and booze that they rarely enjoyed at other times. Everything hinged on that one log. As legend has it, enslaved people even believed that immunity from misfortune for the coming year might be theirs if they just handled that log with the proper respect.

But the legend goes further. Since enslaved workers bore responsibility for selecting this log and lugging it from the outdoors to their master's mansion, they schemed to extend its burning. They measured the fireplace to guarantee their cut log precisely correlated with the maximum length to fit. They searched high and low for perfect Yule log timber, spurning fast-burning softwoods for the slowest-burning, knottiest, hardwood trunk they could find—often a sweet gum, sycamore, or hickory. Should their best option be an already-fallen tree, they picked the greenest downed hardwood at hand. Then they skillfully sawed it to minimize chips flying off the bark and reducing its girth. Most importantly, they presoaked their log in a nearby swamp, pond, stream, lake, or river before they hauled it, now saturated, into the master's "big house" on Christmas Eve for its lighting. Generally, it got them *days* of extra vacation.

This custom began intriguing me some years ago when I first started investigating the Christmas experiences of enslaved people in the South before the Civil War and found descriptions of it in two of the most important books ever written, respectively, about slavery in the South and the history of Christmas in America—Eugene D. Genovese's *Roll, Jordan, Roll: The World the Slaves Made* (which won Columbia University's prestigious Bancroft Prize for history) and Stephen Nissenbaum's *The Battle for Christmas* (a Pulitzer Prize finalist selection). Genovese explains that sometimes "the length of the holiday depended on the burning of a log, with the slaves scurrying about to find the largest and slowest-burning candidate." Nissenbaum explains which southern subregions followed Yule log customs, how long enslaved workers submerged Yule logs in water, where in the master's dwelling the log burned, and what determined when a Yule log was done burning. This is the way he puts it:

> There was at least one ritual, practiced in the "low country" of Maryland, Virginia, and North Carolina, that allowed slaves to exert at least symbolic control over the length of the holidays: They were to last as long as the "Yule log" continued to burn in one piece. Slaves would choose the largest possible tree, chop it down a year in advance, soak it in water for the entire year, and light it early on Christmas Day in the hall of the Big House, where it would be the "back-log." The holidays would be over when the Yule log finally burned into two pieces—a process that could take a full week.[1]

By the time my book about slavery and Christmas appeared in 2019 (*Yuletide in Dixie: Slavery, Christmas, and Southern Memory*), I had also read a scattering of much older accounts of the role Yule logs played in slaves' lives, including the reminiscences of two elderly ex-slaves recalling their early lives in bondage. When questioned in the late 1930s by the Federal Writers' Project of the New Deal's Works Progress Administration, these once enslaved interviewees emphasized the importance of Yule logs in their Christmas holidays while they were enslaved as children.

When an interviewer in Texas caught up with Jenny Proctor, an ailing, white-headed woman who had been born into enslavement in Alabama back in 1850, to document her remembrances of her youth in bondage, she told him that she could not recall any "good times" prior to gaining her freedom. Still, she conceded that her owner provided his enslaved laborers with a Christmas work break so long as a back-log burned on his fireplace, though she qualified her point by adding that the only thing special about the holiday besides getting relief from labor was that her master killed a hog beforehand and gave each laborer a piece, which was "sumpin'" (because enslaved laborers in the Old South rarely received meat rations as part of their daily diets). With some specificity, Proctor indicated which trees made for good Yule logs and touched on how long they burned. Noting that her fellow slaves spent the entire year hunting for the "biggest sweet gum we could find" to down, she added that when they came up empty-handed, they pragmatically chose their next best alternative—a faster-burning oak, which allowed for a three-day work break. Whichever they chose, however, her master resented his own concession because it cut into his profits by letting laborers off work. So, he sabotaged his slaves' preparations by adding fast-burning kindling to the fire: he would "sho' pile on dem pine knots, gittin' dat Christmas over so we could git back to work," she mused.[2]

Like Jenny Proctor, Tom Wilson, who carried out odd jobs like dish washing while growing up on a small Mississippi cotton place while his parents labored in the fields, recalled for his interviewer the abuses African Americans endured under the antebellum enslavers' regime. As a youth, he had seen his mother and fellow Black laborers "git whuppins" from the leather strap of his master. Wilson also recalled that at night his mistress liked sitting on the porch of their seven- or eight-room "Big House" and making the "li'l culled chillun dance an' sing" for her own amusement. Still, when Christmas came, things changed for the better. The holiday ushered in a "mighty glad time," when slaves got extra food to eat and time to "kick our heels." Echoing Jenny Proctor, he specified that the slaves' vacation was circumscribed by how long a sweet gum log took to burn. His master would select "one er [of] de cullud mens" to choose the log, and enslaved people on his place would afterward presoak it in a stream so that it would burn for an entire week.[3]

After *Yuletide in Dixie* came out, I couldn't resist the temptation to discover the full story of this quaint custom because all the accounts I had seen of Old South Christmas log traditions merely amounted to a few sentences or a paragraph or two. And one of the first things I learned was that Genovese and Nissenbaum had not been the only historians to write about Yule logs on southern plantations. Others had done likewise, sometimes identifying the custom with southern states, counties, and cities in the pre–Civil War South that did not match with the Maryland-Virginia-North Carolina geography that Nissenbaum laid out. James Benson Sellers's history of slavery in Alabama, to give one example, reported that Christmas there before the Civil War "lasted as long as the Yule log on many plantations." The most authoritative encyclopedic work on southern culture, the massive twenty-four-volume *New Encyclopedia of Southern Culture* edited by Charles Reagan Wilson, similarly expands the geography of southern Yule logs, stating they mandated the beginning and end of Christmas for virtually *every* enslaved person who toiled on a southern plantation before the Civil War. "The slaves' holiday lasted," explained contributor Allen Cabaniss in his Christmas entry, "until the Yule log burned, which sometimes took over a week."[4]

I also soon recognized that well before serious historians discovered Yule logs, the tales were already insinuated within America's popular culture, sometimes surfacing in ways and places that I never anticipated. In 1919, for example, in a full-page advertisement in an obscure lumber industry

Figure 0.1. Jenny Proctor.

Source: WPA Slave Narrative Project, Texas, container A931, vol. 16, pt. 3. Courtesy of Manuscript Division, Library of Congress.

magazine published in Chicago, a Memphis company asserted that it had been a custom in "the old slave days in Virginia and southward" for plantation slaves to be relieved of work over Christmas. As a result, they carefully selected black gum logs for their "slow burning properties" before rolling those back-logs to "spacious" fireplaces in mansion houses. When the log then smoldered for up to a week, enslaved people celebrated their liberation from labor with music and dancing.[5]

Heading into the football season of fall 1930, a North Carolina newspaper cautioned readers not to expect too much from Duke University's team since with its disproportionate numbers of inexperienced sophomores the "Blue Devil backfield will be as green as a well soaked yule log." The next year, a flower magazine published in New York reported that before the Civil War many plantations dismissed enslaved field workers from holiday labor "as long as the Yule log burned" and that the "Negroes" resultingly selected the "slowest burning" large log they could find and submerged it prior to the time when it was required "to be taken into the house." There it "smouldered for while the Negroes delighted in their 'prolonged holiday.'"[6]

The story's tenacity got an important boost when it was taken up by the prolific mid-twentieth-century popular writer Harnett T. Kane (1910–1984). This New Orleanian gave Yule logs considerable play in his *Southern Christmas Book*, first published in 1958 and then reissued in 1997. Ever colorful and stylistically accessible, Kane explains how southern slaveholders before the Civil War customarily sent slaves out to "cut down the finest and most stalwart tree in the woods." Intriguingly, Kane reports an implicit collusion between enslavers and their workers about what happened once the tree fell and found its way to the master's fireplace:

> As long as the Yule log glowed, servants were freed from work. Even if the wood burned for eight or nine days, the master usually kept his promise. In time the attendants developed a clever scheme for prolonging the delightful period . . . they soaked the log, so that it would last day after day. Master and household knew of the stratagem, and secretly chuckled over it, as did the servants themselves. When he came upon a tree trunk that had lain for a long time in the swamp edge a man might grin: "This one's got as much water as a Christmas log."[7]

Kane's account influenced other holiday publications and cookbooks to describe southern Yule log traditions—books like Hallmark Cards's *Complete Book of American Holidays* (1972), Mary Gunderson's *Southern Plantation Cooking* (2000), and Tanya Gulevich's *Encyclopedia of Christmas and New Year's Celebrations* (2003).[8] But these are just some of the holiday books and cookbooks that have recycled tales of slaves and Yule logs, and not all

of them mention Kane's work as an inspiration. For example, a lavishly illustrated 1990s coffee table guide to Southern Christmas traditions by North
Carolinian Emyl Jenkins—an antiques appraiser especially known for her
guide to appraising and her mystery novels—explains, without citing Kane,
how slaves lengthened Christmas breaks by submerging unseasoned black
gum logs in three to four feet of mud until they became fully saturated with
moisture.[9]

In the years after Kane's book appeared, the tale also made its way into
holiday season issues of *North Carolina Roadways* and *Outdoors in Georgia*,
the latter being the monthly magazine of the Georgia Department of Natural
Resources. Even the U.S. Army found the story too good to resist. In the
December 1979 number of the *Journal of the U.S. Army Intelligence &
Security Command*, an enlisted woman explains that in the colonial South,
the slaves of "plantation-owner masters" would "normally be granted time
off from their duties" while their Yule logs burned.[10]

Later, a burgeoning southern tourist industry put these legends into
service. Many southern historic tourist spots run special programming at
Christmastime, and Yule log stories infiltrate their publicity and docents' presentations. In late 1999, the birthplace of North Carolina's colorful Civil War
governor Zebulon Vance (often a thorn in Confederate president Jefferson
Davis's side), a modest two-story log house in the town of Weaverville, North
Carolina, staged an "1830-style Christmas." Speaking in advance of the opening, former site manager Sudie Wheeler highlighted Yule logs without specifically mentioning enslaved people as their beneficiaries, despite the Vances
being slaveholders. Rather, she vaguely said that "they could celebrate" so
long as the log persisted, without identifying the race of her "they." Similarly,
when the Schiele Museum of Gastonia, North Carolina, put on its annual
(now discontinued) eighteenth-century Yule log event in 2012, research
specialist Suzanne Simmons, citing "oral tradition," told a local paper that
"servants didn't have to work" while their Yule logs burned. Tweaking the
phrasing a bit, an education coordinator at the Historic Arkansas Museum in
Little Rock reported in 2020 how it was a tradition in "'a lot of places, as long
as the Yule log was burning, they would be off.'"[11]

One South Carolina site dwelled regularly on folkloric renditions of Yule
log traditions in the Old South, though publicity for its 2001 programming
might well have perplexed readers. In promoting Christmas tours at the
Redcliffe Plantation State Historic Site on Beech Island in South Carolina
(once the stately Greek Revival residence of the controversial slaveholding
Palmetto State governor and US senator James Henry Hammond), the park
manager confidently assured a reporter that one of Redcliffe's customs had
been burning a Yule log. So "long as the log burned, the slaves did not have
to work." I wondered, in reading this, whether anyone at the time noticed the

confused and contradictory nature of the manager's elaborations, including the notion that masters "would soak the wood in water before setting it afire." This was surely a case of misspeak, since virtually all other such accounts attributed Yule log soakings to Black schemers. Worse, the park manager contradicted his main point by saying that site historians had uncovered proof that "Gov. Hammond provided a four-day vacation for his slaves." Think about this a moment. If Christmas labor was scheduled for a rigid four-day period by Hammond, it hardly could have varied by how long a log burned. It also struck me that Yule log customs could have only affected slave life at Redcliffe for a few years, if it really did so. Construction on the mansion did not begin until 1857 and the Hammonds did not even occupy it until 1859, the year before their state seceded from the Union.[12]

Still, Yule log programming went on year after year at Redcliffe. It is unlikely that visitors to the site's "Christmas in the Quarters" program on December 21, 2008, would forget the event since they were invited to participate in the reenactment of "bringing in a Yule log into the plantation house." Interpreter Elizabeth Laney, in period dress, informed guests that the log held significance because it determined the length of the slaves' Christmas "big times" after their "hard-spent year." They learned from Laney, additionally, precisely when and how the log soaked. Following any given Christmas, she explained, "the slaves would take a log, bury it in a marshy creekbed to soak up mud and moisture and dig it up again next Christmas for a slow-burning Yule Log." In other words, the logs soaked for nearly an entire year prior to their burning! By the 2009 program, reflecting changing racial sensibilities nationally and a growing reaction against romanticizing antebellum southern life and the Confederacy, Redcliffe highlighted that it wanted its programming to illuminate "the darker side of Christmas" in antebellum times and the power that masters exerted over enslaved people. The site, moreover, had hired Black reenactor Kitty Wilson Evans to illuminate a slave's role in the estate's Christmas planning. Still, on that year's tour, interpreter Laney repeated the broad outline of the soaking story as in the past and asserted that the Yule log, once taken to the mansion, burned in the master's bedroom.[13]

Eventually, my research led me to yet another corner of American popular culture, the field of children's literature, where biographies of iconic Black activists in the antislavery movement and Underground Railroad, including books intended to inspire youthful readers, serve up this legend. Dickson J. Preston, in *Young Frederick Douglass*, says that by "tradition," Christmastime for enslaved people on Maryland's Eastern Shore—where Douglass had been held in bondage—"lasted as long as the Yule log burned in the great house." In Frances T. Humphreville's *Harriet Tubman: Flame of Freedom*, Humphreville relates, using Tubman's slave name "Minty," that Minty and her father watched while the slaves brought in the great yule log for the Christmas holidays. It took several of them to drag the big log from the forest to the slave quarters. When it was ready, they would carry it up to the hall fireplace for the folks at the Big House. The boys and men put water on the wood and soaked it for two days.

When Minty queries her father why they soaked the log, he answers that the plan is to make it burn slowly because the longer it lasts the better their luck will be the next year. And in Deborah Hedstrom's *From Slavery to Freedom with Harriet Tubman*, fictional Quaker narrator Joshua Whitaker extracts Tubman's explanation as to why she chose to rescue Blacks from enslavement over Christmas. Her response: "It's the only time that slaves don't work. As long as the Yule log burns, they can stay in the cabins. If I time it right, the masters don't know the slaves are gone for two days."[14]

None of those books, however, match the impact of the most acclaimed illustrated children's book about the enslaved Christmas experience in the American South, *Christmas in the Big House, Christmas in the Quarters*, by Patricia C. McKissack and Frederick L. McKissack. Here, readers discover that the Christmas "Big Times" lasted, according to "Massa's" orders, just so long "as the Yule log burns." Naturally, slaves at this story's imagined setting—a Virginia James River plantation over Christmas 1859—decide "a water-soaked stump down by the creek can simmer from Christmas Eve to New Year's" as their Yule log selection. The McKissacks' book won the prestigious Coretta Scott King Book Award of the American Library Association in 1995 and has influenced readers ever since with its unromantic take on Christmastime in the Old South. The McKissacks' enslaved characters know how to party, to be sure. But they keep tabs on who has run away in their neighborhood, know about John Brown's raid on Harpers Ferry and his hanging, detest the idea of returning to work after New Year's, and expect slavery to end soon.[15]

✳✳✳

So why this book? Why rehash a custom that has been repeatedly verified by scholars, popular writers, and public history sites? Part of my problem with all this is that my instincts caution me that Yule log tales of slaves besting masters in setting the hours and days of their labor are too good to be true, too at odds with my own understandings of the horrors of bondage in the American South, understandings based on decades of teaching, researching, and writing about the history of that part of the country. I am willing to confess to having been initially charmed by these tales of underdogs myself—handfuls of disempowered slaves outfoxing their whip-toting masters and growing not only their personal holiday time through intelligence and artifice but also extending the Christmas vacations of the entire slave communities in which they lived. But it gradually dawned on me that these accounts might well be fictional.

Perhaps the most significant red flag behind my skepticism had to do with a seeming lack of hard evidence that southern masters and mistresses, and the overseers who often enforced their rules in their crop fields, timed Christmas by giant fireplace back-logs or that plantation laborers presoaked those logs to retard their burning speed. In the many slaveholder and overseer letters and diaries I had consulted when writing *Yuletide in Dixie*, I never saw a single allusion to a Yule log in that context. Nor had I encountered Yule logs impacting the Christmas privileges of slaves in antebellum novels or short stories, or in Black antebellum newspapers or the autobiographies of fugitive slaves who published their life stories after reaching freedom in the North. Those nineteenth-century autobiographies often did describe enslaved peoples' Christmas experiences, but burnings of Yule logs were not among them. Given that the whole holiday experience for slaves allegedly revolved around the duration of a single Yule log's flames, this disconnect nagged at me.

Given my puzzlement, I decided to revisit Nissenbaum's *Battle for Christmas* to check the documents undergirding his claims. What proof, I wondered, did Nissenbaum have that southern slaves had soaked Yule logs and tricked their masters? Nissenbaum's note for that assertion lists three sources: post–Civil War reminiscences in magazines by white North Carolina author Rebecca Cameron and the Maryland physician, poet, and journalist John Williamson Palmer, and a third magazine piece, this one in the early twentieth century, by the famed Black leader Booker T. Washington. Palmer's *Century* magazine piece recalled that enslaved laborers in Maryland "waited the whole round year" for holiday time to arrive. At Christmas, "with unerring judgment," they "chose the burly backlog, and solemnly soaked it in the creek, that in the great chimney-place of the dining-room it might show a brave front of glowing coals to the merry company, while its back remained unscorched for a week at least."[16]

Checking Nissenbaum's sources, though, did not resolve my questions. Note: all three of Nissenbaum's sources were published after 1890. None were published before the Civil War. They gain plausibility by being cross-racial. That is, two are authored by white memoirists, the other by an African American memoirist. But their transracial concurrence, to me, seemed overshadowed by their turn-of-the-twentieth-century publication dates. Their time distance from the events they describe weakens their reliability: all three magazine articles draw on happenings thirty or more years prior to publication. Recollections warp and become embellished over time, and personal stories are influenced by what people experience, discuss, and read between their original experiences and their retellings of those experiences.[17] They can also be fabricated out of whole cloth for a panoply of reasons, one of them being that colorful stories sell in the publishing world.

With Nissenbaum's failure to specify a single eyewitness account of Yule log soakings dating from pre–Civil War times in mind, I began paying more attention to other historians' writings on the subject and the sources for their information. What I discovered was that in the rare instances when documentation of the custom was even attempted, the "proof" always pointed to post–Civil War primary sources like Jenny Proctor's interview, which occurred *seven decades* after human bondage ended in the United States.[18] I simply could not turn up books or articles about antebellum Yule log–soaking customs that quoted or credited even a single source written or published from before the Civil War. Not one slaveholder's or overseer's diary or letter. Not an escaped slave's autobiography. Not a single travel account by a Yankee or a Brit going through the South at Christmastime before the Civil War. Not a newspaper or magazine article.

Given this paucity of hard evidence, I could not help but suspect that all the historians and popular writers who had written about Yule logs and Black life in the South before the Civil War had simply recirculated the same Yule log tales over and over, without ever digging up verifying evidence. And if that was the case, I began to wonder, should I think about plantation Yule log tales as folklore rather than recorded history, a highly agreeable yarn that got passed along, mouth to mouth, article to article, book to book, with perhaps a detail or two tweaked each time, but the fundamentals always constant? This is, after all, the way folktales spread. No verification required. They feed on themselves.

In fact, I reached the point of wondering whether there was a single documented instance from any of the fifteen states that would still have slavery at the outbreak of the Civil War, or from America's colonial days when all thirteen English colonies allowed slaveholding, of Black laborers soaking Yule logs or of a master scheduling slaves' winter holidays by how long an unsoaked log burned. If not, it would be hard to resist relating my findings to the truthfulness issue regarding another problematic belief about Black lives under enslavement. Not many years ago, critics debunked claims that slave-sewn quilts provided maps for enslaved people hoping to reach the North and freedom via the Underground Railroad. Supposedly (according to proponents of the quilt theory) black spots on slave quilts indicated homes where fugitives could stay safely on their journeys to freedom; and, during the Civil War, slaves hung their quilts on clotheslines in ways that divulged information to other slaves about troop movements in their area.[19] But there was no hard evidence for such claims. I pondered whether Yule log stories represented a parallel case of a fictional tale masked as historical truth infiltrating American popular culture.

And these thoughts led me to even more provocative questions. If Yule log tales originated after slavery ended, just who invented the story and how and why did it spread? What explains its longevity, its durability, to the present time? Could it be that mapped quilts and Yule logs tell hopeful stories—that enslaved people found ways to "master" their owners? And then, if that is so, do we pay a price for feel-good folklore? Do such stories misleadingly soften the horrors of human bondage? Is it too easy, in dwelling on the fun that enslaved people enjoyed at Christmastime and how they tricked their masters into permitting much of it, to overlook not only the yearlong cruelties attending slave labor but even during the holiday season? Not all slaves got Christmas off. Not all slaves escaped whippings and were exempted from other physical punishment and deprivation over the holiday season. Slave sales continued during the last week of December. So did shipments of enslaved people to new masters and rentals of slaves for the upcoming year that would necessarily break up slave families for the rental period. None of this stuff penetrates southern Yule log stories.

I even began pondering, in this regard, whether accounts of tolerant southern masters allowing their enslaved people to trick them into long Christmas vacations play into the very excusal of slavery in the Old South and southern secession from the Union that are implicit in blowback today against efforts to expunge the Confederate Lost Cause from American life—especially calls to preserve Confederate place-names and monuments, celebrate Confederate Memorial Day, and permit Confederate flags in public spaces. That Confederate flags appeared as rioters stormed the US Capitol on January 6, 2021, made my concerns more compelling.

Today, we sometimes use the term "urban legend" for the folkloric practice of retelling "a story about an unusual or humorous event the way people believe to be true but that is not true."[20] Maybe our Yule log tale about enslaved people will reveal itself as an "urban legend," or, more accurately, as a "plantation legend," since the overwhelming majority of its usages allude to events on antebellum slaveholding estates, always rural settings even when they adjoined southern municipalities. During the two decades before the Civil War, approximately 5 percent of all southern slaves worked in industrial jobs in mining, tobacco production, textile factories, and the like. Large numbers of enslaved people, moreover, lived in urban centers, where they labored as household domestics, hotel servants, artisans, dockworkers, barbers, and a myriad of other tasks. Approximately seventy thousand slaves lived in the eight largest southern cities by 1850. Yet, with very few exceptions, mentions of slaves soaking Yule logs concern agricultural workforces, generally sizable ones toiling under a hot sun while tending one of the Old South's staple crops, especially cotton and rice. So, the phrase plantation *legend* seems in order, should these log-soaking slave stories reveal themselves as imagined.[21]

Suspicions, of course, prove nothing. The only way for me to untangle this mess, to discern whether these tales were true or concocted, I came to realize, was to trace stories about Yule logs and Black slavery from their apparent roots in Old World holiday customs antedating the European settler invasion of North America to retellings in our twenty-first century, keeping in mind historian Catherine Clinton's dictum in a study of southern plantation lore that legends, rather than being discounted as "woven" entirely from false-hoods, are better understood as "selective" retellings of the past for persua-sive purposes that "embroider" facts with inaccurate details.[22]

With that qualification in mind, we need to ask when, why, and where these stories about America's enslaved people were first constructed and then later disseminated so widely that they became inscribed in US popular culture. Did their promoters ever have the "goods" (i.e., historical documents) to verify their tales? Or did they imagine Yule log soakings from the "get-go," or embellish bits of information they never confirmed? And to answer these questions, we will need, in turn, not merely to identify the initiators of these stories but also to discover their personal trajectories, or biographies, since, in Clinton's words, legends tell us "as much about the storyteller" as the events they describe.[23] That might offer clues as to whether Yule log–soaking slave stories should be revered as heroic accounts of Black resiliency against white master oppression, suspected as white southern propaganda justifying the enslavement of African Americans by portraying it as a kind of laid-back, humane system of labor relations, or recognized as some kind of biracial common wisdom based on the genuine realities of how enslaved people expe-rienced Christmas holidays in the American South.

This book is designed to take you along on my research process, a window into my thinking about the evidentiary basis of slaves' Yule log traditions and how my thoughts evolved as I uncovered more and more about the origins and popularity of these tales. As you will see, this was no linear journey for me, and it will not be an uncomplicated one for you. I confess to having my impressions revised several times, as I learned more about these stories and their originators. My wife, Jill, might tell you, I suspect, that I seemed to be changing my mind on an almost daily basis about all this. I would come to lunch or dinner after poring over new evidence and tell her that my opinion about the story's origin and even whether it was true or false had just been altered. I'm going to hold off on my final conclusions in the interest of those of you who don't like to know "who done it" in advance. But I do hope that you'll find in this book something worth remembering about how the history of human bondage in the American South has been interpreted and misinter-preted over time. And I also hope that by the end of your reading, you will, like me, ruminate about the layers of mythology that underlay our historical understandings and public debates. You may decide, in the end, that little is what it seems.

Chapter 1

Colonel Openheart's Great Back-Log

Although his name barely registers with Americans today, William Gilmore Simms (1806–1870) was the pre–Civil War South's literary light. The son of a Scotch-Irish merchant and "a mother of good Southern family," as the historian Drew Gilpin Faust describes her, Simms experienced his share of sadness growing up and in young adulthood. As a youth, he endured his mother's death and father's virtual exit from his life, leaving his upbringing in Charleston, South Carolina, to his grandmother on his mother's side. In 1832, he was dealt the blow of the death of his first wife, with whom he had one child, after barely five years of marriage. And he would always circulate a bit uneasily among South Carolina's vaunted elite society, even after his second marriage and taking up residence at Woodlands—his new wife's family's four-thousand-acre plantation in the southwestern part of the state.

Despite never attending college, however, Simms gained admission to South Carolina's bar and attained elevated literary status, editing newspapers and prestigious southern literary journals and making his mark as poet, essayist, dramatist, nonfiction and short story author, and historical novelist. Best known for his frontier, or "romance," tales of the American colonial and revolutionary periods, in all, Simms turned out a remarkable twenty thousand pages of text and some sixty-five books. And though he was never particularly prominent in the Old South's propagandistic defense of slavery that we call the proslavery "argument," he affiliated with his region's so-called peculiar institution.

In his *History of South Carolina* (1840), Simms lambasted British troops for having "stolen" many thousands of bondpeople from slaveholders in his state during the War for Independence. And although the slaveholder Simms's writings acknowledged some of slavery's abuses, he insisted that Blacks were better off enslaved in the South than on their own in the free North. Their "animal" natures, he argued, could be best held in check under the southern

Figure 1.1. William Gilmore Simms.
Source: South Caroliniana Library, University of South Carolina, Columbia, South Carolina.

labor system. Given such values, it is unsurprising that his stories served up what have been described as "cardboard" enslaved characters who recoiled from the very notion of being free.[1]

Simms begs our attention as one of the South's first authors to mention Yule logs in his fiction. He did so in his 1844 novel, *Castle Dismal*, alluding to the burning of a Yule log each Christmas at a country dwelling visited by his main character, Ned Clifton. A few years later, Simms went even further in his novella *Maize in Milk; A Christmas Story of the South*—a tale first published serially in 1847. In this mellow portrait of an excessively generous and kindly Carolina slaveholder (calculatedly named Colonel Tom Openheart), Simms quotes a Yule log poem for his first chapter's epigraph, waxes for three pages about Yule fires before introducing his main character and describes Openheart burning a massive Yule log during a late-1840s Christmas celebration at Maize-in-Milk (spelled differently than in his title). After sunset that Christmas Eve, the colonel, "emerging from an ancient closet . . . brings forth the rude charred fragments of a half-burned log":

> It is the Yule log of the last year. The hall chimney is carefully denuded of all its fires—the sticks are taken out, the hearth is swept. The great back-log, chosen for the fire of the new year, is brought in, and the fragments of last year's log are employed to kindle it. Our colonel delighted to continue, as nearly as he could with propriety, the customs of his English ancestors; and his own shoulders bore the log from the woodpile, and his own hands lighted the brands of the new year's fire as the sun went down.[2]

This passage is intriguing. For one thing, it gives readers the impression that by the American Civil War, southern slaveholders burned large wood blocks that they *called* "Yule logs" at Christmas and that they attributed their doing so to generational transmissions from English forbears. But it does not clarify when that transmission began. Had southern—or for that matter, non-southern—colonial slaveholders burned Yule logs since white Europeans first arrived on the continent's shoreline? Or did Colonel Openheart's Yule log represent something fresh in southern living, a conscious attempt long after the American Revolution to reinvigorate ancient English traditions? After all, the late 1840s were a time when many southern commentators, in reaction to the growing bellicosity of northern antislavery, were positing the need for a separate nationality of their own based on stereotypes that southern whites descended from different stock than other white Americans. A major trope in these arguments was the claim that southerners carried the blood of carefree pro-monarchy "Cavaliers" of the English Civil War of the mid-1600s, while their Yankee antagonists descended from England's uptight, anti-monarchical Puritans. By inserting Yule logs into his narrative, Simms may have been consciously or subconsciously reflecting on or trying to steer this ongoing cultural momentum, since supporters of English royalty were known for embracing Christmas as a holiday while Puritans rejected it.

Yet Simms's story is even more puzzling because, though Openheart is a slaveholding protagonist, it elides enslaved people from Yule log rituals. According to American folkloric tradition, Black slaves bore responsibility for preparing Yule logs for the big house fireplace. But it is the white Openheart rather than an enslaved house servant or field hand who takes the log from woodpile to mansion hall fireplace. Why would Simms compose his tale in such a way if he and other South Carolina plantation owners were accustomed to assigning the tasks of cutting and hauling plantation Yule logs to Black laborers?

Simms's fiction, then, is helpful as an indicator that by the Civil War some white southerners *might* have been following English Yule log traditions at Christmastime. But it sheds no light on the thorny question of when white southerners first burned Yule logs, if they really did so, or whether their enslaved people soaked such logs in streams and swamps. Clearly, to fully grasp what Simms's tale is or *is not* telling us about Yule logs and slavery in America, we need to step back into colonial times and see if, perhaps, we can uncover something precise about the origins of those customs. If we believe Simms's aside that Colonel Openheart's Yule log derived from "the customs of his English ancestors," we should be able to find evidence that early English immigrants to colonial America burned Yule logs just as they once had in the mother country.

✳✳✳

So, where to begin? Since we are dealing with chronology, there is no better starting gate than the *Oxford English Dictionary* (*OED*). The *OED* not only provides authoritative definitions of English words and terms but also gives the earliest instances of their appearance in print (according to the research of entry authors) as well as examples of later usages. This arrangement helps readers trace how the meanings of words and terms have evolved over time. When I consulted the *OED*, I found a minimalist definition of "yule-log" as "a large log of wood burnt on the hearth at Christmas," with an eighteenth-century first use in print revealing that the term entered the English language a minimum of half a century before the American Revolution. Henry Bourne's *Antiquities Vulgares* (1725), as reported in the *OED*, divulges that the burning of a "Yule-Log" represents a hopeful "Emblem of the returning Sun" as days began to lengthen, and spring lurked ahead.[3]

This was not a lot to go on, but the entry did make me wonder if Bourne reveals more in the actual *Antiquities Vulgares* than the *OED* excerpt indicates. I decided to track down Bourne's original text to see if it could shed further light. In a chapter titled "Of the Yule-Clog," Bourne attributes the term's earliest usages in Great Britain to the Isles' "Heathen Saxon" inhabitants and notes that usages persisted "after Christianity was embraced" by "Our Fore-Fathers" in their "Primitive Church." But that was all.[4]

Further digging led me to an often-recirculated seventeenth-century poem titled "Ceremonies for Christmas" by London native Robert Herrick (1591–1694). Since Herrick died before 1700, the poem indicates, helpfully, that Yule logs existed in the English imagination before Henry Bourne published *Antiquities Vulgares* in 1725, even if encased in a variant term:

> Come, bring with a noise.
> My merrie, merrie boys,
> The Christmas Log to the firing.[5]

Next, I learned from other sources that seventeenth- and eighteenth-century inhabitants of the British Isles were themselves latecomers to Yule log customs. In the mid-nineteenth century, the Troy, New York, church organist Nathan B. Warren declared categorically that the custom of "bringing in and placing of the ponderous Christmas-block, or Yule-log, on the hearth of the wide chimney of the Old English Hall" originated with "the Danes and Pagan Saxons." Much more recently, Ace Collins, the author of *Stories Behind the Great Traditions of Christmas*, emphasizes that Viking invasions during the Dark Ages first exposed the British Isles to Yule log practices, where they took root among Celtic Druids. Other chroniclers reach even further back in time and to other places. William D. Crump's *The Christmas Encyclopedia* traces Yule logs to a New Year's festival in ancient Babylonia, where annual burnings of wooden effigies were believed to fend off the world's death at year's end.[6]

Many Christmas reference works concur that by the Middle Ages the custom reached pagan Germanic peoples in continental Europe, where it easily melded into peoples' superstitious belief systems. Barbara Kissinger's *Christmas Past* explains that written European allusions to "bringing in" an annual Yule log date to 1184, and that in France it became customary to sing a carol to bless the house as a Yule log was carried into it. In Italy, people thought Yule log ashes afforded protection from hail. Significantly, Kissinger relates that in Germanic Europe, a "small remnant of the log was retained" to ignite the following year's Yule log, a practice picked up in Herrick's English take in his poem "Ceremonies for Christmas," which instructed, "With the last yeeres brand / Light the new block." According to another account, it was once common in northern Europe to decorate, bless, and anoint Yule logs with wine and even to scatter seeds on them for ample harvests the coming year. Some accounts connect Yule log traditions to a supposedly magical Norse tree called the Yggrasil.[7]

Figure 1.2.   Bringing in the Yule log. This wood engraving, executed by the famed US Civil War combat artist Alfred Rudolph Waud, depicts Yule log festivities in a wealthy, Old World household.
Source: Historic New Orleans Collection (1977.137.18.291).

Still, histories about the origins of Yule log customs in Europe are glaringly deficient in eyewitness evidence and specificity, so much so that commentators across the Atlantic have sometimes discounted their reliability. On Christmas Day, 1858, the Washington, DC, *Daily National Intelligencer* mused that whether "the 'Yule log' be of Saxon or Scandinavian institution; whether it was brought into England by Julius Caesar, as some have learnedly argued; or whether it was a native growth," were questions best left for "historical Dryasdusts and prosing Commentators." It seems safest, I think, to go with a twenty-first-century Christmas reference work's flat conclusion that "little can be determined for certain regarding the early history" of Yule log celebrations.[8]

✳✳✳

If tracing the origins of Yule log customs is a sticky business, so is deciding whether emigrants from the British Isles or the European continent really transplanted them to England's North American colonies during the 1600s and 1700s, as Simms's fictional tale of Colonel Openheart claims. Other nineteenth-century US commentators besides Simms have suggested as much, but that hardly makes the claim true. In a pre–Civil War short story about King Philip's War, a bloody mid-1670s conflict in New England between English colonists and indigenous peoples, the narrator sets his tale "ere the yule log" became embers on a Christmas Eve, a clear suggestion that there were already Yule logs burning in North America a half century after the beginning of English colonization. A late-nineteenth-century history of Queens County, New York, affirms that down the coast from New England, colonial Long Islanders, too, burned Yule logs at Christmas as their forbears had in "ancient times in 'merrie England.'" And even further along the coast, supposedly, southern colonials did the same. According to one book about southern life before the American Revolution, Yule logs were kindled on "hospitable" hearths in the Virginia colony.[9]

Although none of these sources credited enslaved African Americans for any role in colonial-American Yule log customs, more recent commentators have done so. According to John Baur, author of *Christmas on the American Frontier* (1961), in the colonial period, "household slaves" dragged Yule logs "into the great hall of every Virginia and Carolina mansion." In 1962, many US newspapers carried an anonymously written essay on the holiday's history confirming that on "many plantations" in the southern colonies "slaves were given a holiday as long as the yule log burned."[10]

No wonder, given such claims, that ahead of its 2013 Christmas program at the Bacon's Castle historic site in Virginia, Preservation Virginia promoted the event with a short film in which a costumed presenter explains that colonial settlers burned a "Yule log," which it describes as a "huge piece of wood cut from the property that was then soaked in brandy or rum or some other kind of alcohol and doused with spices." She notes, too, that this log would customarily "burn for the twelve days of Christmas." In a similar vein, each December for some years the Georgia State Park's stunning Wormsloe State Historic Site in Savannah—a locale devoted to Georgia's colonial period (when Wormsloe served as the estate of a prosperous official, Indian agent, and surveyor) and which is notable for its stately live oaks and hanging Spanish moss—has integrated Yule logs into its Christmastime programming. In 1990, a write-up of the event explained how a "1741 Christmas celebration is re-enacted annually at Wormsloe Historic Site. . . . People in Colonial costumes prepare plum pudding and mince pies and carry in the yule log decorated in holly and Christmas berries." With the stereotype still running strong thirty-four years later, the site promised in 2024 that visitors on December 7 would be given an opportunity to "Help find yule logs to be burned starting at 10 a.m." and then later at 4.[11]

✳✳✳

The thing is, none of these claims that colonial Americans burned Yule logs seem based on hard evidence. The closest thing to authentic proof that I have found, and it is not really close, comes in the form of vague *reminiscences* by mid- and late nineteenth-century Americans offering supposedly privileged knowledge that such practices occurred much earlier in American history. Such claims insufficiently resolve matters one way or the other.

Take Nathan Warren's rambling 1895 reminiscence subtitled "Round About the Yule Log." Supposedly, Warren narrated these recollections orally for the first time one Christmas holiday season "in the year 18—" to relations gathered at a farmhouse in Norwalk, Connecticut, as stories that he told on consecutive evenings. Before launching into his vignettes, Warren recalls how boys had once used hand spikes to drag to that dwelling's spacious kitchen hearth a "huge log" from the woods that had been "seasoning" all the prior summer. Warren declares, too, that it had "been the custom for generations in New England to observe Christmas-eve in this manner," as had been done in "Old England." But what does Warren mean by "generations"? Two? Five? There is a big difference. Even five generations back from 1895, the book's publication date, falls short of colonial times. Warren implies that cultural transmissions of Yule log customs from Mother England to North America took place at some early point, but he makes it difficult to pin down the transmission chronology.[12]

Similarly problematic is the autobiographical account of New England Unitarian minister Orville Dewey (1794–1882), who spent his boyhood in Sheffield, Massachusetts. Dewey tells his readers that his primary remembrance from his youth of his father's hired hand Richard "was the point Richard made every Christmas of getting in the 'Yule-log,' a huge log which he had doubtless been saving out in chopping the wood-pile, big enough for a yoke of oxen to draw, and which he placed with a kind of ceremony and respect in the great kitchen fireplace."[13] One might assume, from Dewey's telling, that at least some New Englanders burned Yule logs before the War of 1812, and that it was therefore possible that in doing so they were perpetuating practices inherited from colonial times. Dewey, however, was born nearly two decades after the colonies declared independence from England. We should be wary of stretching his Yule log story too expansively.

Making matters worse, not only is hard proof that Americans conducted Yule log ceremonies during colonial times lacking but there is also scant evidence that they ceremoniously burned Yule logs *after* the American Revolution, despite what Dewey claimed. A day before Christmas in 1824, the Washington, DC, *Daily National Journal* published a piece titled "Reflections of a Student." Its author bluntly stated that the Yule log, despite its reputed origins in northern England, "is not known, I believe, in our country; at least, I have no recollection of having ever witnessed this ceremony in any part of the United States." That claim was echoed by a writer recalling village life along the Massachusetts coastline in the early 1830s. Listeners there were not regaled with stories of Yule logs, nor, for that matter, other

English Christmas customs like "the mistletoe-bough," "the wassail-bowl," or the "boar's head," according to this commentator.[14]

Boston and Belfast, Maine, newspapers boldly asserted that colonial New England's stridently anti-Catholic Puritan settlers had permanently unburdened themselves of English Christmas customs, *including Yule logs*, as emblems of "Popery," though the *Boston Bee* expressed sadness that such hostility to well-meaning holiday "sports" lingered on in Massachusetts. Such contentions seem plausible given well-documented instances of colonial Puritans, mirroring the values of Puritans in the mother country, trying to legislate the Christmas holiday, itself, out of existence.[15]

All accounts of Yule logs in early America, in other words, seem, to use a risky pun, to flame out, though it helps to read between the lines of historical accounts of colonial life to fully grasp the point. Consider this excerpt from a book about colonial Maryland that was published in 1913. Pay attention, particularly, to the words I have italicized:

> At the very period that Maryland was first settled England was making Christmas the merriest season of the year. . . . Hence in Provincial Maryland . . . the great halls of the lords of the manors . . . were decked in holly and rosemary. . . . From the dimensions of the Colonial fireplace, which yawned nearly halfway across the room, *it is quite certain that the yule log in Maryland, as in England, was the center of the Christmas fun.*

If read closely, this assertion is a matter of faith, not evidence. We have proofless causality: if English people burned Yule logs and Maryland aristocrats' homes had immense fireplaces, then colonial Marylanders burned Yule logs too. There is no source listed to support the author's proposition. Nor is there a source for a claim in one late-nineteenth-century book, *The Colonial Cavalier* by Maud Wilder Goodwin, that the kindling of Yule logs on "hospitable" hearths occurred in colonial Virginia. How did Goodwin know that?[16]

It is telling, in this regard, that the rich digitized online resource *Chronicling America*, which offers searchable access to 20,389,221 pages of US newspapers (as of May 8, 2023) dating from 1770 to 1963, gives no hint that Yule log ceremonies had anything to do with colonial America or even Christmas holidays in the early days of the American republic. Despite the size of this database, I was not rewarded with a single hit when, in separate searches, I entered "Yule log," "Yule-log," and "Yule clog" for 1770 to 1828. Yet "Christmas" brings 1496 hits for the same time frame, "Yule" 166, and "wassail" 29.[17] Invisibility in databanks, which have their own deficiencies in terms of picking up search terms in faded or sometimes damaged or incomplete documents and the like, of course, hardly proves that people never burned Yule logs in the United States during the nation's early decades or the last years of America's colonial period. But it invites skepticism.

Another revealing indicator is that the Colonial Williamsburg Foundation, which has been holding annual December Yule log ceremonies at its site since 1940 as part of its holiday programming, concedes on its own website and in its training guide for holiday docents that "there is no record of a Yule log in colonial Virginia." Visually, though, the site, as of this writing, might convey contrary impressions to casual visitors. One of its photographs depicts two adult, liveried African Americans, presumably in the roles of servants in colonial Williamsburg, bearing a Yule log's heavy weight as they carry it outdoors on their shoulders. Costumed white and Black onlookers alike try to touch the passing log for good luck, a custom long prescribed by some Yule log believers according to some accounts, but unverifiable from actual documents dating from the time slavery existed in the United States.[18]

✳✳✳

Of course, if white colonists in English North America never revived Yule traditions from the Old World, colonial slaves would have hardly been given an opportunity by their masters to soak them for longer Christmas vacations. How, then, to explain a book about southeastern Connecticut's African American history published by the New London County Historical Society that connects Yule log traditions to the state's early history? (Connecticut did not even begin to end slavery until after the American Revolution, when its lawmakers initiated its gradual end in the state.) In this 1979 book, coauthors James M. Rose and Barbara W. Brown relate how around the time of the American Revolution, the enslaved Moody family, owned by the white Cook family, had permission as "each Christmas approached" to select and prepare "a huge Yule log" for burning in the kitchen's fireplace. This they did, we learn, under "the understanding that, from the time it was lighted until it was entirely consumed, it would represent a continuous holiday." According to Rose and Brown, this log was "cut and submerged in a large spring" a full year before the Christmas holiday, when "it was brought, thoroughly water-soaked, into the house." There it burned, typically, for a week to ten days. Still, "to make sure that their holiday would last, the Moodys, late at night, poured just enough water on their Yule log" to hinder its consumption. "This custom," Rose and Brown assure us, "was indeed a joyful break in the otherwise laborious life of a slave family."

When I first read these words, I took them as a breakthrough moment for my research. According to Rose and Brown, African American slaves, around the time of America's War for Independence, soaked Yule logs, and probably did so even earlier since there was no indication in the book that the practice was something new at that time. All I needed to make certain of was that Rose and Brown researched authentic documents before relating this story. Unfortunately, that did not prove to be the case, at least so far as I could learn. Rose and Brown helpfully include a source for their Yule log material, but unfortunately that source is merely a history of Griswold, a New London County town, published in 1929, rather than an original document from the Revolutionary War period. Checking the cited book, authored by Daniel L. Phillips, I discovered the same vignette Rose and Brown relate, nearly word for word other than for the addition that the log was "rolled" into the kitchen by the slaves. But Phillips does not provide any source at all for *his* information! I followed up by contacting several local history experts from New London County and Griswold, but none of them could find or knew of a single original document confirming Phillips's (and Rose's and Brown's) tale.[19]

More likely than not, this appealing story about Connecticut slaves soaking Christmas logs around the time of America's War for Independence was merely a literary embellishment to make Phillips's book about Griswold, and later the Rose/Brown account of the Moodys, entertaining for readers. I could only presume that rather than originating in some authentic colonial document, both books derived the idea of enslaved people soaking Yule logs from one of the many Yule log slave stories circulating in print during Phillips's twentieth-century lifetime. As we will learn, there was no shortage of such tales for Phillips to draw from in the 1920s.

✳✳✳

In the end, I was no less skeptical of stories about people in the thirteen English colonies or in the new United States following independence burning Yule logs in elaborate English-inspired ceremonies than when I began my investigation. I had failed to uncover a shard of credible evidence that enslaved laborers during that lengthy time span soaked or otherwise handled Yule logs in ways that maximized their Christmas holiday time.

Ironically, the one seemingly authentic contemporary document I read from those years connecting enslaved Blacks to large fireplace back-logs had nothing to do with Christmas making enslavement more tolerable. Just the opposite. It came from the published travel account of an Englishman named John Davis, who accepted a tutorial position on a South Carolina estate in 1798 and stayed overnight en route at a tavern not far from Charleston. After being ushered into a room with "the largest fire I had ever seen in my travels," he looked on as the tavern owner excoriated one of his "negroes" for "keeping so bad a fire." Not only did the man lambaste his servant Syphax as a "rascal" and tell him to "fetch a stout back log" but he also warned that should Syphax drag his feet he would "make a back-log" of him! The land-lord's wife clarified that her husband was frustrated because another servant had recently run away and that he had already whipped Syphax "till his back was raw."[20] Was it possible, I wondered on reading this travel book, whether unproved legends about slaves tending Yule logs during America's early history have diverted attention from darker and more revealing indications about the circumstances of enslaved people who tended whites' fireplaces in our early history?

Whatever the case, my inquiry was far from over. Just because my research failed to uncover hard evidence that giant, specially designated and deco-rated Yule logs burned in colonial America, or during the decades between the Revolution and the War of 1812, hardly meant that such remained the case afterward. There were a full five decades between the end of the War of 1812 and slavery's end in America following the Civil War. So far, all I knew for sure was that if slave trickery with Yule logs ever occurred in America, it likely got off to a late start. After all, the decades after the War of 1812 witnessed the full maturation of the American South's slave labor system, entrapping new millions of Africans and their descendants in webs of coerced labor.

Chapter 2

Prattville's Soggy Fixed Fact

It came late in the research for this book that I stumbled on seemingly irrefutable documentary evidence from a year before the Civil War that US slaves drenched Yule logs in preparation for Christmas. And I found it, surprisingly, not in a source from the slaveholding South but rather in a newspaper published in Emporia in the Kansas Territory in the nonslaveholding North—a boomtown that as recently as the beginning of 1857 had merely been houseless prairie land. In the short interval of a few years, Emporia had become a magnet for eastern settlers, even as bloodshed over slavery disrupted life in the territory's abundant grasslands.[1]

In that pre-TV, pre-internet time, when almost every US town had a print paper or two, Emporia had its *News*, which began publication in 1859. On the second page of its March 10, 1860, issue, the *News* reprinted an account of a visit to Alabama over Christmas by John W. Ray, the editor of the *Aurora Beacon*, an Illinois paper. In this piece (an installment in a multipart travel account titled "Pictures of Southern Life" that began running in the *Beacon* in November 1859), Ray gave his impressions of the factory village of Prattville, a place that was a far cry from stereotypes of the Old South as an endless expanse of plantation mansions and rows of cotton plants.[2]

Prattville, rather, was a slave state iteration of New England's far better remembered textile villages. In fact, it developed out of the industrial dreams of a New Englander—a tall New Hampshire native named Daniel Pratt, who with his wife had moved to Alabama in 1833 (following some sixteen years in Georgia) with the intention of putting down permanent roots. After purchasing two thousand acres of land along Autauga Creek—some fourteen miles northeast of Montgomery—in Autauga County in 1835, Pratt in 1839 began what by the Civil War became the nation's largest cotton gin factory. Soon after constructing the gin factory, he added a sawmill, blacksmith shop, and gristmill to his settlement, which gained the name of Prattville. Further development included a textile factory (incorporated in 1846 as the Prattville Manufacturing Company) and a foundry, with all these establishments like

New England textile centers depending on water for power. In the case of Prattville, the works drew on a large waterwheel that harnessed the currents of Autauga Creek. Pratt's successes, in turn, enticed other enterprising business and professional types to try their luck there, and by the time Ray's travel account appeared in the *Beacon*, the settlement boasted of druggists, a dentist, a shoemaker, and several general stores and a resident population of 173 households.

Devoted to the modernization of the southern economy, Pratt promoted the construction of a railroad connecting Selma and Montgomery through his area. And despite his New England roots, he so identified with his adopted region and its labor system that he urged a ten-year program of arms production to ready the region for possible war with the North's antislavery Republicans. On acquiring his first few slaves earlier during his years in Georgia, Pratt seems to have expected to divest himself of them within a short time. Once in Alabama, however, he forsook whatever qualms he had about slave ownership. Between 1834 and 1845, he purchased a minimum of eighteen Black males and six women. By the time of Ray's visit, he employed both owned and rented enslaved workers at his gin factory, ironworks, and other businesses, though bondpeople had been declining in recent years as a percentage of his labor force and were down to about 15 percent at the textile plant.[3]

We do not know why Pratt reduced his slave labor force at the mill over the years. Outright worker recalcitrance and other kinds of resistance such as sabotage of equipment and attempts at escape seem to have been rare at his manufactories. Given what our Illinois visitor reported, perhaps some of Pratt's Black workers sabotaged their owner's interests through shoddy work as a way of getting revenge for their subjugation. John Ray, in his reporting, claimed Pratt's slave workers were so unhandy that Pratt confined their labor to producing osnaburg fabric, a scratchy, sturdy textile usually dedicated to slave wear. The implication was that Pratt, from experience, may have come to distrust enslaved people with delicate fabrics, but we do not know for certain that this was the case.

The Illinois journalist, though, noticed more of interest than just local manufacturing to share with his readers about Prattville. A discussion of how Pratt and his slaves slaughtered 115 hogs prior to Christmas for the following year's pork supply segued easily into a brief allusion to back-log traditions in the Prattville area. In 1858, Pratt had purchased a large plantation, where he assigned many of the more than one hundred slaves of whom he claimed ownership at that time. Without alluding specifically to Pratt and his own crop workers, Ray enriched his fact-finding with this colorful aside:

The story is, that the slaves can keep the holidays as long as they can make a back log last; and weeks before Christmas, they go into the swamp, cut a sour gum tree log, let it lie and soak till Christmas, then put it on the fire in the biggest hut. Of course, it is a soggy fixed fact, and when, during the hey days, the master comes in and says, "keep a good fire boys," they say, "yes, massa," and laugh in their dressed up sleeves to think the log will last long past New Years![4]

It is hard to overstate the significance of this account for my investigation, not only for its anticipation of post–Civil War slave Yule log–soaking tales but also because this midwestern editor immediately provides additional details putting enslaved Christmas experiences in Prattville in a positive light. In this locale, the "master" allows every slave to beg a present off him at Christmas and liberally dispenses written passes to his enslaved laborers so they can visit distant towns and plantations during their holiday downtime if they so choose. Intriguingly, Prattville's generic master *wants* Yule logs to burn out slowly to his slaves' advantage even though he is apparently clueless as to how his bondpeople get those logs to burn so long. Why else would the slaves "laugh in their dressed up sleeves"? The master, apparently, is not in on the joke.

I could not help but notice that this piece differed from later Yule log lore in suggesting that the log burned in one of the slave families' huts rather than in the slaveholder's big house. But in other respects, it matched the Yule log legend about the Old South that I was tracking down. Clearly, once I read this 1860 Emporia, Kansas, news story, I had to reconsider my hardening suspicions that Yule log–soaking legends about enslaved life in the United States were unverifiable and likely fabrications. And this reevaluation became all the more urgent when I found a second antebellum document, this one in a *southern* newspaper, confirming the allocation of Christmas holiday time for enslaved people according to Yule log burnings. This second "news" piece, in the 1847 Christmas issue of the Elkton, Maryland, *Cecil Whig*, tucked a tidy allusion to the custom into a lengthy article titled, simply, "Christmas." The *Whig*'s writer suggested that a contemporary custom of burning a large Yule log "more to illuminate than to warm" originated along Maryland's Eastern Shore, where "negroes" had the "liberty to select a back log for the Christmas fire, with a view to its lasting, and are entitled to holidays until it is consumed." Although this earlier essay did not explicitly describe slaves immersing logs to extend their holiday work vacation, it implied as much by mentioning that an "old water-soaked gum" might earn enslaved people an entire week off.[5]

Given the chronological gaps between the two articles, I could assume that the more revealing *Emporia News/Aurora Beacon* piece of 1860 was entirely original and did not plagiarize the first in any way, especially since both Emporia, Kansas, and Aurora, Illinois, are geographically far from Elkton, Maryland. The odds are tiny that the later Aurora journalist read what the earlier 1847 Elkton commentator had to say. And this is significant: two pieces of evidence make for more convincing proof than just one. Everything was again on the table. Finally, I had pre–Civil War Americans relating Yule log–soaking tales. Reconsideration, however, demanded extra digging, not preemptive acceptance of the Yule log–soaking legend on its merits. On the one hand, I had uncovered two late-antebellum news stories about enslaved people in a couple of southern subregions soaking Yule logs. On the other hand, those reports lacked clues as to just how widely Yule log customs were adopted before the Civil War. Who were these tolerant enslavers who allowed themselves to be tricked by their laborers into longer holidays? We don't know. We do not even know if the Aurora, Illinois, editor was implying that Daniel Pratt allowed this custom at his industrial works.

***

Perhaps two cases suffice as proof of slave Yule log trickery, but those instances pale in significance given the enslaved population in the pre–Civil War United States, more than in any other slave society in the hemisphere. The South's enslaved African Americans increased from about two million in 1830 to nearly four million in 1860 when the *Aurora Beacon* article appeared. Given that context, two imprecise reports about Black Yule log privileges are underwhelming, especially considering the explosion in American book and print journalism in the first half of the nineteenth century and the wealth of information being published throughout the country before the Civil War about southern slavery. These publications included verifiable autobiographical accounts (or "narratives") of enslaved people who escaped southern masters and published descriptions of their time in bondage, often compensating for the illiteracy they had been relegated to by enslavement with assistance from abolitionist amanuenses. Such sources must be taken seriously, given that historians have meticulously identified exceptional instances where abolitionists manipulated the stories or made things up for ideological or sales advantages. That did not occur often, as most of the editors of these published autobiographies were professionals such as ministers and historians reputed for their integrity. Some were even hostile to the northern abolition movement or apathetic about it. Generally, scholars confirm the accuracy and honesty of these fascinating sources, double-checking their key details to be sure they can be trusted.[6]

According to a chronological listing of North American slave autobiographies compiled by the Documenting the American South program of the University of North Carolina, ninety-one such narratives are known to have been written between 1800 and 1865, as compared to only fifteen authored between 1740 and 1800.[7] Many of the autobiographies for the 1800s are easily accessible online as well as on the Documenting the American South's website, a good number of them as book publications. A similar point could be made about the vast increase during those same years in the number of slaveholder journals, letter collections, and diaries available to researchers when compared to such writings from earlier times. Many of those, too, are easily accessible in published editions, as well as in manuscript form in libraries and archives, some of which have been microfilmed or digitized. If enslaved men and women made a habit of soaking a Yule log every Christmastime so that they and their peers could gain extra holiday privileges, identifying documents proving such duplicities should be simple enough. Given what I had read in those two newspaper pieces, I now felt a need to look at antebellum materials more methodically than I had so far. Everything remained on the table.

One precondition for my expanded search was to confirm that Yule logs themselves were truly a "thing" in southern holiday life following the War of 1812, since, as we have seen, there is little concrete evidence that they burned in colonial and revolutionary times. If few or no Yule logs burned in southern white households before the Civil War, there is hardly a need to seek evidence that enslaved people soaked them.

Georgia history promoters had no doubts that antebellum southerners annually burned Yule logs when in 1970 they opened to the public their fifty-eight-acre Westville Village living history site near the tiny city of Lumpkin in their state's southwestern reaches, a place dedicated to recreating Georgia village life in 1850. Nor did they doubt that enslaved Blacks soaked them. Beginning immediately, and continuing to do so through 2006, a span of nearly forty years, Westville's promoters held annual Yule log hunts and burnings during their holiday programming, on the assumption that villagers throughout the state really did such things before the Civil War. As the site's researcher Sandra Dixon put it in 1984 to an *Atlanta Journal and Constitution* staff writer, her studies of newspapers, periodicals, court records, and peoples' letters showed that all labor ceased on southern plantations "as long as the yule log burned" and that enslaved people soaked their Yule logs in water whenever they could "get away with it." Some years later, in 2000, the Library of Congress authenticated the Westville programming by incorporating its Yule log ritual into its Bicentennial Local Legacies Project as "a blend of nineteenth century church rituals and plantation customs" meriting recollection.[8]

But researcher Dixon apparently failed to link the Yule log customs to pre–Civil War documents when speaking to the *Journal/Constitution* columnist, since there is no mention of them in the specific pieces of evidence used to justify the Westville ceremony, and the Library of Congress never vetted Legacy Project nominations for accuracy. Indeed, a former president of the Stewart County Historical Commission concedes that the best that can be said about the Westville Yule log program is that people "suspect" Yule logs were burned in southwestern Georgia in 1850, though "there isn't concrete evidence" to support the Westville programming. Insinuating the ceremonies were authentic, of course, did not make them so. Just as late nineteenth-century and twentieth-century historians, novelists, and historic sites have asserted, without evidence, that colonial and revolutionary Americans burned Yule logs, it seems Westville Historic Handicrafts Inc., the nonprofit that operated this living history site, and the Library of Congress operated more on faith than evidence in applying this custom to antebellum southern life.[9]

What does confer some credibility on the Westville ceremonies is that newspapers throughout the South (and other parts of the United States too) mentioned Yule logs in local contexts with increasing frequency for some reason before the Civil War. On Christmas Day 1855, for example, a Fredericksburg, Virginia, newspaper encouraged its readership to apply the Christmas spirit all year long instead of on a single day, advising, "Let the heart be the Yule log, always brightly burning." Two years later, on Christmas Day, the *Charleston* (SC) *Daily Courier* urged that "the Yule log spread a cheerful glow over our faces."[10] Southern newspapers each year around Christmas before the Civil War were filled with such pleasant thoughts.

But did such passing remarks amount to anything? Did the writers of such exhortations expect their readers to take their thoughts literally? Did they assume or know that their readers were accustomed to repeating age-old European Yule log traditions over the holiday season? Possibly offhanded print allusions to Yule logs in the pre–Civil War American press signaled little more than casual banter, given that these were pre–central heating times and people customarily burned large fires in their homes at an especially cold time of the year.

After all, during this very same period of increasing print chatter about Yule logs burning in slave state firesides, other southern newspapers and magazines contrarily maintained that, in the words of the South's leading literary publication, *The Southern Literary Messenger*, "the days of the 'yule log'" had already "passed away"! In 1844, a New Orleans paper urged readers to celebrate Christmas "though the yule-log may not burn on the hearth with us." In 1855, a Virginia newspaper claimed that Americans cherished their Christmas holiday just as folk did "in 'ye olden tyme,' when the yule log" brought "social joy" to all hearts—again implying yule logs were passé. One Richmond newspaper pointedly observed that Pennsylvania coal had knocked all poetry "out of Christmas fuel," suggesting that in the Old

Dominion wood fires themselves were being phased out by the Civil War. No Yule logs there. What are we to make of this?[11]

***

Even if it was true, as William Simms's fictitious tale *Maize in Milk* suggests, that wealthy white southerners restaged English Yule log rituals before the Civil War, we can hardly take for granted that enslaved people ever soaked the giant Christmas back-logs that Colonel Openheart and other plantation owners burned. If Black workers had that kind of responsibility on southern plantations, one would think that Simms, an enslaver himself, might have written it into his story. But he did not, and with the two exceptions already mentioned, neither did the press, even when publishing content dealing with Yule logs and the experiences of enslaved Blacks at Christmas.

Let me give an example of what I am driving at. Just before Christmas in 1858, the Philadelphia publisher Charles J. Peterson published an essay in a Tennessee paper recognizing that Americans observed Christmas variously depending on where they lived, though *none* of them experienced the mirth that English folk did in "the old baronial times" when "crowds of servitors" dragged Yule logs through great halls. It would have been perfectly logical, had Peterson known of enslaved Blacks dragging Yule logs in his own country, for him to have then brought this up, since his article mentioned Black participation in *other* Yuletide rituals at the time in Charleston as well as in Havana, Cuba. In Charleston, "negroes" welcomed Christmas's arrival by lighting firecrackers. Down in Havana, Christmas verged on becoming "a Saturnalia . . . an uproarious negro carnival."[12] That Peterson did not connect Blacks to Yule log customs in the United States is revealing, given his allusion to Yule logs in the same piece.

Peterson's neglect of Black Yule log customs in an article mentioning English "servitors" dragging Yule logs around relates in a potentially illuminating way to a second news piece from the same period. This one, too, mentioned both logs and the Christmas noisemaking of enslaved people but remained silent about Blacks handling *Yule* logs. I found this second article in a holiday season 1858 issue of the *Eufaula Express*, an Alabama newspaper that proclaimed below its masthead, "A Southern Confederacy—The Sooner the Better."[13]

Here, an unidentified writer mentioned the plantation custom of exploding hog bladders as a Yuletide noise alternative to firecrackers, a tradition confirmed in other accounts. Bladders preserved from the hog-butchering that preceded Christmastime feasting were inflated with air blown into them through a reed. Slaves then roasted the bloated bladders over a fire until they exploded with a blast apparently comparable to gunfire. When she was interviewed a long time later for the Federal Writers' Project in the 1930s, Pauline Grice, who had labored on a large plantation in the vicinity of Atlanta, Georgia, confirmed this antebellum plantation custom. Grice recalled that there generally were about one hundred "hawg bladders save from hawg killin'" on her place each year, and that on Christmas night, "de chillen takes dem and puts dem on de stick. Fust dey is all blowed full of air and tied tight and dry. Den de chillen holds de bladder in de fire and purty soon, 'BANG,' dey goes. Dat am de fireworks."[14]

In broaching this noisemaking, the *Eufaula Express* queried whether any southerner could not recall from their childhood "rising at four in the morning, [and] the bringing forth from their hidden receptacles the precious bladders." The author detailed how Black children customarily would yell each time a bladder was roasted over the fire and then stamped upon, causing such a "loud report" that it was dubbed "a Christmas gun!" Interestingly, in the very next sentence, an "old Uncle Peter" enters the narrative, likely an elderly enslaved person (given the white southern proclivity then and long afterward of referring to aging enslaved people as "auntie" or "uncle"). Uncle Peter is making his own ruckus over Christmas by using gunpowder to blow up an "old, knotty, hickory log." Yet, this account, like Peterson's essay, never connected Uncle Peter or any other enslaved person to the soaking of a Yule log. Since many *post*–Civil War accounts assigned elderly Black authority figures managerial plantation responsibilities for getting soaked, knotty, and sometimes hickory Yule logs to masters' fireplaces, one would think a *pre*–Civil War newspaper piece grouping together Christmas fires, a knotty hickory log, and an enslaved elderly Black man would have something to say about holiday log soakings—if they occurred. All the necessary elements were in place. Yet no Yule log–soaking story followed. Rather, the piece shifted from Uncle Peter to holiday customs at "the home of a tobacco planter of twenty years ago," where a master dispensed eggnog and Christmas presents to his slaves.

Consider too a poem titled "Christmas" written in 1849 by Arkansas lawyer, newsman, author, and, later, Confederate general Albert Pike. Pike's poem includes a line wishing the "Yule-log should again be brought by many a stout, strong hand." Who were Pike's "stout, strong" hands? One might assume they were Black crop laborers, given the author's southern background. But Pike's lines show he is musing instead about what it might be like if his poem's readers could celebrate the holiday just like their forbears did under the "Saxton rafters" of "Old England":

> Had we our way, the good old sports
>   should be revived once more
> Again should maiden's little feet dance
>   twinkling on the floor;

> While overhead again should hang the
> dark green mistleto,
> And all lips that strayed under it the for
> feit pay, we know.
> The Yule-log should again be brought by
> many a stout, strong hand,
> And some fair girl should light it,
> with the last year's sacred brand.

Pike's "strong" hands, just like Charles Peterson's "crowds of servitors," signified English white yeomen, not Black slaves. And that is significant because Yule log stories about the Old World in American publications before the Civil War sometimes mentioned the role of free *whites* in handling the preparation of Yule logs in the Old World. In an 1858 *Charleston* (SC) *Daily Courier* article dating Yule log ceremonials to Charlemagne's being crowned Holy Roman Emperor by Pope Leo III in Rome on Christmas Day, AD 800, the author explained that Yule logs were "always selected for the vast chimney" and dragged to the fireplace by "Stout and ungainly yeomen." One Christmas later, the same sheet reported the "ungovernable mirth" erupting "in the olden time" when a "couple of sturdy fellows" would drag "knotty and ponderous" Yule blocks into English parlors.[15]

Given how much European folkloric traditions about white yeomen and Yule logs circulated in America *before* the Civil War, one must consider whether these legends inspired all the post–Civil War accounts in the United States of enslaved southern Blacks earning longer Christmas holidays by soaking Christmas back-logs that lie at the heart of this book. After all, it is well known that prior to the Civil War, Americans found it difficult to wean themselves from a long-standing preference for English books and magazines over the works of their own countrymen, despite nationalistic appeals that Americans should instead support native-born authors and homegrown publications. And these very US-read English writings sometimes reported that it was a tradition in northern England in more "primitive" times to determine Christmas booze distributions among *white servants* by the length of time Yule logs burned, a clear parallel to extra vacation time for slaves according to Yule logs.[16]

Pre–Civil War American magazines and newspapers spread this servant–ale–Yule log connection, along with their mentions of how white servants hauled those logs into baronial halls in the first place. As a Lancaster, Pennsylvania, newspaper explained during Christmas 1848, among the heathen people of the British Isles, servants had been entitled to "ale at their meals" so long as their Christmas or Yule logs "kept burning." Tracing Yule log customs to Druidism, the *New York Herald* in 1859 claimed that Yule logs in ancient days were expected to last from Christmas until New Year's Day. While "the Christmas block lasted the servants were entitled to ale." One Massachusetts paper claimed that before the "heathen Saxons" crossed the English Channel, it was believed "in some of the northern counties of England" that "so long as the log lasted, the servants were entitled to ale at their meals." Could it be, in other words, that American tales of enslaved people tricking their masters with soaked Yule logs originally derived from English literature?[17]

Both English and early American Yule log legends concerned manual workers, the passage of time, and the calculation of labor bonuses. Significantly, both also portrayed employers positively by emphasizing their encouragement of the extra holiday benefits their Yule logs facilitated. Did British legends about yeoman laborers' ale morph once across the Atlantic into American mythologies about slaves and Yule logs? A late-century Montana newspaper implied that process by asserting that, at Christmas, "darkies" in the South "befo' the wah" had been "treated by the wealthy planters much the same as were the tenants on the baronial estates in the early days of Merrie England," including having holiday "as long as the yule log would burn."[18] And so did a novel published in the United States before the Civil War.

Written by a native of London, England, who emigrated to the United States and lived in the South for over a decade, this tale raised the matters of Christmas vacation benefits for enslaved southern Blacks and Yuletide ale benefits for English white servants in consecutive sentences! Released in 1854 by Evans and Dickerson, a New York City establishment on Broadway, William Carey Richards's didactic novel for boys and girls, *Harry's Vacation; or, Philosophy at Home*, taught scientific principles for youthful readers indirectly through its narrative plot. The dropping of a dish by a servant, for example, inspires a digression by one of Richards's characters into discourses on gravity. And that same didactical element governed the novel's appropriation of Christmas holiday traditions across different American regions and on both sides of the Atlantic Ocean.

Harry's Vacation revolves around an extended Christmastime gathering of family and friends of a retired physician and his children at a farm called Beechwood at some distance from an unspecified northern city. At breakfast on Christmas morning, Edward Vivian, a close college friend of another guest, an English immigrant named "Mr. Oldbuckle," interrupts debate contrasting New Englanders' lack of enthusiasm about Christmas with enthusiasm about the holiday in Old England. Vivian insists that southerners in America, at least, took Christmas celebrating seriously. Explaining that he had once passed the entire month of December at the town residence in Charleston, South Carolina, of a college friend, as well as at that friend's father's "Roseland" plantation, a slaveholding of nearly two hundred adult and child laborers,

Vivian reveals his fascination with the Christmas "sports and frolics" of "servants" on the plantation while they were excused from labor responsibilities. Wishing to know more, the English emigree Oldbuckle asks, "Do they have a Yule log in the South?" Vivian's startling answer?: "Oh! yes; and the servants are cunning enough to protract their holiday by selecting the largest and toughest log of black gum which they can find, and by soaking it in the creek beforehand, to make it burn slowly." Upon hearing this, Oldbuckle wonders if his host realizes that "in the northern counties of England, the servants were formerly entitled to ale at their meals, so long as the yule log lasted?" Our host then takes note of the "curious coincidence" between Oldbuckle's point and "what Mr. Vivian says of the southern yule log," before the conversation turns to Christmas decorations in the slave states.[19]

Since *Harry's Vacation* appeared in print seven years after the *Elkton Cecil Whig* published its piece on Eastern Shore enslaved people in Maryland and Yule logs, it would be misleading to imply that this antebellum children's novel originated Yule log–soaking lore in the United States. What is worth noting, however, is that a lot of Americans, far more than ever looked at that *Cecil Whig* column, must have read this story and for that reason it may have influenced literary and news renditions about Yule log soakings later in the century.

In this respect, it is helpful to know something about author William Carey Richards's biography. After arriving in America with his family in 1831, he settled initially in Hudson, New York, while his father served as minister of a Baptist church. However, in 1840 he relocated to the South following his graduation from the Hamilton Literary and Theological Institution (today's Colgate University) in upstate New York. Although William married New Englander Cornelia Holroyd Bradley, a woman who made her own mark as a schoolteacher and published writer, he developed strong ties in the southern literary world following his move to the region, becoming professionally and personally associated with William Gilmore Simms. During his southern years, Richards lived variously in Athens, Georgia, and Charleston, South Carolina, in addition to Penfield, Georgia, where his family had moved in 1834, all the while bent on improving literature in the slave states. A succession of magazines depended on Richards's editorship during his southern years, including *Georgia Illustrated*, the *Orion*, the *Southern Literary Gazette*, *Richards' Weekly Gazette*, and the *Schoolfellow*.[20]

Richards moved back north (to New York City) in 1852, well before *Harry's Vacation*'s release in 1854 prior to Christmas, but he remained a southern literary light in the minds of slave state residents, ensuring his new novel would receive a good share of attention in the South. On December 8, 1854, the New York City correspondent of the *Charleston Daily Courier* notified his paper that "Wm. C. Richards, who is favorably known and esteemed both in this city and the South . . . has just published a pleasant holiday book, entitled 'Harry's Vacation, or Philosophy at home,' and refreshed *Courier* readers' memories with the reminder that Richards had once been "editor of the Southern Literary Gazette" and accomplished much "literary labor . . . during his residence among us." When the book was announced, moreover, it was advertised for sale locally for $1 in leading newspapers throughout the country, including prominent newspapers in Virginia and North Carolina, the two states whose newspapers and magazines later in the century would do more to circulate tales of slaves soaking Yule logs than publications in any other state.[21]

Though there seems no way to prove that American tales about Blacks soaking Yule logs were inspired by legends about Christmas ale for the English working class, *Harry's Vacation* makes one wonder. Its author, after all, was English by upbringing. American-born fiction authors, in contrast, omitted Yule log soakings in their prose, even in scenes involving southern Christmas activities. In the popular and prolific mid-nineteenth-century novelist Emma D. E. N. Southworth's story "Hickory Hall," first published serially in the antislavery paper *The National Era* in 1850 and 1851, her character Ferdinand Field accompanies a Harvard College classmate named Wolfgang Wallraven (the "eldest son and heir of an immensely wealthy Virginia planter and slaveholder") to the Wallraven family's Virginia plantation and shabby mansion Hickory Hall for the Christmas holiday. On arrival, the pair's carriage is greeted at the gate by an "old white-headed negro," and at night, a "blazing hickory fire" warms Ferdinand's bedroom. But no "white-headed negro" nor any other Black domestic tends a "Yule log" during Ferdinand's stay. It would have been so tempting to insert such detail had Southworth known or heard about such a colorful custom occurring in Virginia. She lived in Washington, DC, not all that far away from Hickory Hill's Shenandoah Valley locale.[22]

✳✳✳

Given the paltry amount of hard contemporary evidence, or even soft evidence, that enslaved African Americans before the Civil War coaxed their masters into giving them long Christmas holidays by soaking Yule logs in nearby ponds, swamps, and streams, is it safer to assume that very few if any such instances occurred than to assume that they did? With the notable exception of *Harry's Vacation* and two newspaper items, so far as I can tell southern whites never suggested that such customs repeated themselves annually each Christmas, even when they mentioned Yule logs. A decade after William Gilmore Simms gave the white Colonel Openheart full credit for carrying in the Christmas back-log in his novel *Maize in Milk*, the magazine

Southern Field and Fireside ran a supposedly nonfiction account by one "M. M. Of Walnut Grove," a slaveholding mistress, conveying the same impression that Yule logs in the Old South were large pieces of wood with no special meaning for the South's coerced laborers. M. M.'s piece describes a warmish prior Christmas during which she and her guests debate whether they might dispense with burning that year's designated Yule log, an "enormous" oak. In this article's take, Yule logs were all about white holiday comforts, not Black deviousness. Though M. M. is only making an aside, these few words reinforce the impression conveyed by Simms's much longer account—that enslaved people were divorced from whatever Yule log customs, if any, survived from England in the Old South.[23]

One might protest with the counterargument that, with scattered exceptions, southern laws and white labor management practices before the Civil War denied literacy to enslaved people—the very people who knew the most about what was going on in the Black quarters on their plantations. Such prohibitions on teaching slaves to read and write not only mitigated the danger that slaves could learn how to forge travel passes from their masters that would facilitate their escape from bondage; such denials also lessened the likelihood that enslaved people might gain inspiration from written accounts of how white abolitionists in the North condemned their condition and demanded their emancipation. Had enslaved people been educated, they might well have written how they tricked enslavers into giving them extra-long Christmas vacations by soaking Yule logs. Obviously, however, they could not do that. In fact, even if they had the writing skills to do it, they would have had every motive to keep secret a trick that advantaged them in their daily struggles against the constraints of bondage.

Still, if Yule log–soaking customs were as common on antebellum southern plantations as later legend insisted, it is curious that escaped slaves who reached the North and described their prior experiences in published autobiographies never mentioned them, not even in their sometimes-lengthy descriptions of Christmas holiday time on the places where they had toiled. Nor did Black northern antebellum newspapers pay any attention to Yule log trickery in the South. The antebellum northern Black press appears to have been totally oblivious to the role of Yule logs in enslaved culture in the South. Northern Blacks, so far as we can tell from printed sources, not even those who had escaped from Maryland and Alabama (the sites for those two newspaper reports about slaves and Yule logs), mentioned slave soaking tricks, though they sometimes did comment on other holiday customs involving enslaved people.

When the pioneering Black weekly *Freedom's Journal* of New York City—America's first Black newspaper—ran a story on "The Yule Clog" in

1828, it claimed that such clogs still burned in north English kitchens and farmhouses where drinking, singing, and storytelling accompanied the "ceremony" of bringing these objects "into the house." The piece, however, not only never mentioned the custom being preserved across the Atlantic but also virtually ruled out any insinuation of Yule logs having any bearing on slavery in the United States. How could it, given its specification that Yule clogs in the Old World were always lit on Christmas Eve and were expected to flame out by Christmas morning? If the Yule clog failed to last *a single night*, cottage owners considered it an omen of bad luck to come. (Another superstition, the paper added, had to do with "squinting" persons: if a squinter arrived while the log burned, that too was a bad sign!)[24] One night, I would hasten to add, does not make the week or more of slave vacation time that later yarns connected to southern Yule logs.

Chapter 3

Uncle Ned's Big Laugh

Whether American slavery dates from the arrival of enslaved people in Spanish Florida in the 1500s, John Rolfe's buying "twenty Negars" off a Dutch warship arriving in colonial Virginia in 1619, or later colonial statutes legalizing lifetime bondage, a *minimum* of two and a half centuries passed before Yule log–soaking stories gained traction in America. That's a long time. Beginning in the 1870s, however, as Radical Reconstruction in the South whimpered to its end and resurgent ex-Confederates regained their mastery over southern politics, stories started popping up in American newspapers and magazines about how, before the Civil War, enslaved plantation laborers would soak Yule logs and trick their masters. As a Kansas paper reported, it had been "the custom in some portions of the south" for slaves to enjoy Christmas holidays as long as a maximum-sized Yule log burned. In "one case, in Kentucky," enslaved people even saturated their log with water for extra time off by submerging it "in a marshy piece of ground." The more I waded through late nineteenth-century American publications, the more such accounts I came upon. In number, they dwarfed the three pre–Civil War sources connecting Yule logs to the Christmas holidays of enslaved people.[1]

And in the process of scrutinizing these reports, it gradually dawned on me why they were authored in the first place. As largely refurbished versions of antebellum southern polemicists' proslavery arguments, they were written with few exceptions by white southerners with propagandistic intentions. Without outright demanding slavery's revival, these self-justifying tales reassured white southerners of their own legitimacy and decency as American citizens following their treasonous effort in 1861 to shatter their country and create a new nation dedicated to slavery's preservation and expansion. They belonged to a constellation of regional deterrence tactics designed to help dissuade northern politicians and the northern voting public from ever again intervening in southern race relations as they had during Reconstruction. Lurking behind the quirky, colorful prose of Gilded Age Yule log stories was a deep-seated urge among white southerners to cast themselves, their recent political history, and their racial biases in as positive a light as possible.

Such intent helps explain why one late nineteenth-century Maryland newspaper's Yule log–soaking story drawn from the South's "Dreamy Past" claimed that in antebellum days, "no class of people . . . so much enjoyed the holiday season as the colored folks, especially the slaves." In that spirit, the paper described a supposedly kindly master who rooted for his favorite enslaved person to choose a back-log that would burn slowly so that he would have an excuse to give him an extra-long vacation. He genuinely cared for the people he forced into working for free, in other words. By extension, the story implied that all southern slaveholders were kindly, humane people anxious about their slaves' welfare.[2]

✳✳✳

Although it is difficult to pinpoint when Yule log–soaking stories truly began infiltrating America's popular culture, I would argue that the 1877 Christmas season, the first post–Civil War Yuletide when Yankee occupation could be considered over in all the onetime Confederate states, marked a significant milestone. This was a historical moment when although multitudes of white Americans throughout the country still harbored grievances about slavery, secession, the Civil War, and Reconstruction, legions of others craved an end to the sectional turmoil that had so long roiled the nation. Catering to such yearnings for nationwide reconciliation, American magazines and newspapers across the land opened their pages to nostalgic, highly racist writings minimizing slavery's horrors and stereotyping the Old South's former slaveholding masters and mistresses as benevolent caretakers of helpless Black laborers who otherwise could not have survived on their own as free people. As David W. Blight observes in his classic study *Race and Reunion*, American culture after Reconstruction became "awash in such sentimental reconciliationist literature." In fact, so anxious to appease this national mood were the nation's most popular magazines like *Cosmopolitan* and the *Atlantic Monthly* that they sometimes even solicited southern writers to submit soft-edged stories about pre–Civil War times, pieces every bit as appreciated by northern reading audiences, especially female readers, as by southern readerships.[3]

It was during this Christmas season of 1877 that one of the South's second-tier poets, Innes (formally, James Innes) Randolph (1837–1887), contributed a Yule log–soaking tale to this reconciliationist literature. Randolph's "The Back Log; or, Uncle Ned's Little Game"—an eight-verse poem recounting a chronologically indeterminate antebellum Christmas at a fictional "Thornton Hall" plantation—appeared in the *Baltimore Gazette* the day after

Christmas in 1877. At Thornton Hall, ever since *colonial* times, Christmas's longevity for enslaved people was "measured" by its Yule log's blaze: "For till the back-log burned in two / The darkies on the place were free / To dance and laugh and eat and drink, / And give themselves to jolity [*sic*]." The log itself was huge, knotted, and gnarled, which required "six stout men" to bear it ceremoniously on their shoulders with musical accompaniment and by cadenced steps into the big house's great hall, where the log's flames endured from twilight on Christmas Eve until the hours after New Year's morn.

> He cut the log: for days his face
> > Showed gleams of merriment and craft;
> He often went behind the house
> > And leaned against the wall and laughed,
> > > And called the other darkies round
> > > > And whispered to them in the ear,
> > > And loud the ringing laughter broke;
> > > > For Christmas comes but once
> > > > a year.

And it is Ned who, under the influence of alcohol their master generously provided to Thornton Hall slaves during their holiday from work, admits under pressure from his owner precisely how he had outfoxed his master in the log's preparation, quipping that his admission risked retribution in the form of a whipping from his overseer:

> The revel ceased, the guests went home;
> > The back-log burned in two at last.
> And then old master sent for Ned,
> > Still mellow with protracted grog,
> And asked him where in Satan's name,
> > He picked him out that fire-proof log;
> And Ned with all that dignity
> > That drink confers contrived to speak,
> "I tuk and cut a black-gum log
> > And soaked it nine days in de creek.
> > > I fears it was a wicked thing,
> > > > I'm feared to meet de oberseer;
> > > But den you must remember, sah,
> > > > Dat Christmas comes but once a
> > > > year."

We never learn if Ned gets off unscathed but given the conventions of late nineteenth-century white southern nostalgic literature, he probably would have been excused had there been a ninth verse. Gilded Age/Lost Cause southern writing consistently portrayed antebellum southern slaveholding masters and mistresses as invariably compassionate toward their enslaved people, eliding the cruelties of enforced labor in the South before the Civil War. In such a ninth verse, Old Ned's owner likely would have held his sides, laughed raucously at his slave's effrontery, and shooed Ned back to his lodgings in the slave quarter unscathed. Southern masters, we learn from many tales by Randolph's contemporaries, shared keen senses of humor and liked a good joke, even when the prank was on them.

After all, Randolph's "old master" wholeheartedly displayed such charitable instincts over the holiday anyway, giving his enslaved laborers quite the party, providing them with ample food and drink to feast on, and allowing them to surrender themselves to uninhibited singing and dancing:

> And at the quarter merry ran
> > The fiddle's scrape, the banjo's twang;
> How rhythmic beats the happy feet,
> > How rollicksome the songs they sang.
> No work at all for hands to do,
> > But work abundant for the jaws,
> And good things plenty smoking hot
> > Made laughter come in great yaw-haws,
> > > They frolicked early, frolicked late,
> > > > And freely flowed the grog I fear,
> > > According to the settled rule:
> > > > For Christmas comes but once
> > > > a year.

Randolph's "Back Log" poem rings of a post–Civil War apologia for the Old South's planter class, especially since one of the poem's other verses gives an appealing glimpse of what it was like to be a white participant in Thornton Hall's seasonal festivities. Sleighs come "jingling up across the lawn," bearing "argosies of girls" and "cousins to the tenth remove." Relations kiss each other, cheer each other, dance the Virginia reel, and relate stories about witches and ghosts around the chimney fire.[4]

Whether the poem in any way accurately represents actual behaviors or language by enslaved people before the Civil War, however, is another matter. Even its important refrain "For Christmas comes but once a year," implying that enslaved people had to capitalize on their rare vacation opportunity, lacks credibility as speech originating in plantation slave quarters, though Black laborers could conceivably have appropriated it from their masters and mistresses. That memorable hook derived from a poem by the sixteenth-century English versifier named Thomas Tusser: "At Christmas play and make good cheer / For Christmas comes but once a year." And it is no wonder Randolph plucked this phrasing. The Tusser poem itself had been repeatedly reissued after Tusser birthed it, though its once-a-year refrain had sometimes been recast with slight variations (e.g., "Old Christmas comes But once a year"; "For Christmas came but once a year") in successor poems that other writers disseminated in British anthologies that crossed the Atlantic to the US publishing world. By the 1820s, the refrain was well known enough in South Carolina that one Palmetto State enslaver applied it when writing a holiday pass for a slave named Dick. Dick had permission to seek a wife on another plantation after his own spouse had died on the logic that "Christmas comes but once a year / To give poor nigger happy cheer." A century later, American antiquarian A. S. W. Rosenbach informed *Ladies' Home Journal* readers that Tusser's two lines about Christmas's annual occurrence were "probably the best-known lines on Christmas."[5]

※※※

Who was this poet Innes Randolph? Given the plantation locale for his poem, one might guess he hailed from aristocratic wealth, but this was hardly the case. Innes Randolph circulated on the margins of Dixie's elite aristocracy, despite being a native of Winchester in Virginia's Shenandoah Valley and a member of a branch of Virginia's illustrious Randolph family. This Randolph lineage connected him to Thomas Jefferson and other prominent Old Dominion political and intellectual figures. But it would be a mistake to assume too much from this distinguished genealogy. Innes financial circumstances were relatively modest. He was born the fifth-eldest child in a household that, by 1855, had twelve children.[6]

Innes's parents, whose only slaves in 1860 seem to have been a couple of Black female servants, maintained their residence in Washington, DC, not Virginia, for most of Innes's boyhood and adolescence. There, until 1856, Innes's father, James Randolph Sr., held the minor functionary position of messenger to the doorkeeper of the US House of Representatives. Two years later, James Sr. was admitted to practice law in the federal district's criminal court.[7]

Rather than enroll Innes in a southern collegiate institution, Innes's parents chose to send him north for his advanced education, at a time when southern regional extremists were calling upon white southerners to patronize colleges in their own region rather than enrich the coffers of northern institutions, then a common practice in southern aristocratic families. As a result, in September 1855, Innes enrolled at Hobart College in Geneva in upstate New York, selecting for his concentration its Course of Science and Modern Languages. According to college records, he lasted just two years, leaving little evidence of his time there besides notations on his grades, class attendance, and Geneva Hall residence in the institution's records. Unlike his more accomplished peers, he apparently never gave an oration or performed

musically during public events over the course of his studies. Departing
Hobart degreeless, Randolph turned up next at the State and National Law
School at the Hudson Valley town of Poughkeepsie for some coursework,
before rejoining his family in Washington. There Innes married a Georgetown
woman in her early twenties, Anna Clare King, and began a family; his first
child was born in 1860.[8]

Of course, one did not have to belong to the Old South's plantation gentry
to serve in the Confederate army or contribute to the South's Lost Cause
mythology following Appomattox. After his native state seceded and joined
the Confederacy, Randolph and his wife moved with their young child to
Richmond, and then he and his brothers enrolled in the Confederate army,
with Innes serving as second and then first lieutenant of engineers with post-
ings on General Richard Ewell's staff for part of 1862 and an assignment in
Petersburg that summer. A map of Dinwiddie County, Virginia, that Innes
Randolph signed off on in 1864 turns up in the well-regarded "Hotchkiss
Map Collection" published by the Library of Congress in 1951. But his Civil
War service seems to have been only marginally more noteworthy than his
collegiate studies.[9]

Late in the war, Innes Randolph did receive a lengthy posting in
Richmond, where, according to the reminiscences of Thomas Cooper De
Leon, a Confederate functionary at the capital, he became active in a loosely
organized clique of intellectually inclined men and women known as the
"Mosaic Club," a group that never named officers and gathered irregularly
at "one hospitable parlor, or another." It was during such an assemblage that
Innes first sang a verse he had composed to the melody of "Joe Bowers,"
that would afterward, in January 1867, be published on the eve of Radical
Reconstruction. That piece, titled "The Good Old Rebel," with lyrics identifying their narrator as a soldier in Robert E. Lee's command who had been
wounded three times, would ultimately be reprinted ad infinitum and be
adopted and taken by many as the classic statement of an unreconstructed
southerner who could care less whether he was ever accepted back as a US
citizen with rights restored:

> And I don't want no pardon
>> For what I was and am,
> I won't be reconstructed
>> And I don't care a damn.

In this spunky poem about a Confederate veteran's refusal to accept defeat
or express any humility about the Old South's exploitation of coerced Black
labor before the war or its secession act of disloyalty, Randolph gave vent
to the shockingly bloodthirsty wish that Confederate soldiers had slain an

extra 2.7 million Yankee soldiers before surrendering. He also expressed pride in the Union soldiers he had personally killed, vented his "hate" of the "negro," rebuked the Freemen's Bureau's mission to succor impoverished ex-slaves, and declared loathing for the Declaration of Independence and the US Constitution! The lyrics were over the top. When one Ohio newspaper announced its availability in music stores in Richmond in 1867, it claimed the piece had already been adopted by southern Democrats as a "hymn" to the rebel cause."

In retrospect, that embrace by southern Democrats seems ironic since there are indications Randolph intended the lyrics more as a spoof than as the Confederate polemic it was immediately and long afterward assumed to be. In the 1890s, one of Randolph's boyhood friends went public with a claim that he and Innes had many times laughed over the song's reception since it had been written "in a spirit of humor." The friend also insisted that after the war Innes had been accepted as thoroughly reconstructed as anyone—so appreciated in Yankee circles as to be invited on one occasion to give an address to a reunion of the Union's Army of the Potomac.[10]

Still, even if "Good Old Rebel" was penned to mock Confederate die-hard fanatics, Randolph had served with Rebs, not Bluecoats, during the war. And given that loyalty to the Confederate nation, it is hard *not* to view "Uncle Ned's Little Game" as one of the post-Reconstruction South's opening salvos in the politicization of antebellum Christmas customs as an indirect way of justifying the labor system Dixie's soldiers had just fought to preserve. True, there is a fleeting allusion in the poem to a potential overseer's whipping as retribution for Ned's trick but most people reading this poem would have good vibes about the antebellum plantation-slave's Christmas experience. Its lines deliver a clear message that masters were generous to their bondpeople over the holiday in terms of food, drink, and time off, and that laborers in turn were joyful because of their masters' laxity. Later revisions and elaborations of the Yule log legend would expand on Randolph's suggestion of slave Yule log deceptions enabling all the fun, while refraining from any insinuations that enslaved laborers risked corporal punishment for the soaking and deception.

And it is precisely because "Uncle Ned's Little Game" spins such a pleasant picture that its dissemination strikes me as significant as Innes's better remembered "Good Old Rebel." This is especially so because the Ned poem quickly took hold in Maryland and Virginia, states that would become the localities for a high percentage of later versions of Yule log–soaking stories. Days after Randolph's poem was published in the *Baltimore Gazette*, it reappeared in the Harrisonburg, Virginia, *Old Commonwealth* and the Easton, Maryland, *Star*. At the next Christmas (and later in 1887), it found new life in the *Westminster* (MD) *Democratic Advocate*. Possibly, it influenced an article appearing in the *New Orleans Times-Democrat* in 1883 that described back-log soakings during slave times at George Washington's Mount Vernon estate. According to that piece's writer, in "slave times in Virginia, the custom was that the holidays of the slaves lasted as long as the back-logs placed in the great fire places on Christmas Eve lasted," generally for a full two weeks. The explanation why the log lasted so long? "Weeks before the holiday season," slaves would "cut the biggest gum log they could find in the swamp and soak it in water until the time for using it arrived."[11]

More importantly, the poem found its way into compilations designed as speaking materials for orators at public events, like one John G. James, superintendent at the Texas Military Institute at Austin, published in 1879. Soon, speakers at recitals and school exercises nationwide were performing it, including a "Miss Cox" in far off Butte, Montana, who delivered it during a recital at Butte's Good Templars' Hall. Apparently, it remained popular afterward in the southern states. During the Great Depression of the 1930s, the *Richmond* (VA) *News Leader* ran Randolph's poem once more and the *Nashville Banner* explained its theme in detail in a piece on lingering old southern Christmas customs traceable to colonial Virginia and "'Merrie England.'" The *Banner* credited Randolph for helping to preserve traditional southern plantation Christmas customs.[12]

✳✳✳

A decade after Innes Randolph's tale about Uncle Ned's Yule log captivated readers in Maryland and Virginia, slave Yule log soakings had a second breakthrough in US print culture. In its holiday issue for December 22, 1887, the Boston area weekly magazine *The Youth's Companion*, which dated to antebellum times and boasted a circulation of nearly four hundred thousand,[13] carried an anonymously authored piece titled "The Holly Back Log." This story held many of the elements of racialized Yule log yarns that we are concerned with in this book, starting with its first paragraph.

After divulging that for all "colored people" in slave times a holiday celebration of feasting, singing, and fiddle-playing in the quarters commenced on Christmas Eve and "lasted as long as the back-log burned in the great fire burned in mas'rs kitchen," the writer provided specifics. Enslaved people before the Civil War chose the "biggest back log" that could "do duty" (that is, fit in the fireplace); and in places like Mississippi, where holly trees flourished, the "darkies" shrewdly cut them for Yule logs in early fall, while they remained full of sap, and heaved them into rivers to soak for two to three months. Unsurprisingly, the article explained that enslaved people justified extending their holidays in this surreptitious manner with the rationale, "Christmas don't come but once a year, / An' I tink ev'ry nigger ought to have his sheer!" Since each verse in Innes Randolph's Old Ned poem published ten years earlier had as its last line the refrain "For Christmas comes but once a year," I could not help but wonder whether the *Youth's Companion* piece derived from or was inspired by its predecessor, or whether it drew from familiarity with the Englishman Thomas Tusser's verse. Even one of the ways that the Old Ned poem and the new article differed suggests a relationship. Ned's master was perplexed by his slave's trickery. Although in the 1887 anonymously written version, southern slaveholders were complicit in their slaves' shenanigans, they are so in a way that reveals the second writer may be embellishing on the first: "This practice, at first a trick to deceive the masters, came to be known and winked at by the more generous masters, and was looked upon by the slaves as one of their privileges."

It merits mentioning, too, that in an afterthought, the *Youth's Companion* writer suggested that there remained "colored people" who looked back wistfully "to the old plantation Christmas festivities," though admittedly few would trade their freedom "for all the pleasures of the slavery period." Indeed, the author quoted one unnamed and likely imagined Black commentator who, upon being posed that very question "not long ago," mused pointedly about whether an escaped lark would wish a chance back in the cage for "de nice cuttle-fish they done stuck frew de bars." This clear metaphor for enslavement taught that freedom beat bondage but allowed that the latter had some perks.[14]

And this allusion to enslavement's perks conformed to the tone of the nostalgic literature about the South being generated following the overthrow of Radical Reconstruction. Commonly, authors of reconciliationist stories *implied* the superiority of race relations during slave times while ostensibly disavowing insinuations that emancipation required reversing—an assertion that would have been highly inflammatory and disruptive to the ongoing process of reunion between white southerners and northerners. As the historian David Goldfield puts it in *Still Fighting the Civil War*, white southerners in postwar times, though "publicly" professing "good riddance to slavery," "rarely pronounced" it a "moral evil," because that would have amounted to a renunciation of the Confederacy and values many southern whites still held dear. In fact, it was not uncommon during the late nineteenth century for white southerners to claim that slavery was a burden on masters and mistresses rather than a means for their wealth accumulation.[15]

✳✳✳

It was a big deal that the South's Yule log legend gained traction in such a prominent publication as *Youth's Companion*, given the magazine's recent ascendence in the magazine world, a rise so impressive that its advertising space was attracting takers at the then premium rate of $2.50 per line. By the mid-1880s, the *Youth's Companion*'s subscription numbers overshadowed those of all other US periodicals other than mail-order newspapers, which is really saying something since the number of US magazines increased some fivefold between 1865 and 1885 to a total of 3,300 magazines. Even more noteworthy, the *Youth's Companion*'s readership included adults in addition to the youths it initially targeted as its audience. One can see this evolving readership in one of publisher Perry Mason & Co.'s promotional announcements, made just prior to its first 1887 issue, that "the Special Contributors to the Companion for 1887" would include William Dean Howells, Francis Parkman, and T. H. Huxley. As one small-town Maryland paper observed, the magazine offered "something of interest" for every family member. Of course, it did not hurt that Mason's staff resorted to gimmickry to stir up interest and subscriptions, including offering discounts to first-time subscribers and subscription clubs.[16]

Within days of its appearance, this modest magazine article of approximately a half-column of print was republished without attribution by at least two northern newspapers, and it resurfaced again in newsprint in the twentieth century. Very possibly, too, it inspired a similar account published in the *Chautauquan*, another northern periodical that in 1889 was originating out of a publishing operation in Meadville, Pennsylvania. And though we do not know the regional background of the author of the *Youth's Companion* piece, we do know that the *Chautauquan*'s readers were getting their information from a white southerner whose personal history had commonalities with that of Innes Randolph.[17]

In 1889, Charles W. Coleman of Williamsburg, Virginia, a rising magazine poet and essayist whose mother was the daughter of one of Old South's earliest disunionists (the William & Mary College law professor Nathaniel Beverly Tucker), and whose slaveholding father had been a surgeon with the Confederate army,[18] contributed a short piece to the *Chautauquan*'s April number titled "A Virginia Plantation." Within this story, Coleman purposed to imaginatively revisit a representative Virginia plantation from forty years earlier to rescue contemporary readers from what he believed were misleading stereotypes about Old South plantation life—a world that Coleman held was commonly and simplistically misunderstood as dualistically inhabited by an "indolent, arrogant, pleasure-loving, high living" planter class and by "gangs of negro slaves" who endured "their thralldom with seeming content, even merriment." To that end, Coleman described a prototypical slaveholding sitting in tidewater (coastal) Virginia *or* Virginia's Piedmont. Readers gained a sense of its manor house, its master's daily routine, the love of its enslaved population for laughter and song, and the estate's healthy self-sustaining character. This contained world had its own blacksmith, shoemaker, carpenters, and weavers.

Using this composite estate as his model, Coleman detailed a plantation "Christmas tide" where the masters accorded their enslaved populations an entire week off and offered a new variant of the Yule log–soaking story. In his telling, there was "on record" a Virginia master "who granted absolute freedom [from work] so long as the yule-log burned." Given this assurance, the plantation's astute (Black) woodchopper cut a trunk from a "stalwart tree" and soaked it in the swamp for a month, leading to slave quarter celebrations of "prolonged duration" that year.

Unfortunately, I could not trace Coleman's basis for this Yule log custom, since he left no clues regarding how he discovered the "record" for the Virginian who gave slaves their Yule log holidays. Did he read either the Randolph or *Youth's Companion* iteration, or *Harry's Vacation* from prewar times, before writing his own piece? It's hard to know. But the modesty of Coleman's claim is instructive. Very likely, casual readers drew the impression that southern slaveholders commonly pegged enslaved Christmas holidays to Yule log timetables, overlooking Coleman's implication that only one Virginia planter did so in the entire history of the state! And it was not simply the *Chautauquan's* tens of thousands of readers who could have misremembered the piece, since it was immediately republished in *The Congregationalist*, a prominent Boston religious publication.[19]

✳✳✳

Once southern male authors Randolph and Coleman opened America's periodicals and newspapers to Yule log–soaking stories, the cat, so to speak, was out of the bag. This was simply a tale too good for southern writers to pass up, especially the region's white female authors—a cohort that produced a major proportion of the propagandistic glorifications of antebellum southern life, slavery, and Confederate soldiers' wartime bravery that oozed off American publishers' presses following Reconstruction.

Although before the Civil War, southern white women had been notably less politicized than those of their Yankee counterparts famously associated with the abolition and women's rights movements, they nonetheless did have grooming for becoming literary defenders of Dixie in the late nineteenth century. Not only was creative writing a professional outlet that educated southern women could pursue before the war with some hope of success, but they also sought and regularly achieved leadership roles in benevolent societies and local churches during that time. Meanwhile, in their own homes, many southern women were accorded responsibility over their family's historical records—recording, for instance, the births and deaths of family members in heirloom Bibles passed down from their ancestors. Eventually, in the 1850s, girls and young women in the slave states (especially those from elite slave-holding households) became caught up in the sectional crisis roiling relations between the North and the South, so much so that far more than previously, they actively debated politics. They did so at home and at the academies they attended, as well as in their diaries and journals and in their letters to friends.[20]

Then came the war, providing an added jolt in terms of prepping southern white women for public advocacy. During the fighting, many were compelled not only by their own ambitions but also by the dire needs of their communities to labor outside their homes, especially in hospitals, factories, and as government clerks, in roles that had been mostly closed to them in peacetime. Moreover, when Reconstruction arrived, bringing risks for southern men in appearing unrepentant about secession and the war at a time when federal occupation soldiers were all around, southern white women found they could hallow Confederate heroism more "tenaciously" than Confederate veterans themselves and get away with it. Yankee soldiers felt less threatened by unfranchised southern women than by resentful ex-Confederate soldiers. Surrogacy for their menfolk not only allowed many southern women escape from confinement within the domestic sphere into the public domain but more generally provided them a heightened sense of self-fulfillment. So, in the postwar years, they succored struggling Rebel army veterans and organized between seventy-five and one hundred community-based Ladies' Memorial Associations to reinter fallen Confederate soldiers. They also initiated Memorial Day remembrances to preserve a semblance of the South's crushed bid for nationhood. Later, southern white women stood at the forefront of efforts to raise monuments to the Confederate cause.[21]

Ultimately, in 1894, a group of such southern white women gathered in Nashville, Tennessee and created the most effective single entity for promoting Confederate memory and its underlying racial codes—the chapter-heavy United Daughters of the Confederacy (UDC). This was a "memorial army," as historian Caroline E. Janney aptly dubs it, and it enjoyed an explosive growth, reaching more than eight hundred chapters and some forty-five thousand members by 1912. The founders pointedly limited membership to the female kin of Confederate military personnel, women who served the Confederacy themselves in such capacities as civil servants and the female descendants of persons in those two categories. Members devoted themselves to fund-raiding for Confederate monuments and casting a selective southern and Confederate slant over antebellum and Civil War history through public print materials and schoolhouse teaching. UDC "historical committees" pressured educators to rid themselves of textbooks they deemed misleading, especially those suggesting the war was fought over slavery. And the UDC specially purposed itself to indoctrinating future generations by establishing the "Children of the Confederacy" as an auxiliary for young people and by encouraging children to attend UDC events.[22]

It is not surprising, then, that starting around 1889, southern women should assume the lead role in authoring slave Yule log–soaking tales (though the earlier *Youth's Companion* anonymously authored piece might have been a southern woman's work too). I have identified forty-one book-length and shorter memoirs, novels, short stories, short pieces of nonfiction, and speeches by southern white women published between 1867 and 1922 that softened remembrances of human bondage in the South by emphasizing the joy and self-fulfillment enslaved people universally experienced at Christmastime. These works had in common the following themes about antebellum southern plantation Yuletides, though only a few of these works featured all of them: (1) masters showered their slaves, often in elaborate ceremonies, with sometimes expensive, often individually selected, and always highly appreciated presents; (2) masters gave slaves long work holidays; (3) masters threw elaborate feasts that included many delicacies; (4) masters gave slaves unusually generous alcohol allotments; (5) masters let slaves go where they wished and freed them from tight supervision; (6) masters fraternized casually with slaves both in their mansion residences and during visits to their cabins; (7) slaves who remained on their home plantations for Christmas used their time to dress up, court and marry, and joyfully dance until all hours of the morning. And a few of these forty-one works by southern white women related Yule log–soaking incidents that, by highlighting a custom that portrayed masters as kindly persons tolerant of their slaves' misbehavior, complemented other southern efforts to justify slavery, secession, and the Confederacy.

✳✳✳

Perhaps Anna Alexander Cameron (1843–1903), a North Carolina poet and essayist, familiarized herself with the 1887 *Youth's Companion* Christmas issue or the early 1889 *Chautauquan* issue with Charles Coleman's piece before authoring her own Yule log contribution to what might be dubbed a burgeoning subgenre of southern plantation mythologies. An unmarried, lifelong resident of Hillsborough (aka Hillsboro) in central North Carolina, Anna Cameron hailed from a family background programmed to instill in her a devotion to memorializing the Old South, slavery, and the Confederacy.

Anna Cameron's great grandfather on her mother's side, Alfred Moore, was a Revolutionary War Continental Army and militia officer and, later, from 1800 to 1804, associate justice on the US Supreme Court. The owner of a rice plantation called Buchoi in Brunswick County on a branch of the Cape Fear River about four miles from North Carolina's southern coastal port of Wilmington, he also owned land in adjacent New Hanover County as well as "Moorefields"—an upcountry manor house on a farm about three miles outside of Hillsborough in Orange County. Moorefields became the Moore family's summertime refuge from the heat and malarial conditions prevalent in Buchoi's low-lying coastal locale. Judge Moore seems to have held a significant number of enslaved people at Buchoi throughout his late life. The US Census for 1810 credits him with holding ninety-four persons in bondage in Brunswick County. His will, filed in Brunswick County shortly before his death, meticulously described how he wished those bondpeople distributed among family members or sold following his death.[23]

The judge's will devolved much of his landed property to his son Alfred Moore Jr.—who served as the Brunswick County representative in North Carolina's legislature for fourteen years, rising to the speakership of its House of Commons (later House of Representatives)—a bequest with repercussions for Anna Cameron as her mother, Emma Claire Moore, was one of Alfred Jr.'s five children with his wife Rebecca. In 1820, Alfred Jr., who long survived his wife, held ninety-five slaves in Brunswick County alone, with a smaller force at the Moorefields house and farm in Orange County.[24] Although, as we will see later, Alfred divested himself of Buchoi long prior to his own death on July 25, 1837, he held on to his Orange County properties and took up permanent residency at Moorefields for the final years of his life.

Alfred Jr.'s will, filed in Orange County shortly before his death, provided Emma would inherit one-third of the value of his "negroes" in Orange County when they sold following the division of his estate, as well as one-fifth the value of his real estate there including the Moorefields place. This bequest helped support Emma when in December 1837 she married physician William Cameron, despite a rocky engagement period. (The county's representative in the North Carolina House of Commons, William Alexander Graham, noted in a letter to his wife in February that William and Emma Cameron had just had enough of a "blow up" that William had "emigrated to Alabama to endeavor to dissipate his thought in other scenes.") When the Moorefields estate was broken up a decade after Alfred's death, Emma and William received a tract of some three hundred acres valued at $1,000, which they held on to over the years that followed (while two of her sisters occupied the house itself), until William put the extra acreage up for auction in 1844. Meanwhile, Emma and William established their own household and William's medical practice in the town of Hillsborough, where they raised their five children, three girls and two boys.[25]

Although Anna's grandmother (on her father's side), Anne Call Cameron, provided in her own 1856 will that her enslaved "negro man Christopher" be freed and "sent . . . to some free state or country" following her death in recognition of his "meritorious and extraordinary service," there is no evidence that Anna grew up in an unusually liberal southern household when it came

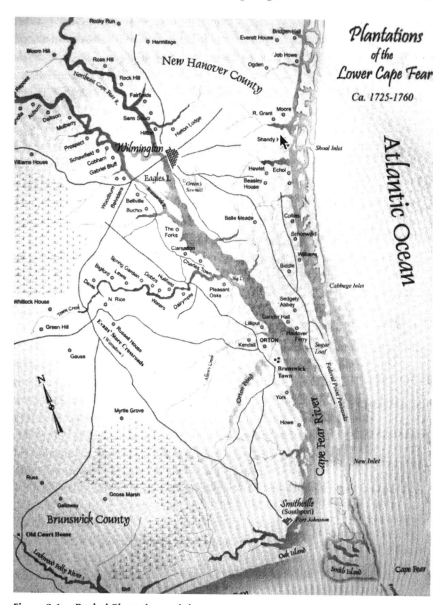

Figure 3.1. Buchoi Plantation and the Lower Cape Fear River, North Carolina.
Source: Alfred Moore Waddell, *A History of New Hanover County and the Lower Cape Fear Region, 1723–1800*, vol. 1 (Wilmington, NC [?]: no publisher indicated, 1909), 39.

to race and slavery. Orange County probate records reveal that her father's William's flight to Alabama in early 1837 had to do with a scheme to establish a new plantation there using as laborers enslaved people held in trust from his father-in-law for his wife and her siblings. Other records suggest that Anna's father lacked moral scruples about selling off slaves to new owners. In 1841, William sold a twenty-eight-year-old slave named John to another North Carolinian for $650. In 1844, a Hillsborough newspaper announced that, on March 25 at the county courthouse, William Cameron would "sell to the highest bidder for cash . . . Six Likely Negroes." In 1850, the US Census taker for Orange County reported a thirty-three-year-old female slave in the William and Emma Cameron household in Hillsborough. A decade later, the last antebellum US Census reported an enslaved Black female aged nine in Anna's parents' house. That nine-year-old was almost certainly the "small negro girl" named Evalina bequeathed to Emma in a codicil to Anne Cameron's 1856 will, to be held in trust for Emma's daughter Sarah Rebecca. Slaves to the Camerons as to most antebellum white southerners embodied chattel property, to be disposed of as they wished.[26]

Anna revealed her youthful support for slavery in a remarkable entry in her Civil War diary that was prompted by an appearance at the Cameron Hillsborough residence of a former family servant. Anna's entry noted how the servant arrived by buggy bearing some oranges from the Camerons' relations at Moorefields, and then lamented how she and her parents and siblings were no longer served by the retinue of Blacks they had commanded in better times:

> "Maum Katie" came to see us this evening. She seems to be so glad when she can come among her former owners. How the old family servants are scattered since our fortunes failed. Oh! I wish we could re-purchase them, but this is impossible in the shattered condition of our *estates*. Poor things how they grieved at being sold.[27]

Clearly Anna Cameron genuinely felt her family had always treated enslaved people humanely and that the people her parents held in bondage appreciated that kindness. But her diary also reveals an obtuseness to the possibility that her family's slaves resented their own situations but rationally feared punishment should they ever unburden themselves to their enslavers. She never seems to have wondered whether her family's servants' despair at being sold had to do with factors other than their affection for the Camerons.

Not only was Anna Cameron from a slaveholding family but her physician father served the Confederacy as captain of the (North Carolina) Orange (County) Light Artillery in 1862 and 1863. And her Confederate connection goes further. One of her first cousins, the University of North Carolina graduate and prewar Wilmington, North Carolina, lawyer, journalist, and local officeholder Alfred Moore Waddell, achieved the rank of lieutenant colonel in the Confederate cavalry. After the war, this same cousin served as a Democrat representing North Carolina's Third Congressional District from 1871 to 1879 and editor, briefly, of the *Charlotte Observer*, before returning to Wilmington. There he gained the city's mayoralty and historical infamy as the white supremacist who spearheaded a horrific 1898 race riot and massacre that ended up in the destruction of the city's Black newspaper and the deaths and expulsions of many Black Wilmingtonians including several who had achieved local political office. That riot put a sudden end to local biracial politics that lasted for decades. Another of Anna's first cousins, James Iredell Waddell, had captained the Confederate cruiser *Shenandoah*—a vessel whose watery and far-ranging rampages from the Atlantic Ocean to the whaling grounds of the South Pacific to the Bering Sea in the final months of the Civil War resulted in the burning of some thirty-two Union vessels and the commandeering of six others.[28]

During the Civil War, Anna, for her part, became so ardent a Reb that she went into a virtual swoon when she ventured to the North Carolina Railroad depot at Hillsborough merely to catch sight of General John Hunt Morgan of the Confederate army who was passing through, and the "hero," though surrounded by a sizable crowd, turned his attention to her ("he clasped our hands in a *hearty* grasp. I was in a whirl of excitement"). Unreconstructed following the war, she wrote in a book review published in 1883 that Confederate soldiers ranked among "the world's most renowned heroes."

Four years later, she wrote Cousin Alfred in 1887 about her continuing resentment that ex-soldiers of the defeated Confederacy had ever felt compelled to eat "humble pie" when speaking about the Civil War for fear of offending northerners. A decade later, in the lead-up to Wilmington's white supremacist uprising, she was described by a sister as "blood thirsty" with anger over Black political power locally. In her later years, she would serve as corresponding secretary of one of the North Carolina chapters of the United Daughters of the Confederacy. Appropriate to her values, the *Raleigh News and Observer*'s obituary of Anna Alexander Cameron would reference the importance to "her heart" of "the cause of her Southland," reporting that her "last active service" to her region had been to help dispense "the Cross of Honor" to Confederate veterans from Orange County.[29]

As part of a regionwide trend toward rehabilitating the reputation of her region's slave regime and its Confederacy, Anna Cameron advanced her own version of Yule log soakings, one far more detailed than the accounts previously appearing in the *Youth's Companion* and *Chautauquan* magazines. She did so in a generously illustrated essay titled "Christmas on the Old Plantation" for the *Home-Maker* magazine's December 1889 issue (a piece republished immediately in a Montpelier, Vermont, newspaper).

She began by maintaining that white southerners recalled antebellum Christmastimes better than any other aspect of the "old plantation life" before the Civil War and explained that her intention in writing was to share those experiences with people who lived in those parts of the country where these customs were "perhaps totally unknown," a comment that hints at soft indoctrination. And in phrasing that exemplifies how the literary reconciliation genre muted all the horrors attending human bondage in the United States, Cameron added that no "history of the negro as he was" would be complete without "a record of the festivals which he enjoyed with an abandonment of mirth and an absolute exemption from care of any sort."

Asserting that antebellum southern plantations were managed similarly at Christmas with modifications depending mainly on the varying wealth of different masters, Cameron universalized Black Yule log–soaking practices as typical throughout the region:

> Early in the fall the negroes searched the woods for the largest tree they could find, felled it, and the first cut was hewed off for a back log, or "yule log," as it was called. Into the creek it was immediately plunged, to soak so that it might resist the action of the fire as long as possible. For just as long as a piece of it remained unburned in the master's fireplace, just so long carnival and holiday held sway on the plantation.

Come Christmas Eve, Cameron explained, slaves extracted these logs from their "watery grave" and hauled them to the master's dwelling, where on Christmas morning they were positioned in the fireplace and ignited amid considerable "ceremony."

The balance of Cameron's piece casts other plantation Christmas happenings in a favorable light, covering slave marriages, dances, and the dispensing of extra provisions and clothing to enslaved people from the plantation smokehouses and storerooms, as well as a game slaveholders played with enslaved house servants throughout the South on Christmas morning widely known as "Christmas gif'"—in which any person taken by surprise on awakening that morning was expected to hand a present to the surpriser (playful contests that masters purposely lost as a way of conferring holiday gifts on and pleasing servants who did unfree labor for them all year long). Additionally, Cameron describes how a white-wigged, enslaved banjo player named "Uncle Mingo" and a "young mulatto" fiddler named Lisburn play the "Virginia Reel" (with Mingo calling the dance steps) at the big house's holiday ball for white gentlemen and ladies, after which the musicians are rewarded by "Old master" with large glasses of apple toddy. Cameron concludes with the annual arrival at plantation mansions of "Coonah" dancers, an allusion to a custom (often called "John Canoe" or "John Kunering") nearly exclusive to coastal North Carolina before the Civil War, when tattered slaves—clothed in rags, animal skins, masks, horns, and other exotic apparel—would turn up

Christmastime at plantation residences amid dancing, horn blowing, the rattling of bones and triangles, frenetic dancing, and the like. Cameron's account has the Coonahs led by a whip-bearing large man and explains that white onlookers threw on the piazza floor "a shower of nuts, fruits, candy, silver coins, and pennies" as tips to satisfy their entertainers so they will willingly move on to other households. In her only comment remotely suggestive that there might be anything disturbing about this ritual, Cameron acknowledges that John Canoers could seem intimidating, saying that southern children regarded the Cooners's dance performances with a mix "of delicious horror and fear" due to the "barbaric" nature of performers' costumes.[30]

Although Cameron, as mentioned earlier, claimed her details about plantation Christmases were representative of her entire region's pre–Civil War customs, it is dubious whether we should take all of them, most especially when it comes to Yule log soakings and revelries, at face value. As we will see, she possibly based her account exclusively on stories about a single plantation that she may never have visited.

*** *** ***

Though by 1890 accounts of enslaved people growing their Christmas vacations by means of Yule log soakings had appeared in US newspapers and magazines, most of those publications had modest circulations and visibility. Publisher Marion Harland's *Home-Maker*, for example, only enjoyed a five-year print run that lasted between 1888 and 1893, never attracting an extensive readership. As a result, this legend had yet to go "viral" in the media of the day. Meanwhile, the country remained awash in Christmastime articles about Old English holiday traditions and casual allusions to Yule logs providing warmth from winter fires. Two days after Christmas in 1890, a Georgia newspaper remarked offhandedly that the Atlanta journalist and state representative Clark Howell had been "toasting his feet by the Yule log" on visiting the offices of the *Augusta Chronicle* that holiday.[31]

The Christmas 1891 issue of the highly popular *Ladies' Home Journal*, however, reached large numbers of readers with a story about enslaved people preparing and soaking Yule logs,[32] a piece authored by Anna Cameron's unmarried younger sister Rebecca, who shared Anna's devotion to Confederate memory and co-resided with Anna and their elder unmarried sister Emma in their widowed father's home in Hillsborough.[33] In her mid-teens when the Civil War erupted in 1861, Rebecca Cameron had immediately identified with the Confederacy, joining a women's sewing circle in Hillsborough that was making shirts for North Carolina soldiers going off to fight and mulling anxiously over the new nation's political setbacks and military casualties. Her early wartime letters bewailed "Outrages" committed by

"Lincoln's minions" at Hampton and Alexandria, Virginia, and railed at the "contemptible" news that Kentucky was resisting secession and remaining in the Union. Upon learning a North Carolina regiment manned by some of her own relations and acquaintances had been "*chopped up*" at Manassas (the first battle of Bull Run), she spewed venom. "Auntie!" she wrote in a letter posted from "*Southern Confederacy*" on July 24, "It makes my heart ache, to think of the noble fellows whom I had an acquaintance with lying cold and stiff on the gory field or maimed and writing in the hospital." And she added that it made her blood boil to contemplate "the *noble* hearts stilled by infamous Yankee bullets." But Rebecca took consolation that the sacrifices had not been in vain. After all, thousands of Yankees had fallen before "our *unerring* bullets" and the fighting had culminated in a "great" battlefield victory.[34]

Following the war, Rebecca wrote pieces for regional publications like *The Southern Opinion, Southern Home Journal*, and *Banner of the South*, including the novelette "Eleanor Staunton, by a Southerner" for *The Banner of the South. Southern Opinion* was edited by the former secessionist and now virulent anti-Reconstruction brother (H. Rives Pollard) of Edward Pollard, the Richmond newspaper editor who in 1866 authored the pro-Confederate tract *The Lost Cause*—the polemical work which originated the phrase that would become so identified with defenses of the Confederacy that it persists to this day in debates over Confederate monuments, flags, and name commemorations.[35]

Shortly prior to the publication of her piece on Christmas in *Ladies' Home Journal*, Rebecca collected funds for and promoted the erection of a monument to honor native Virginian and Confederate officer Randolph Shotwell—who had been captured by Union forces and imprisoned during the war, contested Radical Reconstruction after the war as a Democratic newspaper proprietor in North Carolina, and suffered confinement in a federal penitentiary for suspected complicity with the Ku Klux Klan (though Shotwell never seems to have formally affiliated with it). Shortly after she published her account, Rebecca would serve as Orange County vice president of the North Carolina Monumental Association, a group sponsoring a monument at the state capital in Raleigh to "those who laid down their lives in the cause of the South." Later she would join the United Daughters of the Confederacy, becoming president of the George B. Anderson Chapter No. 335 of the UDC in Hillsborough, a group that chose her sister Emma as its corresponding secretary. And like sister Anna, Rebecca became infuriated at the ability of Blacks in Wilmington to hold political office long after Radical Reconstruction was expunged almost entirely everywhere in the South.[36]

Just weeks before the Wilmington race riot of November 1898, Rebecca sent her cousin Alfred a summons to war against Wilmington's Black political class and their white allies. In an eight-page diatribe almost exclusively devoted to what she dubbed a "bugle cry," she challenged Alfred's southern manliness by telling him that women were "amazed, confounded and bitterly ashamed of the acquiescence and quiescence of the men of North Carolina" at the status quo. She asked why North Carolina's white males had yet to use their shotguns for remediation and intimated she had personally told an ex-major in the Confederate army that the state's white men might as well empty their shotguns "into the hearts of all the decent white woman in the state" if they intended to continue tolerating "Negro supremacy"! Further taunting her cousin, Rebecca quoted Solomon from the Old Testament's Ecclesiastes, particularly his alluding to there being "a time to kill," and tried to inspire action on Alfred's part by bringing up how his forebears on the Cape Fear turned out against British in the War for Independence. Once Alfred made a finish "once for all" of Black officeholding in Wilmington, it would be time for the calling of a statewide convention to "disfranchise, now and forever all the negroes" by means of constitutional alterations.[37]

Southern nationalism and race hatred, however, were hardly the sole drivers of Rebecca Cameron's literary career. Monetary needs also nudged her ahead. In 1867 and 1868, she wrote two letters baring a connection between her literary career and her dependence on remuneration from it. In the first, she pursued a staff position in the magazine business, explaining to a potential employer, "I . . . prefer to make an [exclusive] engagement with one periodical" while emphasizing that she needed to learn "if you *pay* your contributors!" In the second, she informed the literary editor of *The Southern Opinion*, the noted poet and regional defender Paul Hamilton Hayne, that she wished to sever her relationship with the magazine, since for all her contributions she had "never received one cent from Mr. Pollard" and she could scarcely "afford gratuitous contributions." In contrast, she would get reimbursed for her much later holiday article when it was accepted by Edward W. Bok for the *Ladies' Home Journal*'s December 1891 issue (originally titled "Christmas on a Rice Plantation" but published as "Christmas on an Old Plantation"). Bok promised her that the magazine's cashier would "remit" "in due course" for her submission. Financial considerations, in other words, melded into the ideology that inspired the publishing instincts of Rebecca Cameron.[38]

Like her sister Anna, Rebecca Cameron front-loaded her southern holiday essay with an explanation of plantation Yule log traditions, claiming definitively that Christmastime "lasted from Christmas Eve—always a half-holiday—until the Yule log burnt in two after New Year's Day." Then she launched into her version of the custom, contending that the very "first work done in the New Year" by the plantation "negroes" was not anything agricultural, but rather to select their "Christmas back-log," as they termed it, for the "next Christmas fire," while it remained a full year away. This selection process, she told her readers, was managed by the "driver" (an enslaved, trusted laborer who, under the authority of a master or overseer was assigned disciplinary and other field oversight responsibilities on many large plantations). It was this driver who assembled a group of his best "axe hands" and sent them into a nearby swamp to cut down amid much hoopla "the biggest, knottiest, most indestructible cypress tree that could be found." While felling their target, the hands "chanted a part of the 'Coonah' song" that went "'Christmas comes but once a year / Ho rang du rango! / Let everybody have a share / Ho rang du rango!'" Note the reappearance, here again, of Innes Randolph's once-a-year refrain, which raises the possibility that Rebecca Cameron was familiar with Uncle Ned and either consciously or subconsciously plagiarized the phrasing.

After the log was cut, the slaves measured the length of its "butt [fattest] end" to match the maximum length of the hall fireplace in "de gret house." They sawed it off and hauled it to a plantation canal where it would be anchored to soak for the next twelve months. Lest her readers not grasp the obvious point, Rebecca emphasized that the object was "to keep it from being burnt out too soon; for as long as the Yule log burned the whole plantation force had holiday." Then she added that one or two days before the next Christmas, this log was dragged to the big house and bedded in sand temporarily, to drain off excess moisture. Finally, on Christmas morning, the log was carried into the mansion's "holly-wreathed hall" and laid on a bed of wet ashes, before some "fragrant, resinous lightwood and seasoned oak" was placed in the forefront of the fireplace (to crowd backward the Yule log) and ignited. In the balance of her piece, Rebecca, much as her sister had done in her essay of a couple of years earlier, detailed many other features of plantation Christmastimes, including six paragraphs on the "John Coonahs" that Anna's piece had highlighted.

Unlike her sister, however, Rebecca Cameron never implied that her piece represented plantation Christmas customs universally in the pre–Civil War South. Rather, she clarified at its beginning that her descriptions were autobiographical, derived exclusively from what she had observed and experienced as a child visiting her grandfather's Cape Fear River rice plantation in Brunswick County at Christmastime (though she never mentioned Buchoi or Alfred Moore Jr. by name). This was a story about "Christmas holidays on his plantation" alone, though she adds that "Coonah" customs entered South Carolina from Barbados before making their way into North Carolina, and at one time had been known on the Georgia and Florida coastlines and in New Orleans as well as in the Carolinas (implying that enslaved workers in North Carolina were not the only southern Blacks allowed to participate in such celebrations). What she did not reveal in her article was that enslavement was a particularly grim affair in the lower Cape Fear area where Buchoi was situated, with dense populations of Blacks laboring in harsh, isolated conditions to make profits for their owners in rice, turpentine, and naval stores. Her article was designed to reassure readers about the South's racial past, not to inflame passions.[39]

By describing her grandfather as an "amiable, easy going master" whose heart lay more in literature and carrying on the customs of his "English ancestors" than in rice planting, Cameron establishes herself as a witness and casts her essay dually as history *and* autobiography. It was *she* and other children in the big house who were scrubbed by the Moore family's "mammy" "within an inch of our lives" on Christmas Eve so that they would be properly clean for the events of the next day. It was *she* and the other children who were roused by the plantation horn at four o'clock the next morning, hearing as they arose "the men" struggling to get the Yule log through the hallway. It was *she* and the other children who inspected the presents left for them in their stockings by Santa Claus as *her* grandfather prepared to dole out tumblers of just-whipped-up eggnog, first to his guests and then ceremoniously to his torchlight-bearing enslaved people, all of whom were summoned to the piazza by the driver's drum beating. It was *her* grandfather and the women of his household who distributed to the laborers all kinds of Christmas gifts from hampers on the piazza as well as coins for each Black man, woman, and child. It was *her* grandfather, or "ole Master" as the slaves knew him, who, after leading the assembled white "gentlemen" and hounds on a deer hunt, presided over a grand ball for the white guests, during which the slave "Uncle Robin" assumed the role of lead fiddler, looking "absurd" because the Moores had dressed him in the regimental uniform that *her* great grandfather (the Supreme Court judge) had worn in the American Revolution. And it was *she* and *her* relations who during the Cooners appearance "dared not draw a breath" when the performers arrived at the hallway door, as *their* hearts beat tumultuously from anxiety.

Symmetrically enough, Rebecca's ending circles back to her beginning:

> But, meanwhile, the Yule log has been burning out. Uncle Tony, coming in to mend the fire, discovers that the log is only two chunks now. When the family go to dinner he will carry one chunk out, extinguish the fire upon it, and lay it in the path between the house and the kitchen. The next morning he will put it away in the corner of the wood-house to start the next year's Christmas fire. But while it lies in the path it is a sign well understood. Over the plantation has fled the news, "De back log done burn in two, an' Cousin Tony done lay um out!"
>
> The long merry festival has ended. The negroes will dance and frolic all night long, and to-morrow, at daybreak, the overseer's horn will blow; each gang will muster under its head man, and the plantation work begin.

✳✳✳

Given the complementary accounts of the two Cameron sisters, it would be easy to conclude that *both* women were reporting intimate understandings of southern Yule log customs before the Civil War based on their own Yuletide visit or visits to Buchoi during antebellum times. Certainly, this was my reaction when I encountered, initially, Rebecca Cameron's account and then, more recently, stumbled upon Anna Cameron's more obscure earlier piece. I had no doubt, in either case, that the two Cameron narratives were crafted to cast southern slaveholders, especially their own family, in the best positive light imaginable. Grandfather Moore was just too kindly and considerate, and the family a bit too jovial and generous to enslaved laborers, to take everything at face value. But I also had no reason to suspect that these articles were wholly or partially fabricated. After all, both Cameron women had been in their late teens when the Civil War erupted, an age when we would expect them to have been keenly observant of the world around them. Surely the Christmastime events they discussed, including Yule log customs, occurred during their visits, even if they embellished some details to make their narratives more compelling reading. Many contemporary accounts from pre–Civil War times affirm that masters *did* throw feasts for slaves at Christmas, bestow Christmas presents on enslaved workers, and request talented enslaved musicians to accompany their balls, where they were generally rewarded with tips. And there are enough pre–Civil War commentators who mentioned John Cooner performances in North Carolina, including the famous escaped slave Harriet Jacobs, to validate what the Cameron sisters later wrote about them. Given, then, that most details in the Cameron articles squared roughly with known historical knowledge, I initially jumped to the conclusion that their publications strongly indicated that, despite my suspicions, slave Yule log soakings were a thing in the Old South!

Yet, the more I learned about these Camerons, the more I wondered whether my eureka moment amounted to mirage rather than reality. My initial doubts arose when I came across a report from Wilmington in 1825 that appeared in a Boston newspaper, about two decades before either Anna or Rebecca Cameron were born: Alfred Moore Jr.'s residence at Buchoi had just been "totally consumed by fire." If the house had never been rebuilt, its burning obviously would rule out any possibility that Anna or Rebecca had ever been inside its walls. However, reconstruction does seem to have occurred, since in 1838 a newspaper notice alluded to Buchoi's "dwelling house, with necessary outhouses, a large brick barn, and other improvements." Sometime afterward, however, the house met with disaster again. A post–Civil War letter in Rebecca's papers mentioned a woman living in Buchoi's vicinity who had reported that "[w]here Buchoi'[s] residence stood" was now "ploughed and planted in corn," adding that "all of the buildings were burnt you know." Possibly the burning was an allusion to an incident before the Civil War, though it is more likely the destruction was the work of a Union raiding party during the conflict.[40]

In either case, it is plausible that Anna and Rebecca Cameron visited the rebuilt Buchoi main house during the 1840s or 1850s, since the house likely still stood during at least part of their childhoods. The second red flag I encountered, however, was less easy to dismiss: their Grandfather Moore died in 1837. Despite the claim in Rebecca's reminiscence that she (and by extension her sister, since their articles overlapped in many ways) had been eyewitness to her grandfather's customs at Buchoi at Christmas, she could never have witnessed them. She was born in 1845, eight years after her grandfather's death. Nor, for the record, could her older sister Anna have experienced Christmas with their grandfather, because Anna was born in 1843, six years after Grandfather Moore's death! Further mucking the waters, the plantation may not have even remained in the family between the time of Alfred Moore Jr.'s death and the point when Anna and Rebecca were old enough to visit the place and take stock of what they saw. According to records at the University of North Carolina's Southern Historical Collection, Alfred Moore Jr., by a deed dated in 1830, seven years before his death, gave the title to Buchoi to his daughter Elizabeth and his son-in-law Francis Nash Waddell. And twelve years after that, the year before Anna Cameron's birth, a Wilmington newspaper noted that the "valuable" Buchoi rice plantation, already purchased from "F. N. Waddell and Wife" by Alfred Jr.'s son-in-law Hugh D. Waddell, was now being sold at a public auction scheduled for the Smithville Court House on June 7 (1842). Perhaps T. C. McIlhenny was the buyer. In 1858, one Frederick K. Lord bought Buchoi from McIlhenny. At any rate, the place does not seem to have belonged to Anna's and Rebecca's relations after 1842.[41]

Given this sequence of events, it is entirely possible that the Moore sisters imagined every element of their story/stories about Christmas at Buchoi, most likely with Rebecca squeezing a second article out of the topic, and extra remuneration for the family, by embellishing her sister's prior work. Of course, it is entirely possible that even though Anna and Rebecca never shared a Christmas holiday at Buchoi with their grandfather, they nonetheless drew their material from family oral legend, passed down to them from someone in their very large extended family who had passed one or more Christmases at the Cape Fear River plantation. But in that case, the stories would have been, at best, secondhand. Given the obvious lies in Rebecca's piece, it is just as likely they never heard such tales from their relations in the first place. Rebecca was certainly capable of writing fiction. Using the pseudonym H. M. LeGrange, she had already published a novel titled *Salted with Fire*. That work had appeared in 1872, nineteen years before her *Ladies' Home Journal* Christmas piece.

Regardless of whether the Cameron sisters' Yule log tales were fabricated, the younger sister's version, immediately republished in a Gettysburg, Pennsylvania, newspaper, had more staying power than the elder sister's, surely attributable to the *Ladies' Home Journal*'s wide circulation. In 1895, retitled as "Christmas on the Buchoi Plantation," Rebecca's work had a reprise in Raleigh's *News and Observer*. And in 1913, as "Christmas at Buchoi: A North Carolina Rice Plantation," the piece had another public airing, this time in *The North Carolina Booklet*. Three years after that, in an example of how Yule log tales became recycled and embellished, writer Genevieve Tapscott Gill for the (Little Rock) *Arkansas Gazette* published a piece about southern plantation Christmases before the Civil War clearly grounded in Rebecca Cameron's account. Gill started this article by disclaiming originality, reporting that having been requested to write about "Christmas times on a plantation," she had depended entirely on "what someone has told me." Who was that someone? "My friend Miss Cameron of North Carolina tells so cleverly her experiences as a child while visiting her grandfather one Christmas and of the strange custom of some of the negroes called Coonahs." Actually, Gill did more than base her piece on Rebecca Cameron's work. Much of the phrasing is word-for-word plagiarism.[42]

✳✳✳

Although the Cameron sisters deserve the most credit for popularizing Yule log–soaking stories at the turn of the twentieth century, the applauded southern writer John Fox Jr. helped ensure the momentum of Yule log legends into the next century with a lengthy vignette in a full-length novel set during the Spanish-American War. Throughout this novel, Fox's narration glanced backward so seamlessly to antebellum times that his readers might have been forgiven for overlooking that his scenes of Black workers soaking and delivering a Yule log to a Big House was occurring at the end of the nineteenth century, decades after Emancipation, rather than during the heyday of plantation slavery.

John Fox Jr. was born on December 16, 1862, during the Civil War, in tiny Stony Point in Bourbon County, Kentucky, in the state's famed Bluegrass region. One of ten children of local schoolmaster John William Fox and his second wife, John Jr. received a classical education at his father's academy prior to completing coursework at Transylvania University in Lexington and then studies at Harvard, where in 1883 he graduated cum laude. During the interval between his graduation and the outbreak of war with Spain in 1898, Fox worked as a *New York Sun* and *New York Times* reporter, briefly studied law at Columbia, published short stories and a novel, and plunged along with other members of his family into a web of mountain mining schemes and land investments, some of which fared poorly enough to leave the Foxes in a precarious financial position. By mid-1890, he along with his father, mother, and several siblings relocated their family's permanent residence to Big Stone Gap in the Cumberland Mountain range in southwestern Virginia in a quest for fresh investment opportunities and pecuniary relief—a locale that advantaged John Jr.'s literary career by providing him with an intimate familiarity with the culture of southern mountaineers, an understanding that enriched much of his writing.[43]

Although Fox suffered from serious health ailments throughout his life (including, apparently, tuberculosis), his adventuresome tendencies, lengthy bachelorhood, and his family's constrained finances induced him to accept a $364 offer in 1898 from Harper & Brothers, publishers of *Harper's Weekly*, to cover the war with Spain (a salary he supplemented by negotiating a bonus when Harper & Brothers included his wartime dispatches in a subscription book titled *Harper's Pictorial History of the War with Spain* [1899]). Fox's wartime experiences, in turn, inspired his novel *Crittenden: A Kentucky Story of Love and War*, published in 1900 by Charles Scribner's Sons in time for the Christmas book trade, written in part in the expectation that its potential sales would afford relief to his debt-ridden family. "'Crittenden' is to appear on Nov. 10," Fox wrote his mother as publication neared, noting that "Scribners promised me $250 more in advance royalties and I've been waiting for it . . . so that I could send you a checque." More than a war novel, though, *Crittenden* also reflected Fox's experiences growing up in the Kentucky Bluegrass country and his deep knowledge of his native state's history.[44]

Fox starts his action in the springtime of 1898, around the time the United States declared war on Spain, when his white Kentuckian main character, Clay Crittenden, a fictional scion of one of Kentucky's very real most distinguished families,[45] returns from a sojourn in the mountains to his parents' Bluegrass place, "Canewood." Though the novel deems Canewood a "homestead" rather than a plantation, the place boasts ample grounds and retains as "servants" a retinue of "slaves and the children of those slaves" from former times, enough of them to evoke images of antebellum plantations. These include a turbaned "Aunt Keziah" in the kitchen, a "black butler" called "Uncle Ben," and a youth named "Bob" who hails Clay as "Ole Captain"— the form of address, according to the narrator, that all the servants were accustomed to using since the death of "Ole Master," Clay's father. After mulling over the pros and cons of serving in the breaking war, many of them related to his difficulties in romance and the tradition of wartime service by past family in the War for Independence, the War with Mexico, and the Civil War, Clay follows the lead of his younger brother Basil in volunteering for action against Spain.

Figure 3.2. John Fox Jr.
Source: Scrapbook, "Family and Friends" (circa 1870–1919), 19, Fox Family Papers, Special Collections Research Center, University of Kentucky Libraries.

Figure 3.3. John Fox Jr. while covering Theodore Roosevelt's Rough Riders as war correspondent during the Spanish-American War.

Source: Scrapbook, "Family and Friends" (circa 1870–1919), 50, Fox Family Papers, Special Collections Research Center, University of Kentucky Libraries.

The heart of Fox's story relates Clay's military experiences stateside and abroad. After traveling to a major encampment of soldiers and a monument dedication on the old Civil War Chickamauga Battlefield, he makes his way to Tampa where he enlists at the rank of private in a regular US Cavalry regiment (in contrast, brother Basil serves with Teddy Roosevelt's famed volunteer "Rough Rider" dismounted cavalry regiment). Clay participates in the landing of US forces at Siboney, Cuba (the island at that time was still a Spanish possession and it became the primary war theater). Clay proceeds to the front, and both Crittenden brothers find themselves in thick of the action on the one day of heavy land fighting in the entire war. On July 1, 1898, at El Caney and the San Juan Heights, they witness horrific sights, graphically described in Fox's prose. In the end, the brothers prove their mettle in action, with Basil taking a serious wound to his throat and Clay a less alarming one to his chest. Both survive to return to Canewood by fall, with Clay suffering from the recurrent malaria that he contracted in Cuba.[46]

Some modern commentators belittle *Crittenden* more than they do Fox's subsequent novels, two of which were among the first American titles ever to earn over a million sales. One of Fox's biographers lambastes *Crittenden*'s "sentimental rubbish" and mocks its love story as "a complete failure."[47] Nonetheless, the novel merits consideration as historical fiction, and not just because it intertwines genuine figures and incidents from the past with its fictionalized elements.

Crittenden's plot and protagonist Clay Crittenden reflected the Spanish-American War's very powerful meaning within an accelerating reconciliation process for once-estranged white northerners and southerners. The contrast with the Civil War when Americans fought each other in what is sometimes dubbed a brothers' war because it split many families apart, could hardly have been more obvious. Now ex-Billy Yanks and ex-Johnny Rebs serve arm in arm against a foreign power. Fox's messaging was clear enough for the famed western artist Frederic Remington, who like Fox covered the war as a correspondent. He gave the book a rushed reading the month it came out and immediately wrote Fox that its sentiment and truth were so power-ful that it would be a "D—[damned] good thing for an American to read." Of greater interest, though, is *Crittenden*'s racial and racialist messaging, both in respect to the narrator Fox's terminology (e.g., young Black girls at Canewood are "pickaninnies") and Clay's conflicted and gradually more respectful reactions to the idea of Black US cavalry troops participating in the US war effort. A key subplot follows Bob, the young family servant, who stows away aboard the vessel conveying Basil to Cuba. Making his way to the front in the hope of assisting Clay at a dangerous moment, Bob demonstrates loyalty to the Crittenden family and bravery in his own right when he rescues the wounded Basil from the battlefield and extracts him to a field hospital.

As the scholar Gretchen Murphy suggests in *Shadowing the White Man's Burden*, Fox's story sought to assuage the very real fears white Americans had at the time of the war about the government arming and deploying Black soldiers by "affixing Negro character locally, as a plantation 'type.'" Indeed, Fox's southern Black characters remain faithful to their masters, though they are long since legally free, and Bob risks his own life in the action against Spain. Fox thus comforted his contemporary readers by implying that African Americans in the crunch would remain nonthreatening to whites despite their transformed legal status from slave times, even with guns in their hands.[48]

Keeping Murphy's reflections in mind, we need to visit the book's last chapter, which unfolds at Canewood two weeks before Christmas Eve during that same year, 1898. There we come upon the Canewood "negroes" led by the returned Bob and the white-haired "Uncle Ephraim," scouring the woods for as large a fallen oak tree as possible for that Christmas's Yule log. The "wily" Ephraim, we learn, seeks one that would "burn slowly and burn long; for as long as the log burned, just that long lasted the holiday of every darky on the place." Finally, Bob, standing atop the "torn and twisted roots of a great oak that wind and ice had tugged from its creek-washed roots and stretched parallel with the water," yells he has found what they need, and his accomplices rush toward him with "every tooth showing delight in his find."

Fox makes Bob into possibly the most scientific of all the African American characters in all southern Yule log stories in terms of the precision he takes with cutting those logs. When two boys in the group approach the tree with their axes, Bob stops them and instructs them in dialect, "Go back an' git dat cross-cut saw!" The axmen defer to him, but Bob explains, lest any of Fox's contemporary readers be confused by the scene, that the "Fool niggers" did not realize how using a saw would better preserve the log's maximum size than using axes, which would have sent chips flying, thus reducing its mass. The larger the log, all realized, the longer the burn. Best to keep those chips.

Eventually, with a "darky" holding each end of the saw, the cutting begins, with all Blacks present singing this song while the "shining whistling blade" passes back and forth through the thick wood, a log so thick it buried the saw to its handle:

> Pull him 'troo! (grunt)
> Yes, man.
> Pull him 'troo—hug!
> Saw him to de heart.
> . . . .
> Gwine to have Christmas.
> Yes, man!
> Gwine to have Christmas.

Yes, man!
Gwine to have Christmas
Long as he can bu'n
. . . .
Burn long, log!
Yes, log!
Burn long, log!
Yes, log,
Heah me, log, burn long!
Gib dis nigger Christmas
O log, burn long!

It takes them a full hour to finish the job. Then, while the two men get fence rails to use to lift the log, they receive new guidance by song:

Soak him in de water,
Up, now!
Soak him in de water,
Up, now!
O Lawd, soak long!

And the two, of course, do just that. They use the fence rails to roll the log into the dark water, with Bob driving a spike into it and roping it to a nearby hickory, forestalling its potentially floating away in a rainstorm. One "little negro" watching the proceedings expects to get two weeks off from work given the log's soaking.

Subsequently, on cue during Christmas Eve, the heavy log is hauled into the house, "with [the] cries and grunts and great laughter and singing" of the Black workers who are carrying the Yule log "from its long bath" across the snowy landscape. By nighttime, it is blazing and crackling. And what a wonderful Christmas celebration follows! Fox ends *Crittenden* by tidying up key plot strands with Clay and Basil marrying their girlfriends.[49]

***

Unlike Innes Randolph, John Fox Jr. lacked experience in the Confederate army. He had only been an infant during the Civil War. Unlike the Cameron sisters, he lacked membership in an organization memorializing the Lost Cause. Moreover, though his grandparents on his father's side were slaveholders, he grew up in a household without enslaved servants. Still, he invoked common southern white racial stereotypes of and descriptors for African Americans in his writing, as in his "Br'er Coon" tale for the *Century Magazine* in 1898, which referenced the inseparability of the southern "Darkey and his coon-dog." Further, he noted in a brief autobiographical sketch that his "mother's people were all Confederates." And if, as Fox Jr. wrote, his father's relations all identified with the Union, his father may have felt otherwise during the war or later developed Confederate leanings anyway. In 1899, Fox Sr. alluded offhandedly in a letter to John's younger brother James about having "two or three" issues of *The Confederate Veteran* lying around the family's home. Likely, John was accustomed to reading *CV* issues while at the family home, since the magazine's December 1897 issue acknowledged a contribution of one dollar by "John Fox, Jr., Big Stone Gap, Va." for a monument to honor "the hero Davis," a Dixie military paladin. Remembered afterward as the "Boy Hero of the Confederacy," Tennessee cavalryman Samuel ("Sam") Davis had been captured and hung as a spy by Union troops in November 1863. Davis was executed after his captors discovered he was carrying maps of Union fortifications in Nashville and other revealing paperwork and refused to reveal his source lest he compromise Confederate supporters.[50]

Even if Fox had entirely lacked connections with organizations promoting Confederate veterans and the Lost Cause, he had to have been influenced in his writing about Bob and the Yule log by his intimate personal and professional ties to Virginian Thomas Nelson Page, the southern male author who at the time was most identified in the American popular mind with romantic images of the *prewar* South's plantation slaveholders. Page not only delighted southerners with his wildly popular stories; northern readers, too, despite hatreds against southerners engendered by the recent war, embraced Page's warm portraits of the Old South's slaveholding masters and mistresses as well as their enslaved Black laborers. Literary scholar Edmund Wilson declared in *Patriotic Gore* that Page's African American characters come off as belonging to a "lovable but simple race," adoring of their enslavers and fully accepting of the idea of laboring for free for "Old Mass and Mistis and Meh Lady" (as Page's Black characters in dialect fondly called members of the white families who owned them). Noted historian Ed Ayers has reasoned that Page's writings rendered "fantasies, unbridled glorifications of a lost childhood, lost innocence, and a lost civilization." And one should additionally note, those "fantasies" sold wildly in their time.[51]

Though Page never drew directly on accounts of Black Yule log customs that were already circulating in the books, magazines, and newspapers of his day for subject matter in his own writings, his take on antebellum southern plantation life surely helped inspire the Yule log scene and Black dialect in John Fox's *Crittenden* (facets of the novel that Fox's brother James surely meant when he congratulated John on the book's paying "the negro" a "deserved tribute"). Some contemporaries linked Page and Fox together for the very reason that the racial content of their writings overlapped. In a 1906 *Confederate Veteran* article, Chattanooga literary figure Mary Brabson

Littleton associated Fox and Page, along with Joel Chandler Harris (remembered today for his Black dialect-heavy "Uncle Remus" tales) and Kentucky fiction writer James Lane Allen, as prominent practitioners of a "distinctive school of literature" that was "deep-tinted with romance" and assigned "the ex-slave his part and place." Brabson described Black characters within this genre as "unconsciously humorous" and dignified by their loyalty to whites, a description that clearly applies to Bob. One wonders if Brabson had *Crittenden*, published six years earlier and serialized in several newspapers in 1903, in mind when she made these remarks.[52]

Fox first made Page's acquaintance in 1887, well over a decade before writing *Crittenden*, and that acquaintance blossomed by 1894, the year after Page and his second wife moved to Washington, DC, to take up permanent residence. When Fox, in August 1894, sojourned in Ashville, North Carolina, and agreed to give a free public reading of some of his work for a benefit at a local park, the *Asheville Daily Citizen* promoted the event with Page's endorsement of Fox, though it was qualified since Page cautioned that Fox lacked elocution skills. Declaring, "I know Mr. Fox," Page emphasized, though, Fox's "clear musical voice of great sweetness" as a speaking attribute and predicted it would serve him well when reading to a "cultured and refined audience." After this endorsement, the Fox–Page bond deepened. A Buffalo, New York, paper reported in March 1897 that Fox was passing time in the nation's capital as "the guest of his friend, Mr. Thomas Nelson Page"; and in the winter immediately following the war with Spain, newspapers picked up on Fox's spending an extended Christmas with the Pages. During this same period, Fox frequently spent parts of his summers, including the three preceding the publication of *Crittenden*, at the Pages' Rock Ledge summer cottage in York Harbor, Maine. And during the lead-up to *Crittenden*'s publication, Fox may have solicited Page's feedback while it was in manuscript form. In May 1899, Fox's father wrote his brother Jim that John had arrived back at the Big Stony Gap family home the previous night and reported that "Thos Nelson Page had criticized his new story as far as furnished—pretty adversely." The senior Fox thought the remedy would be for John to apply more time to his writing.[53]

Though one of *Crittenden*'s contemporary critics complained that "Mr. Fox's negroes—a necessary adjunct of a southern story" lacked "individuality" and were "a little too African" in comparison to parallel Black characters in the tales of Page and Joel Chandler Harris, the book benefited from Scribner's ample advertising in the nation's leading publications—including the *New-York Daily Tribune*, the *New York Times*, and the *Boston Evening Transcript*. Booksellers proudly announced its availability, and it captured reviews in newspapers and in the nation's weekly and monthly magazines. Among newspapers providing unique reviews, with some merely giving plot summaries and others printing extensive analyses, were the *Kansas City Times*, *Lexington Morning Herald*, *Knoxville Sentinel*, *Louisville Courier-Journal*, *Brooklyn Daily Eagle*, *Richmond* (VA) *Times*, *Buffalo Courier*, *Chicago Tribune*, and *San Francisco Chronicle*. Magazine reviews turned up in *The Bookman*, *The Advance*, *The Dial*, *The New York Evangelist*, and *The Watchman*. *Crittenden* was serialized in the *San Francisco Call* in four installments, got on books-of-the-month and books-of-the-week listings in periodicals like *The Living Age* and *Outlook*, and claimed shelf space in public libraries. By April 1901, it had reached the distant Honolulu Public Library in the new American possession of Hawaii. All the attention, in turn, generated respectable if not spectacular sales. Just in the interval between its November 1900 release and August 1, 1901, the novel sold nearly ten thousand copies. Having survived some twelve decades of culling by library administrators and non-returns by patrons, *Crittenden* remains in the collections of more than six hundred libraries, according to WorldCat and available new from online vendors.[54]

Although the preponderance of *Crittenden*'s contemporary reviewers focused on its love story and Spanish-American War chapters rather than on its plantation scenes, their positive tone encouraged a large readership, especially among male readers enamored with military history. Some reviewers merely praised the war chapters in broad strokes, as when the *Buffalo Courier* applauded "the vivid, powerfully impressive description of the battle front" in *Crittenden*. But two reviewers matched up Fox's combat scenes against a book that even today remains a signpost for fictional representations of the soldier's experience in battle—Stephen Crane's novel *Red Badge of Courage*, which had first been published five years before *Crittenden*. The *Kansas City Times*'s reviewer insisted that "Steve Crane never wrote a line describing a battle that was more forcible than parts" of Fox's tale. And a critic in the *Brooklyn Daily Eagle* thought that *Crittenden* held its own not only against Crane's works but also those of two other masters of military writing at that time, Theodore Roosevelt and Richard Harding Davis.[55]

All this positive publicity, in turn, suggests that turn-of-the-century American readers not yet exposed to southern Yule log legends in the magazine articles of the Cameron sisters and others who had written of Black soaking customs could have learned about them through Fox's story. After all, even readers picking up *Crittenden* for its heralded Spanish-American War content rather than its plantation material would have been unlikely to skip its colorful Yule log chapter. Since Fox's handling of the war absorbs all the chapters immediately prior to the book's Yule log caper at its conclusion, we can safely assume that few readers would put the book down at the end of chapter 14, when the war with Spain fades from the plot, and not read the twelve pages of the Yule log chapter that follows. Finishing the book required minimal effort at that point, and readers absorbed in Clay's romance would especially have had reason to continue reading.

It is also safe to conjecture, I think, that some of John Fox's readers probably misinterpreted that same chapter's tale of Bob and his associates cross-cutting and soaking their oak Yule log so that their Christmas relief from labor would last longer. Meticulous readers, of course, would have kept in mind when reading about Bob's Christmas doings that Fox was describing holiday events long after the Civil War rather than antebellum times when slavery was legal in Kentucky. But Fox's plot flashes back to pre–Civil War history so often that it is not difficult to imagine readers, when they read about Bob's holiday shenanigans, losing sight of the timeline and thinking themselves transported to a plantation in the Old South. As late as 1953, a columnist writing a Christmas piece for a small-town paper in North Carolina mused about *Crittenden* and reflected that the book's depiction of a Christmas celebration on a plantation occurring around 1900 was itself based on "the old-fashioned Christmas that had been celebrated back in the middle 1850s." Eras of time in this reading of *Crittenden* become compressed, conflated. The important thing is that Fox's description of "the Negroes as they search for the Yule log, seeking the one that will prolong the wonderful day to the very greatest extent" remained fixed in this newswoman's memory, and that those "Negroes" might just as well have been enslaved as free. Perhaps others read the tale similarly.[56]

What this Tar Heel State columnist apparently never considered was the possibility that Yule log soakings never occurred at all while human bondage was legal in Kentucky, North Carolina, or the rest of the South. Nor did she consider an alternative explanation for Fox's Yule log–soaking story, one that came to me only after I mulled over a front-page piece by someone identified as "O. B. H." for the Christmas Eve day issue of the *Urbana* (IL) *Daily Chronicle* in 1924. In a column titled "Yuletide in Dixie," the writer recalled a Yule log when describing a huge Christmas season gathering of his/her large Kentucky clan some "two or three generations ago," when over sixty family members "sat down to the festive board." Reporting, no surprise, that Christmas lasted "as long as the yule log continued to burn," the memoirist recounted that it took the hosting estate's entire force of "'field hands'" to cut the tree—always a black gum, hard maple, or oak—"when the sap was up." Then the workers would roll the log, with the help of a yoke of oxen, to a brook or creek for soaking before maneuvering it "up to the big house for the beginning of the festivities on the 'night before Christmas.'" The allusion to three generations initially suggested to me that the author might be describing enslaved field hands, but this was not the case at all. In the article's second column, O. B. H. confides that the described events occurred a full twenty years after Abraham Lincoln's Emancipation Proclamation, setting O. B. H.'s

Christmas event in 1883, earlier than Fox's fictional Christmas gathering but long after slavery's abolition in the South.[57]

I would not have caught the significance of this time frame had I not run across a second relevant news article, this one published ten years after the Urbana paper's piece. It concerned a southern planter's daughter, who in 1934 made news in Greensboro, North Carolina, for speaking to a Sunday school rally in the nearby town of Stoneville. Alberta Whitlock Miller, a child of planter Francis Marion Whitlock Jr., who before the Civil War had owned thirty-five slaves in Chester County, South Carolina, told her audience that at her father's "Riverside" plantation in Union County, South Carolina, it had been the custom for a Yule log to be "cut in the 'woods' two weeks before Christmas day and put into the creek to soak wet enough not to burn out in two weeks or more." Then, during its tenure in the "big house" fireplace, Whitlock's "negro tenants" enjoyed a workless holiday. Miller's use of the term "tenant" and the fact that she was describing a plantation in a different county than where her father planted before the Civil War is suggestive of *post-slavery* times in the South rather than the antebellum years, since Black farm tenantry became prevalent in southern rural areas following slavery's eradication. If the Black workers who soaked Yule logs on her father's place had been enslaved, she would have said so. The term "tenant" gives the game away.[58]

This recognition, in turn, caused me to reconsider *Crittenden*'s messaging. Although John Fox Jr.'s novel may have given the impression that enslaved people in the Old South soaked Yule logs, that may not have been the author's intention. Using O. B. H.'s and Alberta Miller's remembrances as reference points, we should ponder the possibility that Fox's lively Yule log scenes should be taken solely at face value—as a description of the contemporary Christmastime doings of late nineteenth-century Black tenant farmers or plantation wage laborers, nothing more. Then again, Fox was writing fiction and there is even less evidence that postbellum southern plantation magnates set their Christmas calendars by Yule logs and encouraged Yule log soakings than the evidence they did so before Emancipation. And the evidence for *pre*–Civil War Yule log southern Christmases, as we have already seen, is flimsy enough.

Chapter 4

LaSalle Pickett's Deceits

Arguably, the most eloquent testimony to the grip of the Lost Cause on the southern imagination comes in the writing of Mississippi novelist William Faulkner. Through the medium of his character Gavin Stevens in *Intruder in the Dust*, a novel about racial injustice set in Mississippi in the 1940s, Faulkner, in less than a paragraph, powerfully evokes the hold on the southern mind of a single moment in the Civil War—Confederate Major General George E. Pickett's suicidal assault on July 3, 1863, against Union positions on Cemetery Ridge at Gettysburg, Pennsylvania.

Prior to the fight at Gettysburg, nothing in Pickett's military record had been predictive of his everlasting fame in American historical memory. Born in 1825, George was the child of Mary Johnston Pickett and Robert Pickett of Richmond, Virginia, slaveholders who besides their city residence held a plantation down the James River on Turkey Island, where George spent much of his childhood. By his teenage years, George had decided on a military career, and he gained an appointment to the United States Military Academy at West Point, entering the institution in 1842. Though he graduated last in his West Point class of 1846, he demonstrated gallantry in the US–Mexican War during General Winfield Scott's capture of Mexico City in 1847. Just prior to the Civil War, Pickett's dangerously reckless side—seemingly embodied in his rakishly long hair ringlets, goatee, and mustache—manifested itself when he risked embroiling the United States in an unnecessary war with Britain during a sovereignty dispute over the San Juan Islands between what is today's northern Washington State and Canada's Vancouver Island. Not long after this crisis, Pickett, following Virginia's secession from the Union, resigned his US army commission and accepted a colonelcy in the new Confederate army.[1]

In Gavin Stevens's telling in *Intruder in the Dust*, Confederates' hopes of triumph in their war for southern nationhood hinged on Pickett's performance at Gettysburg on the third and final day of the battle, when Robert E. Lee's Army of Northern Virginia suffered such a resounding defeat as to close Lee's invasion of Pennsylvania and send his troops reeling back into Virginia. At the climax of the fighting on July 3, General Pickett and his soldiers charged into withering Union fire up on Cemetery Ridge, where they were repulsed with devastating losses. But until Pickett's immediate superior officer, General James Longstreet, had unleashed Pickett's men in that charge, anything had seemed possible. No wonder white southerners remained haunted many decades later by the Civil War's might-have-been:

> It's all *now* you see. Yesterday wont [*sic*] be over until tomorrow and tomorrow began ten thousand years ago. For every Southern boy fourteen years old, not once but whenever he wants it, there is the instant when it's still not yet two o'clock on that July afternoon in 1863, the brigades are in position behind the rail fence, the guns are laid and ready in the woods and the furled flags are already loosened to break out and Pickett himself with his long oiled ringlets and his hat in one hand probably and his sword in the other looking up the hill waiting for Longstreet to give the word and it's all in the balance, it hasn't happened yet, it hasn't even begun yet.

In a whimsical afterthought, Stevens muses about what might have been had Pickett's attack carried the day: "Pennsylvania, Maryland, the world, the golden dome of Washington itself to crown with desperate and unbelievable victory the desperate gamble . . . made two years ago." The gamble, of course, was the South's secession from the Union in 1861 and bid for independence.[2]

Not all modern historians would agree with Faulkner's insinuation that George Pickett's charge at Gettysburg was the turning point of the Civil War, but few would dispute either its salience in the postwar southern Lost Cause or that the general's place in Civil War memory owed much to the writings and speeches following his death by his widow, LaSalle Corbell Pickett. Skepticism, however, is required not only when considering what she had to say about her spouse but also her colorful accounts of personal interactions with other prominent figures of the Civil War era including Abraham Lincoln, not to mention her rich, colorful revelations about life on southern plantations before the Civil War. LaSalle Pickett was, if truth be told, an inveterate fabricator, a spinner of enticing yarns quite willing to concoct historical drivel out of whole cloth. That she made such a practice of doing so posed a serious complication for me as I sought to determine for certain whether there was any factual foundation for legends about enslaved people in the South ever soaking Yule logs, given that over the first two decades of the twentieth century, the widow Pickett published a lot about this custom. Her insistence on the centrality of Yule log rituals in the antebellum experiences of enslaved people and enslavers alike helped keep these legends in the public eye for decades.

✳✳✳

For all her adoration of George Pickett, LaSalle enjoyed a mere twelve conjugal years with him before he died in 1875, a full fifty years before her own death. A daughter of privilege, LaSalle was born Sallie Ann Corbell on May 16, 1843, into a moderately prosperous Nansemond County, Virginia, household, and she gained eight siblings over the years that followed. Her parents, John David Corbell and Elizabeth Phillips Corbell, resided on a place called Cypress Vale Farm, which LaSalle would later locate as "diagonally opposite Newport News, on a neck of land" near Chuckatuck (then a village, today a Suffolk neighborhood). According to the federal census of 1850, her father and mother claimed ownership of eight and ten slaves, respectively, on the property around the time LaSalle turned seven, with all but three of their enslaved people aged thirty or less. LaSalle would remark later in life on how the property fronted Hampton Roads, a locale that during the Civil War afforded her an eyewitness view for the famous battle of Union and Confederate ironclads in those waters. In her mid-teens, LaSalle's parents sent her westward to the Lynchburg Female Seminary in the foothills of the Blue Ridge Mountains, an institution whose curriculum favored a mix of academic subjects like French and natural philosophy as well as behavioral training in the "deportment" deemed appropriate for the coming of age of a proper southern belle. Curiously, her award for distinction during her junior year came in mathematics rather than in literature, the field she would embrace as an adult.

By her enrollment at the academy, the dark-haired, dark-eyed LaSalle had attracted George Pickett's interest, though the chronology of their relationship cannot be pinned down. She apparently first encountered the previously married George on the beach at Old Point Comfort in 1852 when she was not yet ten years old. At the time, he was on a leave of absence from an army posting in Texas following the death of his first wife during childbirth. Their acquaintance took a romantic turn early in the Civil War when LaSalle, now in her mid-teens, was studying in Lynchburg and he was serving nearby with Confederate forces in Virginia; and they married a couple of months after the Gettysburg battle at Petersburg's St. Paul's Episcopal Church. In 1864, LaSalle gave birth to their son George Jr. All the while, George Sr. continued to serve the Confederacy in North Carolina and Virginia, and he was at Appomattox when General Robert E. Lee surrendered the Army of Northern Virginia there in April 1865.

After the disbanding of Lee's command, times turned hard for the Picketts. Late in the war, federal forces decimated George's family's home on Turkey Island, and Lee's surrender put a sudden end to George's income from his profession at arms. Compounding their challenges, the couple fled to Canada

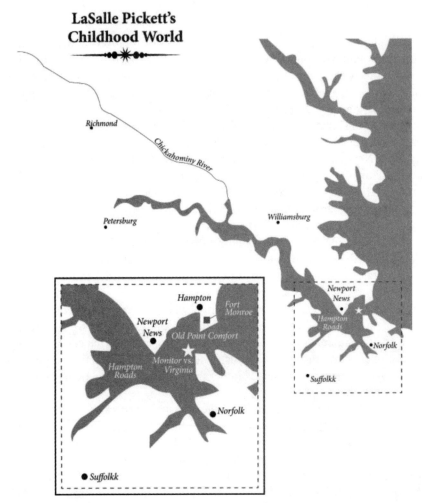

LaSalle Pickett's Childhood World

Figure 4.1.   LaSalle Pickett's childhood world.
Source: Graphic design by Chris J. Brannan.

upon learning that George was under federal suspicion for a war crime involving the hanging of Union prisoners of war in North Carolina (as things turned out, the government never pressed charges against him). There they remained for months before returning to Virginia. Taking up residence at the Turkey Island ruins in December 1865, the Picketts constructed a cottage dwelling and set about rebuilding their lives. Over the following years, George tried his hand at farming and other endeavors before hawking insurance for the Norfolk subsidiary of a New York City firm. The birth of a second child (who

Figure 4.2. LaSalle and George Pickett portrait.
Source: American Civil War Museum, under the management of Virginia Museum of History and Culture (1940.20.349).

would only live eight years) exacerbated the Picketts' financial struggles during their postwar decade together.[3]

Following George Sr.'s death in 1875, LaSalle returned with her living son to Nansemond County where she kept a low profile for several years. Needing additional income for herself and George Jr., she moved to Washington, DC, in 1880. Once she established residence there, she sought employment in the federal government, playing off her status as the needy wife of a famed Confederate general at a time when the southern states were fully restored to their political rights in the Union and sectional reconciliation between the North and South was on the rise. Aided by letters of recommendation (playing on her precarious finances and her status as the widow of a "knightly" southern general) from ex-Confederate officers and Virginia congressmen George Craighead Cabell and George W. Wise, and other allies and endorsers like ex-Confederate congressman now-US congressman Ortho R. Singleton of Mississippi, LaSalle procured a lowly sinecure as a "tallyist" in the US Census Office of the Department of the Interior at a $600 yearly salary. Then she spent much of the following decade clawing her way up the federal bureaucracy. She served as a copyist and then clerk in the Census Office and then copyist and clerk successively in the US Patent Office, the latter at an annual $1,000 salary. Eventually she reached the Pension Office, holding that position until 1904, when she was confined for months due to lingering ailments from an accident alighting from an electric streetcar, a condition that led to her resignation.[4]

It was during the late 1880s, with the idea of supplementing her meagre federal salary, that LaSalle Pickett assumed the persona of exemplary "professional widow," a role likewise assumed by a good number of other wives of fallen Civil War soldiers and deceased veterans in similar straits. By moneymaking and war-related public comments, appearances, and writings, LaSalle and her peers catered to a vibrant national "culture of mourning" to hallow an unspeakably brutal conflict responsible for the deaths of more than seven hundred thousand soldiers. Indicative of her own prominence within this gendered memorial army, historian Richard F. Selcer made LaSalle one of two exemplars of this occupational trend. Selcer's second case, Elizabeth Bacon Custer, interestingly, like LaSalle, was the survivor of a last-in-class West Point alumnus with swashbuckling traits and risk-taking proclivities— Union army general George Armstrong Custer. Custer, of course, gained his own immortal notoriety from his postwar escapades much more than his Civil War exploits, being killed in US cavalry action against Lakota Sioux, Arapaho, and Northern Cheyenne warriors at the Battle of Little Bighorn.[5]

When I scrutinized US newspapers starting in the late 1880s for stories about LaSalle Corbell Pickett, I easily picked up her trail as a national personality and well-published writer and speaker. She made quite the splash in 1887 merely for attending, with her son, a reunion of Union and Confederate soldiers on the Gettysburg battle site, part of her calculated "reconciliation" strategy to play off an ongoing reunion process in which Civil War soldiers sought to reduce lingering resentments about slavery, secession, the war itself, and even Reconstruction among the men who had waged the fighting. Her presence at the July 4 affair came at the invitation of survivors of her

Figure 4.3. LaSalle Pickett.
Source: Virginia Museum of History and Culture (1940.20.349).

husband's division, who in turn were guests at the reunion of veterans of the Philadelphia Brigade that had helped fend off her husband's fateful charge on Cemetery Ridge. The gathering's most dramatic moment occurred when the Philadelphians and Pickett's men performed a symbolic handshake at the spot where the latter pierced the Union positions. Press accounts, though, also paid noticeable attention to LaSalle Pickett. Newspaper coverage revealed how George Pickett's veterans picked up LaSalle's travel expenses to Gettysburg, how during the ceremonies she held a reception on the battlefield near the spot where George had launched his attack, and how she graciously spoke individually to each of George's division's attendees when they reached her in a formal reception line. That evening, for a full hour at a reception, she shook hands with anyone who wished her attention and soaked up the entertainment of a band playing under the auspices of the umbrella Union veterans' organization of the day, the Grand Army of the Republic.[6]

LaSalle would continue to represent her deceased husband and the vanquished Confederacy for the rest of the century and beyond, fusing her romantic words about Dixie's heroes with healing messages that her husband had been a loyal and brave American and that the North and the South needed to recognize that there were well-meaning, gallant soldiers fighting on *both sides* in the recent war. Yanks and Rebs needed mutual respect and sympathy for each other. When Confederate president Jefferson Davis's remains were to be reinterred from New Orleans to Richmond's Hollywood Cemetery in 1893, LaSalle alerted organizers that she would be in attendance. In 1899, the *New York Times* and other papers carried her protest (to the *Washington Post*) railing against a planned sham battle at the next Georgia State Fair of her husband's famed assault at Gettysburg on the logic that it was sacrilege to trivialize "the three most awful days in history," a past "sacred" to the entire nation.[7]

Around the turn of the century, to use modern parlance, LaSalle Pickett "upped her game" as a professional widow. From 1903 to 1911, she worked the lecture circuit, though her voice's projection was possibly inadequate in those pre-microphone times for large facilities. In 1905, a town newspaper in Kansas, reporting on her speech about "southern traditions and ante-bellum reminiscences" at a local auditorium, implied as much. It observed that although she retained, despite her advanced years, the "graceful movements" and "sweet and sunny temperament" that "belles of Dixie were and are so justly famous" as well as a "well-modulated" voice, she could hardly be heard in the outermost seats in the room. Still, under the auspices of various lyceum and Chautauqua bureaus and assemblies, she gave a barrage of talks, sometimes earning nearly $300 a week before deducting for travel expenses. Were you alive in 1907, you could have turned up at one of Pickett's many Chautauqua appearances throughout the South and Midwest for her declamations on "The Battle of Gettysburg" to apparently enraptured audiences. Advance advertising announced her as the name dearest to the public of "all the noted women of the South." During one appearance in Missouri, an orchestra played "Dixie" and attendees waved handkerchiefs as the "Widow of Gen. George Pickett" made her way to the "big platform."[8]

Her public visibility, it should be emphasized, transcended her activism in the cause of her husband's and Confederate memory, though her popularity in southern circles fed on her romanticized take on Dixie's soldiers. There was good reason why the United Confederate Veterans, the counterpart to the Union's Grand Army of the Republic (GAR), asked her to the stage at its 1896 Richmond convention to talk on the heroism of her husband's division at Gettysburg. And though she had only a limited association with the United Daughters of the Confederacy (UDC), its Atlanta branch specially invited her to its meeting in 1898. When it came time years later for her to dispose of her last remaining copy of *Pickett and His Men* (1899), her adoring book about her husband's military career, she sent it to the UDC. Nevertheless, her consistently positive messaging about the decency and gallantry of both sides in the war, especially when coupled with the growing numbers of northern friends she cultivated as her years in Washington lengthened, made her a truly national symbol in her own time. As early as 1890, she was mentioned first in a Montana news report on the most prominent widows in the nation's capital, in a piece highlighting her role in the National Women's Press Association and as a leader of a travel club. In 1906, she gained election as one of the two vice presidents of the National League of American Pen Women. And remarkably, this wife of a Confederate general was invited in 1909 by a GAR post in Boston, before the Civil War an antislavery hotbed, to give the city's annual Memorial Day address.[9]

All the while, LaSalle Pickett had her say in the literary world as an author of both fiction and nonfiction, with several of her books feeding a cultish interest in her husband as a romantic, unblemished, knightly soldier. Years after her *Pickett and His Men* appeared in 1899, she came out with *The Heart of a Soldier: As Revealed in the Intimate Letters of Genl. George E. Pickett, C. S. A.* in lockstep with the half-century anniversary of the Gettysburg campaign in 1913, purporting to be a collection of forty-four letters she received from her husband, many of them from the Gettysburg campaign period. During World War I, she published a volume of autobiographical reflections literally starting at birth ("I was borne in the unconsciousness of infancy through the little village of Chuckatuck and beyond until the carriage drew up at my grandmother's door and Uncle Charles, her foreman, came out with the little negroes running after him to welcome us") titled *What Happened to Me*. Although the southern partisan *Confederate Veteran* published her shorter pieces, so did major national magazines such as *Cosmopolitan* and *McClure's*.[10]

✳✳✳

Unfortunately, it is hard to take LaSalle Pickett's "nonfiction" writings seriously, because she constructed her history on the fly to better market her
books and sell articles to magazine publishers. Though hardly the first critic
of her veracity, Civil War historian Gary W. Gallagher rendered the most
shocking exposé of the widow Pickett in a detailed analysis for the *Virginia
Magazine of History and Biography* in 1986, where he meticulously scrutinized the authenticity of the letters in her *Heart of a Soldier* book, all of
which had supposedly been penned from George to herself between 1861 and
the mid-1870s. Gallagher determined that LaSalle plagiarized every one of
the eighteen letters in the collection that concerned Civil War battles between
Seven Pines in 1862 and Appomattox from Walter H. Harrison's *Pickett's
Men* (1870) and other printed sources. Gallagher also found that she invented
passages—including quoted statements from other Confederate officers—in
the minority of cases where she clearly started with genuine letters from
George. Additionally, entire anecdotes were made up. Gallagher's devastating
call that the letters are entirely "worthless" when it comes to General Pickett's
career is disturbing, to say the least.[11]

Plenty of other LaSalle Pickett's authorial and oratorical embroideries, too,
have come to light, such as her fictions about Abraham Lincoln. She reminisced, for example, that a "'tall, gaunt sad-faced man in ill-fitting clothes'"—
none other than President Abraham Lincoln—stopped at her front door
in Richmond to check on her well-being when he visited the Confederate
capital on April 4, 1865, following the city's fall to Federal forces, supposedly because Lincoln was a friend of George. Since there is no evidence that
Lincoln knew George Pickett personally or visited the Pickett residence in
Richmond, the anecdote is surely fabricated. Likewise, there is little reason
to respect LaSalle's claim that George, while at West Point, received a letter
from Lincoln in which the latter confided his hope that one day there would
not be "'one drunkard on the face of God's green earth'" and asked George to
work toward that vision. Lincoln never affiliated with the temperance movement of the day, so there is little cause to think that even in the improbable
likelihood he wrote to the cadet, he would have asked this of him. Over the
years, LaSalle kept spinning out such whoppers, changing details as convenient, as happened with her baseless claim that the congressman responsible
for George's appointment to West Point had been Lincoln. Of course, relating colorful Lincoln anecdotes played well to lecture and reading audiences
craving a good tale.[12]

Years later, famed southern writer Robert Penn Warren delighted in one of
LaSalle's charming stories, even while conceding it might be untrue. That one
concerned how, in LaSalle's telling, when leading his division to Gettysburg,
George spotted a "little Dutch girl defiantly waving the Federal flag." Rather
than chastise the child for supporting his enemies, the general gallantly doffed

his hat and later explained he did it to honor "'the heroic womanhood in the heart of that brave little girl, and the glorious old banner under which I won my first laurels.'"[13]

***

Given LaSalle Pickett's addiction to fabrication, we should regard her autobiographical writings about antebellum plantation southern Christmas traditions with skepticism. Any attentive reader should detect that she sought to anchor the Old South's plantation class in the American imagination as a cohort of men and women just as chivalric, honorable, pure in motive, and generous in spirit as the southern army officers who ultimately, like her husband George, followed the Confederate colors into battle. Southern masters and mistresses, her messaging insisted, were humane. They cared deeply about the welfare of dim-witted Black people in their trust, as she seems to have viewed most African Americans, and earned their loving appreciation in return. Enslavers' Christmastime generosity was heartfelt and excessive. In other words, though much of what Mrs. Pickett wrote about antebellum southern Christmases and Yule logs professed authenticity, it reeked of propaganda.

LaSalle Pickett lodged her first account of Yule logs and antebellum plantation Christmastimes in a small volume of autobiographical vignettes titled *Yule Log*, released in 1900 by the Neale Company in Washington—a relatively new firm dedicated to the "encouragement and aid" of southern literature—whose first chapter carried the book's title.[14] She filled these illustrated stories celebratory of slaveholder paternalism with Black slaves and emancipated Blacks speaking in quoted thick dialect, often for pages at a clip. The dialogue alone casts suspicion on her content's legitimacy, and only partly because contemporary white spellings of African American speaking patterns in southern literature commonly implied put-downs of Black intellectuality, even if Pickett and her authorial peers believed they were recording what their own ears heard with scrupulous honesty.

Before and during the Civil War, southern white writers had cautioned youthful readers from slaveholding families to resist the seduction of Black dialect and to differentiate themselves from enslaved people in their daily routines like their mammies; and late nineteenth-century southern white writers like Pickett robustly deployed Black dialect to maintain those distinctions in readers' minds. To give one example, such writers generally spelled "there" as "dere" when out of the mouths of African Americans, not because southern Blacks necessarily spelled or pronounced it that way but to represent them as inferior compared to the white characters and narrators on the same pages speaking or writing proper English. Though many southern whites in antebellum times spoke in dialects that varied by place, class, and ethnicity, such

white variations from standard norms rarely evidenced themselves in publications by Lost Cause southern white writers like LaSalle Pickett. Rather,
Pickett and her peers made their implicit case for white supremacy by juxtaposing exotic, skewed, and nearly indecipherable Black speaking patterns
against the straightforward wording of Caucasians speaking proper English.[15]

My main gripe with Black dialect in LaSalle Pickett's Yule log stories,
however, less concerned problematic representations of enslaved peoples'
speech than the passage of time. The only way she could have recalled such
mountains of verbiage word for word decades later would be if she had taken
dictation at the time and on the spot and then preserved those notations in
some kind of notebook or diary. The absurdity of that possibility should be
immediately apparent. Old South enslavers did not take dictation from the
bondpeople they regularly condemned as racially inferior and immature.

Significantly, Pickett used the start of the first chapter of *Yule Log* to frame
her narrative in standard English, playing off contemporary themes of nostalgia for the Old South's rural world at a moment when transformative "business enterprise" was sweeping the region, before turning her story over to
Black dialect. Recalling the "fragrance of the snowy magnolias," she emoted
a pleasing justification of what the Lost Cause, in her evaluation, had been
all about—a contention that Confederate soldiers fought justifiably for a way
of life that benefited and enriched all its members, Black and white. And she
did this with Christmastime stage center:

> In the Southern heart the sacred Christmas-tide is linked with memories of the
> old-time plantation, the merry-making of the affectionate, simple-hearted col-
> ored people to whom the Christmas holidays were the great festival of the year,
> the gratitude which lit up their dusky faces as they received their presents, the
> joy of the pickaninnies in their possession of their new toys. Time has no power
> to remove those pictures from the gallery of the heart.[16]

Once she had her tale sufficiently framed in Old South nostalgia, Pickett
released the rest of her introductory story from the mouth of an elderly
once-enslaved male named Jack, whom, she explains, has returned to the
"war-desolated" plantation of his former bondage (we later learn this is her
husband's family's Turkey Island place). There, Jack reminisces about "the
old plantation Yule log, with its mystic blaze flaming out in response to the
cheerful note of the Yule log horn."

The story spills out in Jack's thick dialect over eight pages. Jack relates
that despite the passage of time, he can still see "dat ole Chris'mus-Ebe
Yule log" being kindled "jes lak as ef hit wuz yistiddy"; and he reports that
his master had been "kilt up dar at Gettysburg, a foughten' long [fighting
alongside] Marse Gin'nl Pickett." Before the war, though, "de Marser would

blew de Yule log horn for all han's ter 'semble at de wood-pile," and then Jack and other slaves would race to bring in their own Yule logs first, often running into each other in their frantic competition. Finally, small hickory logs, chips, and bark would be piled on large brass andirons with a "ser'us [serious] lookin' Yule log" behind the pile, with the ignition being done with a holy candle applied by the youngest child on the plantation regardless of the youth's race, with the child's hand guided by the master. The balance of Jack's remembrance covers how "De niggers" on Christmas spent their time thinking about the Christmas gifts they would get and about roasting pigs on a spit. Most important, Jack waxes about their "ole Yule log; dat knotty, tough ole-brack [back] log" whose flame's continuance ensured "de time dat Chris'mus las's." He adds remembrances of his mistress, General Pickett's mother, describing the Yule log's sparks as splinters from the Star in the East over Bethlehem guiding the "wise mens" at Jesus's birth and informing all present that the log's ashes represented seconds of the old year lost forever.

Intriguingly, in the book's third story, "Wuz Santa Claus a Nigger Dat Yeah?" Pickett covers the "last olden-time plantation Christmas of my youth," spent in 1862 at her own family's home in Nansemond County days prior to Lincoln's Emancipation Proclamation going into effect—a holiday that ended with the entire enslaved force escaping to Union lines, other than a single five-month-old baby left behind. LaSalle remembers, from that Christmas Eve, that the family's house servant "Aunt Serena" told her that "Chris'mus don' come but woncet a yeah," echoing the refrain in fellow Virginia native Innes Randolph's Uncle Ned poem, "For Christmas comes but once a year." Given the improbability that Pickett precisely remembered anything one of her parents' slaves had said forty years or so earlier, my hunch is that she was familiar with either English renditions of that line or Randolph's well-circulated Ned verse and that this was just another instance of her dipping in the plagiarist's well. LaSalle, however, possessed excessive originality as well, the kind that allowed her to also invent verse in Black dialect, which the Pickett family slaves sing on Christmas morning along with their once-a-year throwback:

> Chris'mus comes but oncet a yeah
> E nebby las' nigger has his sheah;
> Rum-stag er Hi-me-ho-me, rinkum er shay!
> We's put by de horg-meat en de corn-pone,
> Ea's a greasin' our moufs wid a tuckey bone;
> Rum-sag er Hi-me-ho-me, rinkum er shay!
> We hankers all de yeh fer de Chris'mus times,
> W'en de nigger sheks his cloze en sheds de dimes;
> Rum-stag er Hi-me-ho-me, rink tum er shay!

Repulsive as this might strike readers today, Pickett knew how to charm consumers in her time. The book *Yule Log* belonged to a set of four short LaSalle Pickett–authored books (holding eighteen illustrated stories in all) in the Neale Publishing Company's "de Miz" series (1900–1901), available as a set for $3.50. The other titles—*Kunnoo Sperits and Others*, *Ebil Eyes*, and *Jinny*—also loaded on "Negro dialect" pleasing to the contemporary southern master of that genre, Joel Chandler Harris. That Georgian praised Pickett's "absolutely faithful reproduction of the dialect of the old southern slave." A review in a Lexington, Kentucky, paper, however, unintentionally got to the heart of Pickett's racial condescension in these stories, noting how these "morsels" revealed the Virginia plantation "darkey, his pathos and humor, his picturesque use of words, his faithfulness, courtesy and philosophy."[17]

***

Three times more, in her later years, LaSalle Pickett's storytelling revolved around Yule logs in the antebellum South. The first instance came within Pickett's remembrance, published with illustrations in the January 1907 issue of *Harper's Bazar*, of visiting her widowed grandmother's place as a child for a holiday family reunion. Although Pickett never attaches a specific year to this gathering, it seems to have occurred when she was a very little girl. I base this conclusion on her describing herself at the time as being old enough to dance the Highland fling during the Christmas Day family dance while at the same time alluding to being young enough to need carrying up a "wide stairway" to her "little elder-downy trundle-bed" by her own "black mammy" when she wore out on Christmas Eve and Christmas night.[18]

A mere two sentences after her article's title line, "An Old-time Virginia Christmas," Pickett sets her scene with lengthy commentary on the annual family Yule log, cut from a hickory tree. She explains that it enters the dwelling, long seasoned by sunshine and "mellowing rain," upon the shoulder of "the strongest negro on the plantation, followed by a rollicking troop of Christmas revellers, white and black." She adds that everyone "from the master to the most impish little pickaninny" feel affectionately about their log, that a fragment will be preserved when it burns out to serve as the next year's Christmas "lighting-torch," and that the log's ashes are believed so sacred and magical that they will be preserved for lye to be used in later soapmaking. She also relates how the "plantation servants" dub the piled corncobs and wood-chip kindling their "light 'ood" and elucidates how the complicated privilege of lighting the fire fell to the youngest child on hand regardless of race, with the assistance of her grandmother's elderly enslaved cook "Aunt Dilsey." Additionally, she describes how "Old Santa's rack" for the hanging of stockings was placed "over and in front of the mantelpiece." And then, scene set,

Pickett devotes her story to convince readers of the charms of prewar southern plantation life for her family and their enslaved people.

We learn that another elderly slave, "Aunt Serena," has knit the stockings for Santa Claus, which she brings to the fireplace singing "Christmas comes but once a year, en black en white befe has dar shear" (Black and white both have their share). We appreciate how the gracious, generous master's family members not only hang stockings for themselves but also in memory of deceased relations and that the latter will be filled with money to be distributed to the needy; we learn that Pickett's grandmother marked that Christmas Eve by telling tales about "old-time Yule-tides" in France when she was a child; and we find out that guests related ghost stories to enliven the evening. About halfway through the vignette, Pickett describes what happened the next day, Christmas morning, as she awakens to the sounds of horns and firecrackers. Now she watches her mother and father, accompanied by family guests, arrive on a carriage laden with gifts and notes that afterward the whole white ensemble attends a decorated village church to hear the special Yuletide sermon. She also describes the holiday attire of her family and their Christmas dinner and dance, and she recalls overhearing male family members outside in the "yard" laughing and swapping yarns about fox hunts and the like.

Weaving through the vignette are her family's enslaved people, always in contexts implying that Blacks were treated generously and with kindliness and respect as integral parts of her family, and that in return they were appreciative of their bondage. Of note are "servants" (very possibly field hands despite the implication they were domestic help) who have been hired out to other whites for the year but allowed to return for Christmastime. Slaves expect gifts of tobacco plugs, pipes, and handkerchief bandanas from their owner but also bear gifts of their own intended as "tributes of affection to the master and his family." Enslaved people beg additional Christmas gifts on the arrival of the carriage of family and guests on Christmas Day and relish the family's dinner leftovers, which supplement the slaves' own feast that same day of possums and potatoes. Presumably "Fiddling Jim" who played minuets and Virginia reels while "the Yule fire burned" away was Black, though his race is unspecified. But there is no doubt about the racial identity of Black twins named Arabella and Mary Frances, who beg to stay up late on Christmas Eve. Here, Pickett plays to persisting beliefs in the turn-of-the-century white South that slavery was humane, by mentioning, in a brief but chilling (to the modern reader) aside that these twins had once been her own "first Christmas presents," an admission that, for all their professions that their enslaved people were regarded as family, African Americans embodied legitimate property to many white southerners. More than forty years after the Civil War, Pickett could casually allude to her childhood *ownership* of African Americans with the most casual phrasing imaginable.

One assumes that after engaging LaSalle Pickett's pleasant tales and memories most readers conveniently lost sight of the essential role of compulsion, punishment, and white greed and racism in the enslavement of southern Blacks. How telling it is that the actual term "slave" is unused in LaSalle Pickett's memoir. Rather, Blacks are "servants" or "negroes." It is almost as if they worked voluntarily and happily for their room and board, and possibly even for wages. And within this stilted take on human bondage, everyone got along, with whites genuinely regarding their workers with affection.

Pickett's next contribution to southern Yule log lore, this one a fable with Christian overtones, appeared six years later in the December 1913 issue of the magazine *Pictorial Review* as "The Origin of the Yule Log" and was reprinted in many US newspapers immediately and then again for the 1914 Christmas season. The tale, supposedly being related during the Civil War at a Christmas encampment somewhere in Virginia on a snowy Christmas Eve in 1863, concerns an elderly and very infirm Black man living in a heatless, Spartan shack on a mountainside who hears a child crying in the snow. Bravely dispensing with his crutches, our hero speedily traverses the snow to the little boy on what today we would call pure adrenaline and brings the infant to his cabin to warm it up and save its life. Miraculously, from nowhere, a "great log" rolls through the old man's doorway and up to his fireplace, which the child miraculously sets on fire with gleams of light from his eyes. This fills the room with "radiance and warmth that brought a glow to the soul as well as to the body." After the flames form the shape of a cross, a table appears in the cabin out of thin air laden "with a Christmas feast such as had never been spread before his eyes." Rewarded for his courage and humanity, the old man, we are told at the end, will never be hungry or cold again.

Given this story's setting and that Pickett never identifies her hero as either free or slave and fails even to identify the race of the infant, it would be a mistake to read much of anything into this yarn other than that Pickett, having already used Yule logs in her publications, found it convenient to return to the same well. Still, toward the story's end, she jarringly turns over the narrative from her authorial voice to a "Brer Simon" for a single paragraph. And that paragraph disrupts the tale's flow in a way that could be taken as a metaphor endorsing race mixing if one were so inclined to interpret it. Surely, that is not what Pickett intends when, describing the fire, Simon exclaims: "De flames . . . a lippin' up higher and higher; firs' a lil blue blaze would come, den a yaller one, den a bright red one would flare up, end en de blazes would all mingulate together . . . wid de kindleeation colors or de rainbow."[19] But there can be no confusion about LaSalle Pickett's messaging when she brings up Yule logs one last time four years later in her autobiography.

Chapter 8 of Pickett's 1917 memoir *What Happened to Me*, titled "Yuletide," returns to the topic of Christmas in antebellum times at her grandmother's place, with added details. We now learn that her grandmother's home was a brick building fronting the Nansemond River, that its mistress was her mother's mother, and that the property was known locally as "Holiday's Point" because of all the holidays afforded the servants during her deceased "grandfather's day." After describing the house's layout, she explains that her mother brought her there on Christmas Eve day so she could witness the igniting of the Yule log—a ritual that had been one of her "greatest joys" since the time as an infant when she was granted the privilege of holding the candle that started the fire as the youngest child on hand.

Though Pickett briefly turns her attention to the foreman Uncle Charles's arrival atop a cart bearing Christmas gifts and foodstuffs including New Orleans molasses, cases of figs, barrels of nuts, and the like, and after noting the sense of mystery all the barrels and boxes inspired among the "colored children," she quickly revisits her family's Yule log customs, unashamedly pillaging her *Harper's Bazar* account, even down to the "golden sunshine and mellowing rain" and the light "'ood'" kindling, though she adds that her younger brother was now accorded the honor of lighting the Yule fire (still with Aunt Dilsey's assistance). This detail clarifies that her parents made it a custom to spend Christmas at her maternal grandmother's place, not just the particular Yuletide she recollected for *Harper's Bazar* or in her earlier *Yule Log* book. And, as might be expected, she gives ample treatment to the gift-giving and feasting accompanying the occasion, almost all of it lifted word for word from the earlier piece.

Curiously, none of LaSalle Pickett's memoirs on antebellum plantation Christmastimes reinforced contemporary claims in American magazines and newspapers that enslaved people soaked Yule logs for longer Christmas holidays. Instead, she undercut that notion by noting that her grandmother's workers believed a year of disaster would follow if the log failed "to give itself wholly to the sacrifice," and thus worried that the log might *not* fully burn rather than that it would not burn long enough to get them a lengthy holiday. From her telling, enslaved people mostly cared about Yule logs because of the lye produced with their ashes. These they used later "to kill evil spirits and free themselves from the sins they had committed during the year." Blacks in the antebellum Pickett household, in other words, were superstitious but not tricksters when it came to the burning of Yule logs, at least as she remembered them. Still, Pickett's book *Yule Log* reinforced contemporary notions about their importance for enslaved holidays by having the Turkey Island plantation slave Jack state that Christmas lasted while the yearly log burned. And she did emphasize that logs were waterlogged, in that her memoirs made a point of noting how Yule logs were well exposed to rain during their seasoning process.

Without embellishing soaking legends, LaSalle Pickett put an authorly spotlight on Yule logs in four publications, making her the legend's over-achiever. Moreover, her reminiscences embedded in American popular culture impressions that enslaver–enslaved relations were harmonious and reciprocal and that those relations, framed within annual Yule log rituals, reached their apogee at Christmastime. After all, once her white family fin-ished their Christmas feast, all the "good" leftovers were sent on for the ser-vants' own feast in the mansion's weaving room, in which all the looms had been discreetly hidden by mistletoe and holly decorations. What more could any forced laborer have wanted?[20]

✳✳✳

Even as LaSalle Pickett went public on the private Yule log customs in antebellum plantation households, retrospective glances at antebellum slaves handling Yule logs began to permeate her country's popular culture more than before, even in the North. It was during the early twentieth century that Philadelphian Jean Leon Gerome Ferris (1863–1930) executed in oil *The*

Figure 4.4.   Distributing Christmas presents to servants. Stereotypical 1855 etching titled "Christmas Gifts." It depicts a white slaveholding woman and, presumably, her daughter distributing presents to Black household servants.
Source: Maryland Department Photograph Collection, Enoch Pratt Free Library, Baltimore.

Mount Vernon Yule Log for his ambitious seventy-eight-scene series depicting American history, a painting that reinforced notions that eighteenth-century southerners burned Yule logs and that enslaved Blacks did the work of preparing them for burning. As Ferris envisioned his scene, George Washington, on horseback, watches on as two Blacks riding a yoke of oxen and heralded by a Black fiddler haul Yule log and Christmas tree to the front of his mansion. A lumber company's full-page illustrated advertisement in the Christmas 1919 issue of a Chicago trade journal explained, with a similar focus on Virginia, that the Old Dominion's slaves before the Civil War preferred black gums for their Yule logs since the wood burned so slowly that they might get a week off for idleness and dancing. Similarly confident a couple of decades later about the actuality of such practices, the *Zebulon* (OH) *Record* stated during the 1937 Christmas season that, before the Civil War, slaves, following Saxon customs, soaked Yule logs in cypress swamps for longer holidays. Around the same time, Harold E. Christie, a freelance journalist, highlighted in the *Indianapolis Star*, with derogatory racist coding, the subterfuges resorted to by slaves to extend their logs' life span:

> Back in slavery days, the blacks were permitted a Christmas celebration which included the burning of a Christmas log. The feast and freedom would continue as long as the log continued to burn. The darkies devised many ways to make the log burn longer. They chose the knottiest and largest green log they could secure. Frequently they soaked it in water before bringing it into the house. And at the end of the ceremonies, the darkies flocked about the fire-place, collecting the ashes from the log. It was preserved throughout the year as good luck charms.[21]

But if scattered northern voices embraced southern Yule log tales, white southerners still dominated storytelling ranks, though pinning down regional affiliation can be tricky. In 1909, Scipio Africanus Kenner, an elderly Mormon known for his journalism and influential prominence in his state's bar, made the sweeping claim in a *Western Monthly* article that before the Civil War, soaked green Yule logs eighteen inches in diameter lengthened the Christmases of all "Colored people" throughout the South to "the greater part of a month"! One might chalk Kenner up as the rare westerner relating Yule log stories. But Kenner (b. 1946) had passed his entire childhood and nearly all his teen years in the slave state of Missouri. The popular early twentieth-century New Jersey writer J. Walter McSpadden presents a parallel case. In his 1926 young adult novel *Indiana*, McSpadden had the hostess of a Wayne County farm's Christmas gathering ask guests if they knew that "in the old slave times" "farther south" enslaved people-soaked green logs in creeks to lengthen their holidays. Since McSpadden resided in New

Figure 4.5. A lumber company spreads southern Yule log myths. This Memphis lumber company's advertisement appeared in a lumber industry trade magazine published in Chicago. The advertisement contends that black gums provided the slaves' preferred timber because they burned slowly.

Source: *Harwood Record*, December 25, 1919, 67.

Jersey for much of his adult life and published *Indiana* with J. H. Spears in Manhattan, one might think him a Yankee appropriating a southern legend. But McSpadden was a native of Knoxville, Tennessee, who never shed his southern sense of self.[21]

What most changed over time were the sources for these tales. As generations passed away, there were fewer and fewer chroniclers who could, like the Cameron sisters and LaSalle Pickett, profess recollections of having themselves witnessed Yule log tricksters at work. Rather, southern white Yule log chroniclers now attributed their knowledge to conversations with older family members or other acquaintances who had been alive before the Civil War. The more time separated Yule log–tale tellers from the events they described, the more storytellers certified their secondhand credentials for telling the tale.

When Mississippian Louise Campbell Miller delivered a paper to the Washington County (Mississippi) Historical Society in 1913 relating how enslaved people soaked Yule logs on her grandfather's Argyle Plantation, she credited two aunts as her source. "Being asked to tell of Christmas times on a plantation, I must first tell you that my story must be only what someone has told me," admitted Genevieve Tapscott Bill, in her Arkansas newspaper Yule log account in 1916. "There are a few old people still living who like to talk about the good old antebellum days and Christmas on the southern plantations," mused Walter E. Campbell, before explaining Yule log traditions in a Greensboro, North Carolina, paper in 1938. Such survivors confided to him that each year's back-log was sized as large as possible for the master's fireplace, cut around the first frost, and then soaked in a creek or pond until Christmas. Then the "bringing in of the Yule log" became "the occasion for a great annual ceremony when all the plantation help lined up behind the bearers to see the log placed in the fireplace." Before relating to a different Tar Heel State paper's readers how giant Yule logs were cut from hickory trees, soaked for months, and borne to their burnings "on the shoulders of four husky men," Mary Alice Blackmore assigned her particulars to her grandmother.[22]

In one instance, a Yule log information trail resembles the game of "telephone" for its sequential transmissions. In a piece for a Raleigh, North Carolina, paper in 1955, writer Nell Battle Lewis explained that Anne Batchelor Meekins had said to her that Plummer Batchelor, Anne's father, "used to tell about how slaves on his family's plantation in Warren County made a big thing of going out to get the Yule log." They were sure that if allowed to carry it into the house they would gain immunity from witchcraft for the next year. Lewis, clearly, was twice removed from her evidence.[23]

Although all these Yule log story recyclers attributed their knowledge to white informants, Quimby Melton Sr. (1890–1977), the publisher of a Spalding County, Georgia, newspaper, the *Griffin Daily News*, broke that mold. Melton cited an African American as his source. The newsman related that during his boyhood he had a Black acquaintance, one "Uncle LeGrand," who much earlier in life had been enslaved on an Alabama plantation. Melton gained LeGrand's acquaintance when LeGrand "worked around the old girls college in Tuscaloosa" (the Alabama Central Female College), where Melton's father Fletcher served as president. One day, when asked by Melton for a Christmas story, LeGrand answered that he and his enslaved peers had always enjoyed ample time for a holiday partying because Christmas lasted "as long as the big backlog burned in the big fireplace in the big house." LeGrand divulged that one year the slaves chose and soaked so heavy and tough an "ironwood tree" that it required "many an ax" just to bring it down as well as oxen to drag to the "big house." Their payoff for a subterfuge which, LeGrand chuckled, only "a few of us on the place" knew about? A more than two-week vacation.[24]

Unfortunately, pretenses of authenticity and objectivity in twentieth-century southern white renditions of Yule log legends demand juxtaposing against the racist and self-serving sectional propaganda infusing these same writings. Melton, to give one example, was a notorious segregationist who gained attention statewide and beyond for his vehement opposition to the US Supreme Court's fateful school integration decision in the *Brown* case in 1954. In fact, he helped spearhead the reactive initiative that in 1956 (two years before he published his Yule log article) embedded the Confederate battle flag within Georgia's state flag. Nearly a century after Appomattox, Melton was as fanatically pro-Confederate in his ideology as one might imagine. Repeatedly, he took to speakers' platforms at Confederate Memorial Day events and meetings of the United Daughters of the Confederacy, where listeners heard him rail against Yankee bayonets responsible for freeing Georgia's "deluded negroes" from their masters during a civil war that ended with the destruction of all Georgian Confederate soldiers' homes and their crop fields turned to weed. His polemics had victorious Yankees, carpetbaggers, and scalawags unconcernedly abandoning Blacks immediately after the Confederate surrender, so that former slaves found themselves "staggering" along Georgia's streets "drunk on Yankee booze and the promise of 40 acres and a mule." Melton praised the UDC's campaign to replace the "War of the Rebellion" with "War Between the States" as the standard terminology for what today we usually call the Civil War (implying misleadingly that the war was fought over regional disputes over states' rights rather than slavery) and declared that history never saw "finer soldiers" than the followers of Confederate generals like Robert E. Lee and Stonewall Jackson. He also declared that Confederate women established a standard for heroism "equalled [*sic*] by no other group in the world's history" and dubbed the UDC the "greatest organization of its kind the world has ever known"![25]

When describing Yule log customs before the Civil War, Melton implicitly endorsed the Old South's labor system by emphasizing how in the Tuscaloosa area "Negroes" from "all over the neighborhood" cherished their Christmas holidays and their annual "dance in the quarters"—summed up in Uncle LeGrand's declaration that "Christmas back on the plantation was something shore nuff." That Melton describes LeGrand condescendingly

as a pipe-smoking "Uncle Remus" type who told "tall tales" in the vein of
Remus, however, undercuts the credibility of this story, not just because tall
tales are definitionally fiction but, more importantly, because the fictional
Remus held no outward grudges about once being enslaved and retained
only agreeable recollections of that phase of his life. That Melton quoted
LeGrand's word for word, decades after LeGrand told him the Yule log story,
further tarnishes the columnist's credibility. One quoted passage ran a full
one hundred words.

Consider, likewise, the way in which the best-selling Kentucky fiction
writer Janice Holt Giles framed her 1973 Houghton Mifflin memoir of her
childhood, based on what her grandmother Catherine Babb taught her grand-
children "about the old days in Mississippi before the war and how gracious
life was then." According to Giles (who defensively claimed Babb "held
no brief for slavery"), her grandmother had "staunchly insisted that slaves
belonging to her [Giles's] grandfather and to her own parents were well
treated" and "catered to." Within that context, Giles explained that enslaved
people received extra provisions, clothing, and whisky for eggnog making at
Christmastime and that slaves had surcease from labor so long as the Yule log
burned. Those logs were green and oversized, and they were presoaked for
several weeks in water. According to Babb, sometimes the logs took as long
as two weeks to be reduced to ashes.[26]

A high proportion of twentieth-century expositors of Yule log legends, moreover, were direct descendants of Confederate veterans, which clearly influenced their perspectives on antebellum southern Christmas customs. John H.
K. Shannahan Jr., a Sparrows Point, Maryland, resident, published an article
in 1907 about slaves' Yule log soakings in the *Baltimore Sun*'s "Romance of
the Eastern Shore" series. Shannahan's father was a Confederate veteran who
had joined up with the Chesapeake Light Artillery when the Civil War began
and served in Lee's Army of Northern Virginia for most of the conflict; and
Shannahan Jr. would accept the duties of historian of a Sons of Confederate
Veterans chapter in 1917. Fondly reflecting that in antebellum times a planter
in the Eastern Shore might live like "a veritable Norman lord" with more than
a thousand acres and quarters for his slaves, Shannahan divulged that come
Christmas the master would receive his "black henchmen" on the veranda.
Once all were assembled, he would give each slave "some trifling present,
while the delighted blacks bow and scrape with a 'Thanky Marsa.'" And a
Yule log "kept soaking in a neighboring swamp since the previous Christmas"
ensured the holiday would linger for some time.[27]

In a stunning example of neo-Confederate excess, Montpelier, Louisiana,
native and history buff John Milton Tate wrote for a small Louisiana paper
that in the pre–Civil War South, weeks prior to Christmas, a slave "whose
business it was to make the fires" went out to cut a "huge green log" in the

woods prior to soaking it in a pond for a long holiday. Shockingly, given modern perspectives on enslavement, Tate, the son of a Confederate veteran, prefaced his findings by declaring that the South's "negro slaves were the happiest and most contented people on earth"—so "carefree" they never worried about the future! Here we have a Confederate descendant suggesting, implicitly, that not a single enslaved person in the entire South before the Civil War ever worried about whippings, sexual abuse, the sale of family members, or not having enough to eat or warm enough clothing![28]

And we should not overlook how many of the southern white women who recounted Yule log traditions held leadership roles in the United Daughters of the Confederacy. In fact, there was a near perfect correlation between Yule log storytelling by southern women and UDC affiliation. Louise Campbell Miller's father, William Reynolds Campbell Jr., volunteered for a Washington County, Mississippi, volunteer cavalry company to fight for the Confederacy in 1861 and remained with it at the rank of corporal after it was folded into the Twenty-Eighth Confederate Cavalry Regiment in 1862. Campbell made certain in her county historical association speech to report that Yankee soldiers burned her grandfather's colonial style mansion at Argyle. Possibly, her father told her at some point about the later humiliation he experienced in seeking a pardon from President Andrew Johnson immediately after the war for his role in the recent "rebellion," revocable should he "hereafter, at any time, acquire any property whatever, in slaves." Perhaps she belonged to the UDC by the time she read that paper in 1913. In 1930, she would gain notice in the *Jackson Daily Clarion* for giving a paper about Confederate general and Jefferson Davis's nephew Joseph R. Davis to a monthly meeting of the John T. Fairly (Mount Olive) UDC chapter 1156. In 1940, that same paper spotlighted her throwing a tea party for the officers of the Mississippi Division of the UDC and alluded to her service as director of the UDC's affiliate group Children of the Confederacy. Eventually she became vice president of her chapter.[29]

Mary Alice Blackmore presents an even clearer case of the association connecting Yule log lore and UDC activism. A never-married, native North Carolinian whose father had a long career as Warsaw Township justice of the peace, Blackmore spent the greater share of a lifelong business career as a bookkeeper for a Warsaw (NC) wholesale company. In her free time, she threw herself into the affairs of the local James Kenan Chapter of the United Daughters of the Confederacy, serving it as chapter historian and "Recorder of the Crosses of Military Service." Around the time she published her Yule log account in 1949, she attended a statewide UDC convention, agreeing there to serve as state historian for the following year. And she garnered a state UDC loving cup trophy for one of her essays.[30]

Author Janice Holt Giles's adoration of the Confederacy began when she was six or seven years old and had a lot to do with her parents each summer taking her to Arkansas to visit her grandfather on her paternal side, James Knox Polk Holt (named, of course, for America's slaveholding eleventh president). At the age of seventeen, "Grandpa" had volunteered for Confederate service in the Nineteenth Arkansas Infantry Regiment on October 19, 1861, and (according to Giles) served in Confederate ranks through almost the entire Civil War, suffering a wound at the battle of Pea Ridge. Each of her family's visits to her grandfather's place during her childhood by design was timed to coincide with the annual reunion of local Confederate veterans in the small town of Charleston, near the farm where her grandfather lived, which was quite the celebration, with a carnival, veterans' parade through town, and picnic at a local, wooded park. She had thrilled, Giles remembered, how her grandfather, always donned in a "battered old gray uniform," led the sixty or so veterans through town carrying the Confederate flag, while a band played "Dixie" repeatedly. And more revealing still of her own ideology and affinities, she noted that the UDC, "to which most of the women in our family proudly belonged" helped run the cold drink and food stands at the reunion and that her grandfather to his dying day had persisted in his belief that the southern states had conformed to the US Constitution in seceding from the Union. "I grew up saturated in this belief," she volunteered.[31]

Such obvious biases invite skepticism about the veracity of these Yule log storytellers. One can just imagine how often, when Christmas came around, speakers at holiday meetings of chapters of the United Daughters of the Confederacy reinforced their members' racial biases with pleasant, mellow mythmaking about bygone times when Blacks knew and appreciated their assigned roles as coerced laborers on southern plantations and happily rolled Yule logs into their beloved generous masters' dwellings to kick off Christmas holiday festivities. After all, these masters and their wives were warmhearted souls apparently unfamiliar with the whip, as Louise Miller implied in her historical society presentation by noting that slaves soaking Yule logs for longer holidays "was a joke known and tolerated by the Old Marster and his wife."[32] Implied in such messaging was not only that the South's enslaved laborers got away with their prank but also that they had no cause for complaint about their bondage, given the leniency and tolerance of their owners.

Three months after being installed in 1950 as a UDC chapter historian, Lola Silman Wood played to southern racial stereotypes by presenting a paper titled "Christmas Customs Peculiar to the Southern States, Particularly Those of the Past" to the holiday meeting of the Warren Rifles UDC in a Front Royal, Virginia, Presbyterian church's social room. Well before Christmas in the years before the "War between the States," Wood explained, plantation "darkeys" chose a black-gum log, soaking it and turning it daily in a creek so it would be "near fireproof" for its Yuletide burning. Invariably, they succeeded, sometimes so completely that "the holidays would be over before it kindled and burned through" (an unintended and probably overlooked admission that undercut the axiom that enslaved people never returned to labor until the Yule log's flame was extinguished). Men selected for the task of hauling the heavy log to the big house, she continued, felt so honored they joyously sang spirituals and carols as they approached the building. Then the plantation fun truly kicked in, with a "velvet dressed negro butler" ready at the door to welcome guests. On Christmas Day, "little black kinky headed" children watched the game of "'Kismas Gif'" being played with white family members, before all the slaves received ample presents from their owners. Some even enjoyed the rare privilege of taking a meal in the big house kitchen instead of their own quarters. "Joy was rampant," speaker Wood reflected confidently, "from the oldest darkey to the youngest pickaninny."[33]

We can be sure, I think, that no one in the room disputed the content or skewed, insensitive tone of Wood's presentation. Nor is it likely that anyone raised reservations when another very active UDC member, Dorothy C. Dixon, told the 1957 Christmas season meeting of the Richmond, Virginia, "Stonewall Jackson" chapter that enslaved Blacks in the Old South successfully lengthened their Christmas hiatus by diligently soaking a huge, green log for a whole half year before Christmas. Similarly, Bessie Croswell, a UDC officeholder including chapter president and sometime Virginia UDC Fifth District conference delegate, presumably met no backlash when she informed a chapter holiday meeting in 1972 not only that slaves enjoyed long Christmas breaks in the old South because their Yule logs "mysteriously" lasted longer than they should but also that "of all those who enjoyed Christmas then, no one had a better time than the slaves."[34]

It is doubtful that UDC members like Wood, Dixon, and Croswell ever even tried to retrieve the perspectives of enslaved people before drafting their presentations on Yule log lore. But Dixon did note that her findings were based partly on forays to Confederate museums and by reading the works of Robert E. Lee biographer Douglas Southall Freeman (which so far as I know do not mention Yule logs at all!). Balanced history, we can safely guess, was not Dorothy Dixon's holy grail, nor the goal of others relating stereotypical white southern Yule log lore to receptive public and reading audiences at the very moment when the civil rights movement was challenging the South's entrenched system of racial segregation. That a Greensboro, North Carolina, paper in 1971 quipped, after repeating standard white southern Yule log lore, "What would the boss say if you didn't report back to work for several days after Christmas and gave as the excuse, 'The Yule Log was still burning'?" shows how shallowly white southerners parsed the custom and how ill-prepared they were to unpack the meanings of Christmas for enslaved Blacks. It is instructive that Mrs. Dixon's husband, Fred, when serving as principal of Richmond's John Marshall High School, had no problem accepting the donation of forty books on southern history to his school's library from chapter members of the Virginia UDC and Sons of Confederate Veterans. Although we do not know the authors and titles of these books, we can guess that they did not include the *Narrative of the Life of Frederick Douglass* or any of the volumes of W. E. B. Du Bois. I have yet to encounter a piece of evidence indicating that a southern white author or speaker puzzled over whether the enslaved people cutting and carrying Yule logs would have gladly traded the experience for the freedom and wealth of their masters and mistresses.[35]

Chapter 5

A Sorcerer's Revelations

By now, it should be apparent that the decades between the end of Reconstruction and World War I birthed southern Yule log mythologies. It was not until then that a wave of widely disseminated accounts of this purported tradition caught the attention of literate Americans. And it should also be clear that this surge of Yule log stories was nearly entirely the work of white southern men and women, many of them Virginians or North Carolinians by birth or residence. White Americans, not Black Americans, owned Yule log–soaking legends.

It dawned on me early in my research for this book, in fact, that prior to 1901 African Americans had nothing to say about this custom, at least in print. This, despite its suggestive meanings for Black behaviors, aspirations, and community solidarity under enslavement. Although the white-authored Yule log stories of the late nineteenth century and early twentieth century varied in their particulars (e.g., which timbers were preferred, the room in the master's mansion with the Yule log fireplace, and the month or season logs were submerged in swamps or streams), they implied group solidarity and especially male bonding among enslaved communities in the Old South. Yule log tales suggested it took a team of Black men working collaboratively to pull off a stalling caper. The Yule log soaker was no lone wolf. Black publications could have drawn significant empowering meanings from these tales, had they been so inclined.

Yet, just as Black publications had been silent about plantation Yule log traditions before the Civil War, they remained so afterward. Such avoidances persisted despite a growing number of potential literary outlets for such stories. The post–Civil War years witnessed a stream of newly published ex-slave reminiscences that coincided with a marked decline in Black illiteracy (from 70 to 30 percent between 1880 and 1910) and a proliferation of new magazines and newspapers aimed at Black readers. In 1898 alone, African Americans founded eighty-one newspapers, more than twice as many as Blacks had founded in the entire pre-Reconstruction history of the country.

Yet, both ex-slave memoirists and the Black press avoided mentioning Yule logs in the context of slave holidays.[1]

The same held true with Black fiction. There was no African American literary counterpart to John Fox Jr., who featured Yule log–soaking lore to enliven a novel. Black short fiction writers, too, ignored the tradition. Bettye Collier-Thomas's two-volume *Treasury of African American Christmas Stories* features thirty-one short stories and poems about Christmas authored by African Americans in the late nineteenth and early twentieth centuries. A few were set in the South and had content about slavery. But if you check these tales, you will search in vain for mention of Yule logs.[2]

When in 1897 the *Afro-American Sentinel* of Omaha, Nebraska, republished a widely circulating article touching briefly on Yule logs, those logs had nothing to do with the enslaved experience in the Old South. Rather, the article covered European "Old Time Customs." The author explained how in Europe large logs had been "brought into the house with great ceremony on Christmas Eve" and ignited with a brand salvaged from the previous year's log. It also mentioned the superstition that if the log did not burn for *one* entire night, it was an omen of bad luck. Most enslaved people in the Old South, of course, if we are to take white Yule log tales about Blacks as literal truths, would have considered one that burned a single night a mockery of their hopes for a lengthy holiday respite from labor.[3]

Meanwhile, the magazines of Black institutions of higher learning overlooked the Yule log–soaking legend, even at holiday time. During Christmas in 1900, a writer for Howard University's magazine, in an article titled "Customs and Legends of the Yule Tide," asserted that it had been a tradition in England for Yule logs to be "brought in by the servants" (as onlookers sang Yule songs and drank spiced ale), without making the logical extension that southern enslaved people before the Civil War might have adapted English Yule log customs to their own ends.[4]

Similar silences prevailed at the Hampton (VA) Normal and Agricultural Institute (today's Hampton University), or so I assume based on the February 1897 issue of the *Southern Workman and Hampton School Record*, its official magazine. Situated on the southeast tip of Virginia's James-York peninsula not far from Hampton Roads, the institute, founded during Reconstruction, sought to educate future Black teachers and uplift the area's African American population through a program emphasizing industrial and agricultural training, with the latter goal especially pushed at the school's donated former plantation tract called Shellbanks. The February 1897 *Southern Workman* issue described activities at the Shellbanks farmhouse during the recent Christmas, including a student apple-biting contest and a procession from the grounds into the farmhouse parlor. The latter was led by two torch-carrying students and followed by fellow students bearing a Yule log trimmed for the season.

According to the magazine, the students upon reaching the fireplace met up with a teacher who read verse just written for the ceremony, including these bland lines:

> Give to the flames your Yule log
> And may its burning light.
> With richest Christmas blessing.
> Fill every heart tonight.

Then the students cast the log into the flames. Although this ritual presented the perfect time for Hampton teachers or administrators, or a selected student, to provide educational remarks either before or after the ceremony enlightening participants on the historical meaning of Yule logs in the lives and community cultures of southern African Americans *had that been the case*, no one said anything of the sort. Instead, school officials turned students' attention immediately to a "heavily loaded [Christmas] tree" in the same room and singing a song to welcome Santa Claus into their circle.[5]

Still, a few years after this ritual at Hampton, that same institution's most famous graduate, Booker T. Washington, would say plenty about Yule logs as markers for the enslaved Christmas experience, and his statements would resonate so widely that a Louisiana newspaper would claim in 2004 that historians "gleaned" that the country's "Yule log tradition" was rooted in American slavery from the "writings of Booker T. Washington."[6] By publishing authoritative pronouncements about enslaved people and Christmas log customs, Washington paved the way for the story's cross-racial appeal later in the twentieth century. Following Washington's revelations about Yule log traditions, African Americans for the first time would claim the legend for themselves.

✳✳✳

A contested figure whose seeming passivity in the face of escalating racial segregation in the late nineteenth-century South caused critics, then and later, to mock him as an "Uncle Tom" (for the enslaved Uncle Tom in Harriet Beecher Stowe's *Uncle Tom's Cabin*),[7] Booker T. Washington (1856–1915) achieved a prominence nationally unmatched by any other Black leader during his lifetime, except, arguably, Frederick Douglass or W. E. B. Du Bois. When Washington connected Yule logs to enslaved Christmas experiences in Virginia in his inspiring autobiography *Up from Slavery* (1901), it resonated not only with white Americans who held him in high esteem but also with admiring Black Americans.

The son of an enslaved cook and a white man whose identity has never been indisputably established, Washington spent his early years in bondage on James Burroughs's modest 207-acre tobacco farm in the foothills of Virginia's Blue Ridge Mountains some twenty miles southeast of Roanoke. Burroughs's holding was nothing like the grand plantations at the heart of Yule log lore about the Old South. He only owned a small number of slaves and worked side by side with them in the fields prior to his death in July 1861 shortly after the Civil War began. During his enslaved years, Washington was housed in a small split-oak log cabin, went barefoot until the age of eight, and was tasked with the menial work of fanning away flies from the Burroughs table at mealtimes.

Covetous of an education from an early age, Washington took advantage of available night classes and serendipitous learning opportunities that came his way after the Civil War when his Black stepfather removed his now-free family to the Kanawha River Valley town of Malden, West Virginia, and pursued work at nearby salt furnaces. Ultimately, Booker's desire for further education and his anxiety about winding up as a coal miner if he remained undereducated led him eastward across Virginia to the Hampton Normal and Agricultural Institute, where he earned his admission by sweeping a recitation room and matriculated in 1872. As an enrolled student while working part-time as a janitor in lieu of paying tuition, he excelled at debate, absorbed the Hampton philosophy of "industrial education" (gaining proficiency in a trade along with traditional academic coursework), and graduated in 1875 with a certificate confirming his competency to teach school.

After trying his hand not only at teaching but also waitering at a hotel in the North and attending a Baptist seminary in Washington, DC, Booker got a pivotal career break in 1881 when he was twenty-five. On the recommendation of the Hampton Institute's founder and principal Samuel Armstrong, he gained appointment as the first principal of the Tuskegee Normal School (which in 1889 became the Tuskegee Normal and Industrial Institute) in Tuskegee, Alabama—an institution for the training of Black elementary school teachers in academic subjects supplemented by the kind of industrial education emphasized at Hampton. Washington wanted students not only to master practical skills like brickmaking, carpentry, sewing, printing, blacksmithing, and farming but he also saw the advantages of having students as part of their coursework apply their learning to the improvement of the institute's physical plant, a shrewd approach given Tuskegee's Spartan budget and constant quest for funding. Bricks for new Tuskegee buildings, to give one example, were produced on-site.[8]

Over the next decade and a half, Washington parlayed his accomplishments as Tuskegee's principal into remarkable power and notoriety for an African American in the Deep South. His success contrasted sharply with the circumstances of most Black southerners, whose opportunities often contracted rather than expanded during the same period. After overthrowing

Young Women's Department, with Industrial and Dining Rooms.
[Virginia Hall stands just in rear of the above long wooden building, which will eventually be removed.]

Teachers' Residence.

Hampton Creek.

Barn and Store-House.

Young Men's Department, with Assembly and Recitation Rooms.

Hampton Normal and Agricultural Institute.

[BEFORE THE ERECTION OF VIRGINIA HALL.]

Figure 5.1. Hampton Normal and Agricultural Institute. A depiction of the Hampton Institute at the time Booker T. Washington was a student.

Source: Frontispiece, Catalogue of the Hampton Normal and Agricultural Institute, Hampton, Virginia, 1871–72 (Hampton: Normal School Press, 1872).

Radical Reconstruction in the mid- and late 1870s, white southerners, through legal measures reinforced by intimidation and violence, reversed many recent Black advancements—especially in the right to vote and hold office—and imposed rigid segregation of the races in *unequal* public accommodations, schools, and churches. Washington's story, though, was quite different.

Washington achieved his influence by shrewdly cultivating the support of white Alabama newsmen, local political bosses, and legislators, by convincing white philanthropists to invest in his school's development and by courting the distinguished figures he invited to the Tuskegee campus for speeches. Additionally, he lobbied vigorously for funding on behalf of his institution at the state and national levels and through his own publications and voluminous letter-writing. After he issued a call in 1900 leading to the founding of the National Negro Business League in Boston and gained the new organization's presidency, his stature only grew further.

Washington's efforts, however, would have faltered without the "sorcery" he applied to his initiatives. Had he not figured out how to manipulate the prominent white figures he met through his marked personal charm and bargaining skills, his institution and career might have failed in tandem, since the institute so depended on outside funding. Given that Black civil rights were in retreat after Reconstruction and that many of his school's biggest backers were northern industrialists, he calculatedly condemned labor union organizing and strikes and avoided speaking out publicly against the ugly race riots and racial discrimination thwarting Black progress not only in the Deep South where Tuskegee was situated but also elsewhere in the nation.

Never truly an "Uncle Tom" in the sense of being entirely compliant regarding segregation and disfranchisement, Tuskegee's principal occasionally entered the civil rights fray. Behind the scenes, he raised money for a legal test by the recently formed National Afro-American Council against Louisiana's new 1898 constitution's "grandfather clause" imposing literacy requirements for voting upon otherwise eligible Blacks while exempting most white Louisiana voters. Additionally, Washington tried to negotiate with railroad company executives to secure better conditions for Blacks on segregated railroad lines. Still, it is significant that he masked his identity in the Afro-American Council's records (where he turns up undetectably as "X. Y. Z.") and consistently resisted the temptation to push back publicly against white bigotry. He condoned the 1883 decision of the US Supreme Court (the "Civil Rights Cases") that overturned the Reconstruction Congress's landmark anti-segregation measure, the Civil Rights Act of 1875, and opposed federal legislation proposed in 1890 (the so-called Force Bill) to compel federal supervision of southern elections to ensure the upholding of Black voting rights. On campus, Washington remained remarkably even-tempered when visiting white politicians used racially derogatory terms and insulted him to his face. Maintaining an iron grip on his students' out-of-class lives, he repressed their engaging in active protests on race issues, even on the lynching question.

It was Washington's public compliance with white segregation norms that led to the highly flattering invitation he received to address the 1895 Cotton States and International Exposition in Atlanta on its opening day. This address, delivered before a racially mixed but segregated and mostly white assemblage, would be the most consequential speech of his life—his infamous "Atlanta Compromise." In relatively brief remarks celebrated by ecstatic white segregationists in his audience and elsewhere once the speech was disseminated by the news media, Washington touted a southern racial rapprochement between whites and Blacks in such easily grasped and powerful language that he was "catapulted," according to his biographer Louis R. Harlan, "into national prominence as a Negro spokesman," however much it alarmed militantly integrationist Black activists. "He said something that was death to the Afro-American," declared one Black newspaper editor.[9]

Washington started his Atlanta address by suggesting that southern Blacks had been too ambitious in seeking political office immediately following their enslavement. Instead, they should have been acquiring the industrial and agricultural skills that they would require to sustain themselves economically in

Figure 5.2.   Booker T. Washington at his Tuskegee office.
Source: Library of Congress Prints and Photographs Division.

the long term: how shortsighted it was to fall for the seduction of "the political convention or stump speaking" during Reconstruction when they might have been occupied developing dairy farms and truck gardens. Elaborating on the theme that incremental racial progress beat quixotic quests for instant political justice, Washington urged his "race" to befriend southern whites holding the strings in their regional economy and to be content with whatever modest opportunities those whites provided them. For the time being, Blacks should cast their "buckets" in farming, industry, the professions, commerce, and, for women, "domestic service"—seemingly a plea that Black women considered laboring as maids in wealthy white households, performing tasks barely different from the routines of house slaves before the Civil War.

Still, there was a quid pro quo in Washington's deal. For both races to benefit from his program, whites needed to facilitate Blacks' access to economic opportunities. Directly addressing white southerners on their responsibilities, Washington condemned initiatives in the southern states to replace Black laborers with immigrant workers who spoke "strange" words and behaved in unfamiliar ways. Conversely, white southerners should employ the "eight millions of Negroes" already there—people "whose habits you know, whose fidelity and love you have tested"—and better appreciate their docility. Unlike foreign workers, Blacks eschewed "strikes and labour wars." Surely, if southern whites merely provided Blacks with the modest opportunities needed to get ahead, they would be rewarded for their wisdom. They and their families would be "surrounded by the most patient, faithful, law-abiding, and unresentful people that the world has seen." Washington then elaborated what such fealty would involve:

> As we have proved our loyalty to you in the past, in nursing your children, watching by the sickbed of your mothers and fathers, and then the children, and then following them with tear-dimmed eyes to their graves, so in the future, in our humble way, we shall stand by you with a devotion that no foreigner can approach, ready to lay down our lives, if need be, in defense of yours.

And then, once he had gotten off his chest his claim that Blacks bore no bitterness for being enslaved in the South for generations, Washington rendered a fateful concession that would forever tarnish his legacy: if whites aided Blacks economically in his envisioned pursuit of "mutual progress" for both races, *segregation was tolerable.* In "purely social" human relations, whites and Blacks could remain "as separate as the fingers"![10]

How easy and convenient it was, as Washington finished his remarks, for whites in his audience to mull over those concluding words, even as his prior beseeching of whites to offer Blacks employment opportunities faded from their memories. How easy it was, over the succeeding months and years, as his Atlanta comments were disseminated nationally, for upholders of segregation, based on this speech and some of his other, similar, public remarks, to claim that Washington *opposed* Black voting and officeholding and *endorsed* segregation, which was a gross distortion of his position. And for the very reason that Washington's speech resonated so powerfully with whites, his national stature grew noticeably, so much so that when Theodore Roosevelt became president he consulted with Washington on Black political patronage and invited him to dine at the White House—a variance so extreme from the day's race protocols that it sparked angry blowback, especially from white southerners. Unsurprisingly, Washington's accommodationist ideas sparked resistance from more confrontational African American figures such as W. E. B. Du Bois, who would later help found the National Association for the Advancement of Colored People (NAACP) and William Monroe Trotter, publisher of the *Boston Guardian*. But multitudes of other African Americans across the country, especially in the South, revered him as a race leader who had achieved nationwide prominence and acclaim. By the time the Doubleday, Page & Company publishing house in New York City released Washington's *Up from Slavery: An Autobiography* in 1901, his fame and what today we might deem his favorability ratings were at their peak, ensuring his memoir a very strong biracial and nationwide readership.

✷✷✷

Washington's fleeting passage about Yule logs in *Up from Slavery*, a preview of a more elaborate account he would author in 1907, said nothing about enslaved people soaking back-logs, an omission he would reverse in the later piece. Washington did, however, reinforce the notion that the length of Christmastime for enslaved Blacks in the Old South had nothing to do with the desires and whims of enslavers and everything to do with the burnability of Yule logs. In *Up from Slavery*, Tuskegee's famed principal implied that nothing mattered when it came to Christmas holidays for the Old South's people in bondage but whether one log would burn slowly or quickly. The needs and conveniences of enslavers were immaterial, in Washington's telling, when it came to putting limits on Christmas celebrations.

Washington brought Yule logs up in the context of relating his family's experiences during their first Christmas at Tuskegee in 1881 following his appointment as principal. After reporting that throughout the very early morning hours on Christmas Day family members were awakened and intermittently reawakened by Black children rapping on their doors and demanding "Chris-mus gifts," he digressed into a contrasting glimpse of antebellum southern Christmastimes, a natural segue because house servants had commonly made similar demands of their enslavers and their children

DINNER GIVEN AT THE WHITE HOUSE BY PRESIDENT ROOSEVELT TO BOOKER T. WASHINGTON, OCTOBER 17th, 1901

Figure 5.3.   Dinner given at the White House by President Roosevelt for Booker T. Washington, October 17, 1901.
Source: Halftone photomechanical print, Library of Congress Prints and Photographs Division.

on Christmas mornings before the Civil War. "During the days of slavery," Washington explained, "it was a custom quite generally observed throughout all the Southern states to give the coloured people a week of holiday at Christmas, to allow the holiday to continue as long as the 'yule log' lasted. The male members of the race, and often the female members, were expected to get drunk."[11]

Washington's digression in *Up from Slavery* was significant. After gaining their freedom, Frederick Douglass and other once-enslaved southern Blacks had written about how masters and mistresses encouraged and, in some instances, compelled alcohol consumption by their enslaved people over Christmas. Washington, however, was the first prominent African American that I have been able to identify who also remarked in print that there was an equation between enslaved people's Christmas holidays and how long Yule logs burned. That he did so in one of the most impactful and popular books ever written by a Black US author is equally significant. Large numbers of people read Washington's autobiography when it first appeared, either in its prepublication serialization in *Outlook* magazine or afterward as a book. Since then, vast numbers of adults and schoolchildren over many generations have enjoyed its engaging prose and theme of triumphing over adversity through perseverance. Its staying power is remarkable, and it would be a mistake to dismiss Washington's memoir as irrelevant because its upbeat tone so varies from modern emphases on systematic and long-standing institutional barriers to Black progress in this country.

Still widely available at the end of the twentieth century in various printings and formats, *Up from Slavery* ranked number three on the prestigious Modern Library's "100 Best Nonfiction" works of the twentieth century (1999). Moreover, twentieth- and twenty-first-century anthologizers of Christmas writings often appropriate *Up from Slavery*'s out-of-copyright Christmas vignette, using all or part of the Christmas chapter—"Anxious Days and Sleepless Nights"—but in either case always including its Yule log segment. The most significant of these compilations is the one assembled by the Chicago Public Library's nationally prominent African American children's literature expert, Charlemae Hill Rollins. She placed "Anxious Days" near the beginning of her 1963 collection *Christmas Gif': An Anthology of Christmas Poems, Songs, and Stories Written by and about African Americans*. "Anxious Days and Sleepless Nights" also finds its way into anthologies of autobiographical and African American writings.[12]

Washington's 1907 elaboration of his Yule log teaser in *Up from Slavery*, which appeared in the magazine *Suburban Life*, was just as significant as his autobiography in terms of influencing popular understandings of American holiday traditions, and one must wonder why he chose to write about this topic for a second time. Was it inspired by a new and very colorful account by a white southern woman of enslaved people soaking Christmas logs that had appeared in the interim since *Up from Slavery* came out? Of course, Washington could have read any prior publication with the Yule log–soaking legend, but this piece deserves mention as possibly his inspiration because it appeared in a magazine he presumably read regularly—his alma mater's *Southern Workman*—whose editorial slant aligned with his own insistence that enslavement brought benefits as well as evils to southern Black people.[13]

Almost since its founding, and at General Armstrong's prompting, the Hampton Institute had committed itself to the study of African American folklore, including the collecting of African American plantation-slave work songs, as performed by the Hampton Student Singers. Although Hampton's faculty was exclusively white during its early years, many staff members such as Robert Russa Moton, its longtime commandant of cadets and a close associate of Washington's in national fundraising initiatives for Black normal schools, were African Americans committed to the institution's folklore emphasis. And the folklore emerging from Hampton melded into Washington's own recollections about the viability of Black culture and joy of Black family life under slavery, the decency of slaveholding whites, the familiarity and cordiality between enslavers and their enslaved people as they went about their daily routines, and the reluctance of Blacks to indulge in bitterness over enslavement. That merging of white and African American folkloric perceptions about plantation life helps explain why, in the early 1900s, the *Southern Workman* published a series of nostalgic "tributes to the 'old-time Negro'" by southern white women, one of them in the form of a fictional vignette recalling antebellum Yule log customs.[14]

Since taking his position in Tuskegee, Washington's ties with the Hampton Institute had remained tight, and we can trace those bonds in the *Southern Workman*. In 1909, for example, the magazine published Washington's article "Negro Public Schools in the Gulf States"; and in 1902, it carried a biographical piece titled "Booker Washington's School Days at Hampton." After Washington visited the campus to speak at an event there in May 1905, the *Southern Workman* published extracts from his remarks, including his declaration that there was "no spot save one, and no State save one that are so dear to me as Hampton Institute and the State of Virginia."[15] So, it is very possible that Washington read the *Southern Workman* with regularity and encountered the fictional story "Aunt Kitty" in its November 1904 number by one of the parade of white southern female authors featured in the magazine, Rosa Fairfax Lee (1881–1960)—identified in a note as a Hamptonian and "niece of Judge Baker P. [Perkins] Lee." Recently deceased, Judge Lee resided in Hampton for parts of his life (including the years preceding his death). A lawyer and newsman before the Civil War, he attained the rank of major in the Confederate army and following the war was a Democratic journalist and politician, in addition to serving as a circuit court judge for Virginia's Warwick and (what was then) Elizabeth City Counties.

I have been unable to discern how close Rosa Lee was to her uncle and how much he influenced her attitudes, but I have discovered that the judge was known for honoring Confederate veterans and that one of his children was named Dixie. Then, too, Rosa's own father, Wills Lee, had served in the Confederate army for the entire conflict, mostly with the Richmond Howitzers of the Second Virginia. He, too, was caught up in memorializing the Confederacy. In 1896, the *Baltimore Sun* reported that Wills Lee had just gained membership in the United Confederate Veterans' Franklin Buchanan Camp. Whether or not Rosa Fairfax Lee fully absorbed pro-Confederate attitudes within her own family circle, she clearly held stature in traditional southern elite circles. Contemporaries recorded Lee's standing as one of the best-connected Virginia socialites of her day. When she married a nationally prominent college football coach two years after publishing "Aunt Kitty," the *Philadelphia Inquirer* reported that she hailed from the famed "F. F. V.'s of Virginia" (the so-called First Families of Virginia). In the same vein, the *Richmond Times Dispatch* (alluding to her descent from Maryland founder

Lord Baltimore) dubbed her wedding, attended by "prominent people" from cities up and down the Atlantic coast, "the most important nuptial celebration of the Easter season."[16]

"Aunt Kitty" is set in "one of the few old manor houses left standing in the South" after the Civil War, and Lee relates how a fire warms a large room with a four-posted bed and weighty mahogany furniture. Lee mentions that the property's slave quarters had previously been "all bu'nt up," seemingly implying its destruction by Union forces during the war, though she fails to make the point explicit. Within the room, two white children entreat their "red-turbaned, white-aproned" "ole mammy," Aunt Kitty, one of two "dark-ies" remaining with the family, to relate, as she had so often in the past, a "'fo de wah'" story, suggesting they most wanted to hear again her tale about the "bringing in the Yule log."

On cue, Aunt Kitty recalls the wonders of antebellum Christmas celebra-tions in the house, when "dese here halls be plumb full ob flowers" and household members played "Chris'mus gif'" and joined guests from other mansions attending the yearly Christmas ball staged there. Then Aunt Kitty reminds the very attentive children that "ole Marse" always timed the holi-day by how long the dining room fire, tended by an enslaved youth named Scipio, kept burning. Scipio knew how to maximize that time. Aunt Kitty explains that Scipio would carefully measures the fireplace before he and an accomplice cut a log big enough to take up all but an inch from each end of the hearth. Then he and his partner would haul it to a stream and let it soak for a week, a soaking so effective that after being ignited for Christmas it would still linger after two weeks, frustrating "Massa." Aunt Kitty says that Massa is impatient for the log to be consumed completely, and he threatens to "wollop 'em both!" Of course, we learn, he did no such thing. Rather, his solution to the problem was to have the boys remove the log and chop it up to be used in the kitchen fireplace. Abusive punishment would hardly have conformed to the Hampton ideology of racial harmony under the Old South's slavery régime!

In late 1907, three years after Rosa Lee published "Aunt Kitty" in Hampton Institute's magazine, Washington offered his own rendition of the story that Virginian white writers like Lee had been peddling to American readers for decades about how conniving enslaved people outwitted their masters by soaking Yule logs at Christmastime. Washington's version came toward the end of his article "Christmas Days in Old Virginia," published in the December 1907 issue of the magazine *Suburban Life*,[17] a piece that also had much to say about the preparations that went into antebellum south-ern Christmas celebrations—including corn shuckings and hog slaughter-ings—and the roles enslaved people played in their advance preparations. Throughout, Washington's account reeks of a disturbing yearning for antebellum times coming as it did from a once-enslaved youth, especially its musings that there had been a "certain charm" during Christmastime "in the old slave days" when a "peculiar fragrance" filled the air. Washington reports, in fact, that his best Christmas presents ever came not after he gained his freedom but rather during the "last Christmas I spent in slavery" (which would have been in 1864 toward the end of the Civil War). "[C]reeping over to the chimney" at four o'clock on Christmas morning, he had discovered to his delight that his stocking had been "well-filled with pieces of red candy and nearly half a dozen ginger-cakes," as well as small wooden shoes with leather tops. Toward the end of his piece, Washington laments the "stiff and staid" Christmas customs prevailing in his own times, particularly in large cities, when juxtaposed with the richer ones under Virginia's slave régime.

A signal part of those preferred antebellum customs had to do with Yule logs, which Washington spells out in richer detail than he has in *Up from Slavery*, with some of his specifics differing from most other accounts regarding when the logs were cut and when ceremonial songs were sung. As in *Up from Slavery*, Washington reports that Christmas lasted until a Yule log burned in two, but in this later retelling he maintains it took a week's time, sometimes more, and elaborates on *why* it took so long to burn a single log. Significantly, in spelling this out, Washington attributes his frame of reference not to the modest Burroughs farm where he spent his own boyhood but rather to his state's much larger plantations. On such grander places, Washington explains, enslaved people customarily soaked Yule logs for a full year in advance of their being needed:

> On many of the plantations in Virginia it was the custom for the men to go out into the swamps on the last day of the Christmas season, select the biggest, toughest and greenest hardwood tree they could find, and cut it in shape to fit the fireplace in the master's room. Afterwards this log would be sunk into the water, where it would remain the entire succeeding year. On the first day of the following Christmas, it would be taken out of the water; the slaves would go into the master's room before he got out of his bed on Christmas morning, and, with a song and other ceremonies, would place this log on the fireplace of the master, and would light it with fire.

Washington adds that another round of singing followed the expiring of the Yule log's last flame, marking that the holiday had come to an end. Regrettably, Washington never specifies what songs the slaves sang before and after the log burned.

If Washington bore any resentment about enslavement, he fails to expose it in his *Suburban Life* article. Rather, he emphasizes how most Virginian Blacks received presents of new shoes or new clothing when Christmas rolled around. He also relates that field hands as well as household slaves had the privilege of hanging their Christmas stockings in their mistresses' and masters' bedrooms, implying an intimacy between enslavers and their bond-people. And he even displays some Virginia chauvinism of his own, suggesting approvingly that the Old Dominion made more of Christmas than "most other states," if not in the present, then at least during its rich antebellum past.

Although Washington's Christmas piece in *Suburban Life* achieved less exposure than *Up from Slavery*, it was released almost simultaneously in Tuskegee's student magazine as well as in the *Presbyterian Banner*, a weekly published in Pittsburgh. A century later it was anthologized under the title "Plantation Christmas Days" in the collection *A Very Virginia Christmas*. And since 2000, it has guided the National Park Service's educational Christmas programming at the Booker T. Washington National Monument, situated on the site of the Burroughs farm where he spent his enslaved childhood.

In the first decade of this century, the National Park Service staged historical Christmas programs almost every year, sometimes explicitly as "Christmas Days in Old Virginia," and in 2000, 2001, 2002, and 2007, event promotions explicitly promised "a special reading of Booker T. Washington's 'Christmas Days in Old Virginia.'" In 2019, prior to COVID-19 shutdowns, the monument staged an original play by its senior park ranger as part of its holiday program that, playwright Timothy Sims explains, drew both from Washington's autobiography and Washington's "Christmas Days" article. Two years later, with COVID-19 restrictions being lifted in much of the country, the site revived its Christmas function, assuring attendees that they would "step back in time into a mid-nineteenth-century Christmas . . . as Dr. Booker T. Washington described it in his 1907 article." In 2023, the Park Service further disseminated Washington's Yule log stories by republishing the "Christmas Days" article on its website. Additionally, Washington's "Christmas Days" remains easily accessible in volume 1 of Louis R. Harlan's authoritative edition of the *Booker T. Washington Papers*, dedicated to Washington's autobiographical writings.[18]

Unfortunately, Harlan distorted Washington's account of Christmas and Yule logs when treating Washington's childhood in the first volume of his two-volume biography of Washington, *Booker T. Washington: The Making of a Black Leader, 1856–1901*, winner of the 1973 Bancroft Prize. Whereas Washington had asserted that on "many of the plantations in Virginia it was the custom for the men to go out into the swamps on the last day of the Christmas season" to get their log, Harlan specified that "[o]n the Burroughs place and other farms of the neighborhood, the men slaves went into the woods on the last day of the Christmas season" to cut their log. Washington never said that. Rather, he had only suggested that the practice was common-place on Virginia plantations, with no insinuation he had personal knowledge of the custom. Although it is extremely doubtful readers have ever noticed Harlan's wording sleight of hand, his esteemed biography gives an especial stamp of authenticity to Yule log lore about enslaved life before the Civil War. Anyone reading *Making of a Black Leader* would naturally assume that Washington had witnessed the Yule log customs he described, which likely is far from the truth. I certainly imagined he had the first time I read it, just as I initially assumed that the white author Rebecca Cameron had observed such scenes at her grandfather's North Carolina place. But it becomes clear on closer inspection that the messaging is ambiguous. We cannot rule out Washington's having had personal familiarity with Yule log–soaking customs, but there is also no reason to assume he did.[19]

***

Booker T. Washington was hardly the first American to write about the importance of Yule logs in the lives of enslaved people before the Civil War, but he was the most prominent. Further, he was the first African American writer to highlight enslaved peoples' Yule log customs, and this mattered. Washington's story took time to seep into African American popular culture. When Harlem Renaissance litterateur (H.) Wallace Thurman published a piece on Christmas for New York City's Black monthly, *The Messenger*, in 1925, he described how ancient Saxons of the "northland" in honoring their god Thor had initiated the custom of burning Yule logs, with apparently no awareness of that ceremony's bearing on the far more recent lives of southern slaves. Two years later, a writer in *The Crisis*, the official NAACP magazine edited by W. E. B. Du Bois, followed suit, informing readers that the burning of Yule logs began with sun worshippers and that in feudal times the hauling of a Yule log to a "fireplace in a great baronial hall" provided a joyful Christmas Eve activity.[20]

Eventually, however, other African Americans followed Washington's lead in relating tales about the importance of Yule logs in the lives of the South's enslaved people before the Civil War. It is, of course, possible that Washington's successor testifiers knew of what they spoke from personal experiences. But it is also conceivable that Washington's autobiography and *Suburban Life* accounts of slave Christmas traditions became the conduit for a transference process by which folklore invented, regularly reinvented, and popularized by southern white champions of the Lost Cause values, became absorbed, by the 1930s, into African American culture.

It was late in the 1930s, three-quarters of a century after slavery ended, that for the first time Black Americans began giving recorded oral testimony indicating the role Yule logs had played as markers of the holiday leisure of enslaved people in the Old South. It was during these late Depression years that Jenny Proctor and Tom Wilson described to Federal Writers' Project (FWP) interviewers how the duration of Yule logs governed Christmas holiday time during their enslavement. And it was in 1937 that the racially moderate Black Fisk University sociology professor Bertram Wilbur Doyle, a native of Lowndesboro, Alabama, covered southern plantation Christmases in his influential Depression-period book *Etiquette of Race Relations in the South* (1937). This volume declared that in the antebellum South, custom "decreed" that Christmas lasted so long as a Yule log burned. Significantly, although Doyle cited sources in addition to Washington's *Up from Slavery* in his note documenting his assertion, Washington's autobiography was the only one of his cited sources covering Yule log customs.

Although neither Jenny Proctor nor Tom Wilson mentioned Washington in their FWP commentaries, we cannot rule out the possibly that either or both read Washington's Yule log stories or otherwise became familiar with them, perhaps in conversations with others, prior to their interview sessions. Although Wilson implied that he did not attend any of the schools established for formerly enslaved people during Reconstruction, Proctor professed she had so craved an education when enslaved that she had sought one in defiance of strictures against slaves learning to read and write. To that end—Proctor told her interviewer—she and her fellow laborers pilfered a spelling book that they studied late at night by torchlight. Now she could credit herself with "some" reading and writing ability.[21]

It was also in the late 1930s that Alabama native, educator, columnist, and Harlem Renaissance figure Ellen Tarry, who had been steeped in Booker T. Washington lore throughout her life, reported the Yule log legend's tenacity among poor Blacks in rural North Carolina, though there is no way to know if that familiarity influenced her discoveries in the Tar Heel State. Tarry mentioned the famed Tuskegee educator seven times in her fascinating 1955 autobiography *The Third Door*, emphasizing his inspirational stature among southern African Americans and testifying to his omnipresence in her own life story. Thus, she noted that a trustee at the Tuskegee Institute and "good friend" of her father was also friendly with Washington and that a calendar mailed to her by a "Negro insurance company in Atlanta" included Washington's likeness. She recalled that the woman who gave her the first book of poetry she owned held a job at Birmingham's "Booker T. Washington Branch Library" and that in her own newspaper editorial "Mr. Hoover and Jim Crow" published during the 1928 presidential campaign, when praising Herbert Hoover for ending segregation in the US Commerce Department during his tenure as secretary of commerce between 1921 and 1928, Tarry had suggested that Hoover possibly "believe[d] that the same God that made him made Booker T. Washington." Tarry certainly had familiarity with mentions of Yule logs in *Up from Slavery*. While an elementary school teacher as a young woman, she found that although her fifth graders were unaware of the Crispus Attucks story, they "knew enough about Tuskegee Institute to appreciate the well-known story about Booker T. Washington walking many weary miles from his home in Franklin County, Virginia to Hampton Institute and being told to sweep a classroom as part of his first examination." On deciding to prepare herself for a literary career, she naturally made certain to "reread Booker T. Washington" as part of an exploration of the prior works of distinguished Black writers.[22]

After working on the Federal Writers' Project in the 1930s and developing a gnawing realization, as she put it in *The Third Door*, that "much of the unwritten history of the Negro in America would be lost when 'the old heads'" died, she decided to travel through the South with the idea of talking to elderly Blacks and absorbing their stories. Of particular importance to us, given how much North Carolinian whites figure in the literary history of southern Yule log traditions, is her finding that "field Negroes" in the Tar Heel State had entirely different attitudes than the ex-"house Negroes" (former mansion servants, we should presume) Tarry spoke with in Alabama. It was in North Carolina, she remembered, that she "picked up" on a story embodying the distinction—a "tale of the 'backlog' and how it had been used by slaves to prolong the celebration of Christmas on the southern plantations." Never previously, Tarry reflected, had she heard that Christmas celebrations were timed to the burning of Yule logs in the "open fireplace of the 'big house.'" Never before had she been clued in about how slaves tasked with the responsibility of choosing that log would try to find the tree with "the hardest bark and greenest wood, cut it to size, and soak it in a secluded stream." Then, she wrote, the big log was placed on the back part of the grate and set on fire on Christmas, initiating a holiday that might bring six weeks of rest to enslaved field workers.[23]

✳✳✳

To the best that I can tell, Ellen Tarry's discovery of Yule log remembrances among rural Black North Carolinians earned no attention, at the time she published them or later, from either the media or from historians. In contrast, Black Coloradoan and former IBM marketing executive Katie Brown Bennett received ample media coverage when she similarly highlighted the story of North Carolina's enslaved plantation workers soaking Christmas logs in her exhaustive genealogical history of her own family, *Soaking the Yule Log*, published in 1995.

This privately published 514-page book, which had a very small print run, recounted Bennett's quest to uncover her own very complicated and racially complex family history, part of which involved people who were compelled into involuntary labor on the Rowan County, North Carolina, plantation of one Jacob Booe. According to Bennett, Booe's fourth great grandson Paul Griffith, a white descendant, told her that Jacob Booe timed his laborers' Christmas holidays by the burning of a Yule log that slaves soaked in a creek. Bennett introduced the section of her book about the Brown branch of her family tree with the Yule log tale, condensed to two sentences, and subsequently used the tale as a guidepost. In telling about her paternal second great-grandmother Malinda (who had been enslaved in Tennessee before being removed from her mother at the age of fifteen and relocated to North Carolina after being sold to a new owner), Bennett surmised that Malinda "thought of her lost family often and reminisced about some of the experiences they had shared—singing around the fire at the end of a tiring day, soaking the Yule log at Christmas." This passage, seemingly unsupported by evidence, apparently represented a case of authorial license.[24]

Prior to and following its release, Bennett's research process and book became the focus of feature articles in American newspapers, most notably pieces disseminated by the Knight-Ridder Newspapers chain under such titles as "NC Author Searches Slave Records to Find Her Genealogical Roots" and "Search for Slave Ancestry More than 'Roots' Sequel." In all, I have identified forty pieces about the book in US newspapers between October 1996 and May 1997, as well as another two in 2016 and 2017, and there were probably others. Although *Soaking the Yule Log* never caught the attention of the general reading public,[25] some of the most prominent papers in the South, including the *Memphis Commercial Appeal*, *Raleigh News and Observer*, *Fort Worth Star-Telegram*, *St. Louis Post-Dispatch*, and *Atlanta Constitution* carried these articles, putting Yule log lore before many readers previously unfamiliar with the Christmas story.

Further indications that Yule log lore had gained credibility in twentieth-century Black American culture come from the official records of the National Association of Colored Women's Clubs (NACWC), an umbrella federation of Black women's organizations—founded by, among others, Harriet Tubman, in Washington, DC, in 1896 in response to a recent uptick in racially motivated lynchings of Black Americans. According to a letter in the organization's files, in both 1959 and 1960, the veteran civil rights activist Pauline Myers, remembered especially as executive secretary for Black leader A. Philip Randolph's aborted march on Washington in 1941 to pressure the government against segregation in the American armed forces and discrimination in defense industry employment,[26] related a "Yule log story" as part of the NACWC's annual Christmas program. Apparently, Yule log storytelling was included in the NACWC's holiday scheduling from at least 1959 to 1967. In 1964, during the Christmas holiday season, the *Philadelphia Tribune*, a Black newspaper dating back to the 1880s, reported that the "traditional yuletide tea and symbolic lighting of the yule log took place on December 20, at 4 o'clock at the National Association of Colored Women's Cultural Center" on R Street in Washington. Around the same time, the NACWC's headquarters secretary thanked a West Virginia affiliate for contributing to the organization's first "Yuletide Tea," whose program included listening "to the traditional story of the Yule log." During the NACWC's 1967 "annual Yuletide Tea and Tree Lighting Service," the Yule log story was related yet again.[27]

Frustratingly, none of these documents identify which Yule log story was told, or whether Myers might have learned her version from someone in her own family, because her grandfather on her father's side had been enslaved.[28] One would think, given the racial identity of the NACWC, that it was the now-three-quarters-of-a-century-old soaking tale. But it could very well have been a retelling of Yule log legends about Great Britain or Scandinavia unconnected with slavery in the South. And it could even have been a retelling of LaSalle Pickett's story about the elderly Black in the Virginia mountain shack who risked his health to rescue a child from the Christmas snows. We cannot write off the latter possibility, because Pickett's tale lacked content intrinsically offensive to Black readers. Indeed, in 1949 prior to Christmas, the *Baltimore Afro-American* reprinted Pickett's story, introducing it with an assurance that sharing the tale was a long-standing Virginia tradition and would customarily occur as family members on Christmas Eves sat by their own Yule logs sipping eggnog. The *Afro-American* seems to have been oblivious to Pickett's stature as a prominent spokeswoman for the Confederate Lost Cause and the racial mores of the Old South. Very possibly it was unaware that the wife of a Rebel general had authored the story, given that some of its prior reprintings had failed to provide its author's name.[29]

Equally baffling is an earlier news piece by prominent Black educator Mary McLeod Bethune for a different Black paper. Following Christmas in 1937, the *Pittsburgh Courier* ran Bethune's submission, in which she described herself luxuriating under palm trees and thinking back on the glorious recent holiday days. During that period, on the Bethune-Cookman College campus, there had been a night program in which the girls had "presented our most unique event—the 'Yule-Log Ceremony.'" Unfortunately, Bethune gave no hint of just what the formalities entailed.[30]

Whether or not Booker T. Washington's endorsement explains the growing hold of Yule log stories on Black memory in the twentieth century, there can be no denying the staying power of these legends for African Americans into the twenty-first century. Just before Christmas in 2005, spokesperson Anita Singleton-Prather for the Penn Center Gullah Studies Institute on St. Helena Island off the South Carolina coast gave voice, yet again, to this story when speaking to a newspaper interviewer. According to this native of Beaufort on

Port Royal Island and Howard University graduate, enslaved Africans in the area were accustomed to calling Christmas "a week of Sundays" because of the vacation bonus they gained from Yule logs. "Enslaved Africans would ask," she explained, "How long do we have off?" and their masters would reply, "As long as the Yule log burns." And over that same holiday season, the Bethel African Methodist Episcopal Church in Lancaster, Pennsylvania, a church whose congregation dates from the early 1800s and whose pastors had been active in the Underground Railroad, put on a play titled *Christmas in the 1800s: The Saga of Mama CeCe's Family*. In describing the play to a press interviewer, its main character's actor noted how owners of plantations permitted their enslaved people to call on family members held in bondage elsewhere so long as a Yule log held out on their fireplace.[31]

The hold of Washington's Yule log stories on Black memory persists to the present day. In 2019, the Atlanta History Center's blog ran a story, reposted in 2023, on "Historic Holiday Traditions," with a section devoted to Yule logs. After claiming that Americans adopted western European winter solstice celebrations as part of their own traditions in the nineteenth century, the story went on to emphasize how it "became customary across parts of the antebellum South for plantation owners to provide enslaved peoples a yule log." Treading more cautiously than most white champions of this legend, the center explained how on "some plantations" Black laborers gained relief from labor while the "log burned in the hearth" and that for this reason, in instances when they were accorded the chance to fell the tree themselves, they chose "the longest, slowest burning trees available—sweetgum, for instance." Further, they sprinkled water on the log while it was burning to slow things down. The center noted what Federal Writers' Project interviewee Jenny Proctor had to say about this custom, as well as that Booker T. Washington wrote about it in *Up from Slavery*.[32]

Conclusion

I Allow Three Days at Christmas

On the evening of December 27, 1852, the Mississippi cotton farmer Everard Green Baker summoned his small force of enslaved laborers to give them the word that their Christmas holiday was drawing to its conclusion. He had granted them days off from farm labor due to a promise he had made to himself to keep his "negroes joyous & happy." He was pleased they had been "enjoying themselves" with "a contented hearty good will" during their time off. But their toil on his soil could only be deferred for so long. "I told them," he explained a day later in his diary, "the work we had before us compelled our hollidays to close & made a few remarks to them as to their duties the following year." In that same entry, he noted matter-of-factly that he (really meaning his enslaved people) "recommenced work today."[1]

It is remotely conceivable that on December 27, just before calling together his workforce, Baker had either witnessed or been told that a giant Yule log his workers had soaked in a swamp nearby had just expired in his family's fireplace. There were swamps around his place. Such musings, though, fail the "smell" test. Baker likely did not mention Yule logs in his diary because he never designated a particularly big log as anything special in the first place or expected one to determine when his workforce rested and when it toiled as the New Year approached.

Nowhere in the antebellum South, from what I can tell, did enslavers massage the terms "Yule log," "back-log," "Christmas log," or even "Yule" into their private Christmas holiday vocabulary, not even when their diaries mentioned holiday fires. "Weather cold and cloudy—snow on the ground," noted lawyer and diarist William Valentine, while residing on his father's Oak Lawn plantation near Bethel, North Carolina, one December 27, before adding, "Life is passed off in doors by a good fire in humor and enjoyment." And when North Carolina diarist Jane Evans Eliot—married to lumber mill owner Alexander Eliot, heir of the "Ellerslie" estate in Cumberland County—reflected about her Christmas Day in 1858, she observed that her "happy fire-sider circle" was "unbroken," without any intimation that her fireplace held some especially significant back-log.[2]

Not only did the private writings of white southerners fail to suggest anything noteworthy about individual logs in their fireplaces but they also rarely even took notice of logs being brought into their dwellings at Christmas. There were no ceremonies with singing and other ceremonial touches like those supposedly mandatory on such occasions in Merrie Old England. Logs were simply logs, taken for granted and burned. And it is particularly difficult identifying allusions in the Christmastime private writings of white slaveholders and their overseers to enslaved people even fetching fireplace wood, much less a specially designated log. Consider, in this regard, what the Lowndes County, Mississippi cotton planter William Ethelbert Ervin had to say about slaves and logs at Christmas. On Monday, December 26, 1842, Ervin jotted tersely in his plantation journal that although it was the Christmas holiday, his "men got logs for house." Not only does Ervin treat those logs mundanely but he also does so on the wrong day according to American plantation legends. According to lore, slaves retrieved their giant logs on Christmas Eve at the holiday's start. Yet Ervin's enslaved secured them two days later. Note too that Ervin said nothing about those logs being of unusual proportions, decorated, or conveyed to the house by singing or chanting, as post–Civil War Yule log stories by LaSalle Pickett and others sometimes suggested. We can presume that Ervin's logs were, simply, undifferentiated logs, nothing more.[3]

And there are miscellaneous other signals in pre–Civil War sources that log sizes and their flammability were irrelevant to the length of enslaved workforces' Christmas breaks. When a Virginia Superior Court judge provided information about slavery in a letter to the native New York writer James Kirke Paulding prior to Paulding's publication in 1836 of *Slavery in the United States* (a book one authority categorizes as "one of the most important theoretical defenses of racial slavery of its time"), he starkly exposed the irrelevance of Yule log soakings by declaring, cryptically, "I allow three days at Christmas."[4] This declaration provided no time for fudging, no leeway, say, for laborers then to linger on holiday should they luck out with a well-soaked log. We should pay attention.

✳✳✳

Despite authoritative pronouncements for the last century and a half that enslaved people in the Old South cleverly soaked freshly cut logs in ponds, streams, and swamps to earn long Christmas holidays from indulgent masters and mistresses, the evidentiary record is problematic. It amounts to little more than (1) hearsay reports by a couple of white newspaper commentators before the Civil War; (2) one antebellum novel by a native Englishman; (3)

recollections by white southerners between the Civil War and the 1930s, many of whom were devotees of the Old South's racial order and the Confederacy; (4) a claim by African American leader Booker T. Washington in a magazine article that never explained how he knew about Yule log customs among enslaved people; (5) the recollections of two Federal Writers' Project (FWP) interviewees three-quarters of a century after their bondage; (6) an unspecified number of Black North Carolinians relating Yule log tales to Ellen Tarry during the Depression; and (7) a smattering of other problematic accounts, like the one family lore genealogist Katie Bennett picked up from an enslaver's distant descendant about a North Carolina plantation nearly two hundred years previously. All told, these sources add up to a suspiciously small body of evidence for a custom that we are led to believe determined Christmas calendars for hundreds of thousands of slaveholders and millions of enslaved people. Booker T. Washington's own state of Virginia alone had more than fifty-two thousand slaveholders in 1860.[5]

No wonder, given that the documentary proof for Yule log soakings is so flimsy, that the legend's very disseminators sometimes betrayed a lack of confidence in it by adopting the passive voice or qualifiers in their writing. When, during the Great Depression, a North Carolina newspaper conjectured that ancient Scandinavian Yule log ceremonies had been reimagined in the Old South, it claimed that slaves "had holiday while the log lasted" up to twelve days and nights but cautiously added that "*it is said* its endurance was much aided by being soaked in water for days" prior to removal to the "big house" (italics mine). Just who said this?—we might interject. A Louisiana columnist once explained, in a similar vein, how in "writings of Booker T. Washington, historians have gleaned that the Yule log tradition has roots in American slavery." On the one hand, this newsman cited a source, which is more than can be said for many popularizers of Yule log–soaking slave tales. But that source never provided proof to substantiate his claims.[6]

In other words, hedging bets is in order. The Atlanta History Center, as we saw in the last chapter, wisely used the descriptor "some" for the number of antebellum plantations adhering to the tradition, which could hardly be more ambiguous given the thousands of plantations and millions of slaves in the Old South. Distinguished historian Eugene D. Genovese in *Roll, Jordan, Roll* showed similar restraint, saying that in "some cases" the length of Christmas vacations for slaves "depended on the burning of a log." Even Katie Bennett in *Soaking the Yule Log* couched her argument cautiously. She never said outright that she *knew* Jacob Booe tied Black holidays to Yule logs. She only reported that "Legend" had it that way.[7] And that is good, since she offered no documents to substantiate a case.

Perhaps the classic example of such hesitancy appeared in a Greensboro (NC) Christmas season news article by director Christopher Crittenden of the

North Carolina Department of Archives and History in 1964. Note my italics, here, and you will get my drift. Crittenden so gingerly tested Yule log waters. "*It is stated*," he explained, "that in the Old South the workers requested that they be given a holiday as long as the yule log kept burning. As one of their chores was to obtain the log, *it was rumored* that they would get the heaviest piece of hardwood they could find and then soak it in water." Crittenden's vague phrasing covered his tracks. He was undoubtedly aware his archives lacked evidence of the custom.[8]

✳✳✳

Although it is possible, given the lack of eyewitness evidence, that no African American slave in the thirteen English colonies or the later United States earned a Christmas holiday break timed to the burning of a Yule log, it would be unwise to stake so absolute a claim, since there is no way to rule out all possibility that someone might eventually uncover just the kind of eyewitness account that I never came up with. But I think it is safe to pose a slightly more modest proposition here—that even *if* some enslaved people got their Christmas vacations according to the longevity of Yule logs, they likely represented the tiniest fraction imaginable of the total slave population, no more than groupings of Black laborers in a few scattered southern locales just before the Civil War. I say this because in contrast to the three pre–Civil War secondhand accounts I found about Yule log soakings in the South, there are piles of documents from those same years, like the farmer's diary and the judge's letter opening this chapter, proving that Yule logs had nothing to do with the Christmas holidays of enslaved African Americans.

One such body of evidence lies in the accounts of travelers to the Old South who passed through or briefly stayed in the region over Christmas. They provide an illuminating entry point into the customs and routines of southern life before the Civil War, given that they are so descriptive. Northern and foreign visitors and short-term residents on southern plantations in the pre–Civil War decades sometimes took considerable interest in the partying of enslaved people at Christmastime that they happened to observe, as well as how slave-holding masters and mistresses treated and interacted with their bondpeople over the holidays. Yet they took no notice of Yule logs.

A richly descriptive letter dated December 26, 1859, that one young woman from New England posted to her mother from the Louisiana plantation where she had been tutoring white children clearly reveals this tendency among visitors to the region. "Christmas eve we had dancing in the [slave] quarters," she reported, before continuing:

I went to see them for two hours, never was more amused. One played the banjo, another "<u>patted juba</u>" and the dancing was superior to any I ever saw among white people. The singing was very amusing and consisted of a few words with a chorus interspersed in which all join. The main singer stands in the middle of the ring and the chorus singers join hands and dance around her all the time of the singing.

In the same letter, our writer details the hanging of Christmas stockings, how Black servants and their children reacted to fireworks, and how some white family members donned hideous costumes to enliven the evening by scaring servants and other onlookers. What she did not mention was seeing any servants ceremoniously lugging in and setting on fire a giant log of any kind, much less singing or chanting as they performed that task. And this is significant if we remember that Christmas Eve was the very moment in the holiday plantation calendar, according to legend, for the great Yule log lighting to occur on southern plantations. Was our pre–Civil War New England chronicler temporarily distracted at the very moment that a soaked Yule log arrived at the big house that she somehow missed this holiday milestone? It is more likely one never turned up.[9]

Other visitors to southern plantations at Christmastime also left Yule log ceremonies unmentioned. British naval officer Basil Hall visited a Georgia Sea Island cotton plantation in March 1828. In a travelogue he published in Edinburgh the next year, Hall told how all 122 "negroes" on the place were customarily allowed "three holidays [days off] at Christmas, when they have plenty of beef and whisky." Captain Hall gave every impression that the Christmas vacation time for enslaved men, women, and children, including four "superannuated" slaves (presumably elderly Blacks too feeble for farm work), was preset year after year at the same three days, nothing more, nothing less. Similarly, Rhode Island native Lewis W. Paine reaffirmed slaveholders' control while reporting on Georgia slaves' Christmas holidays. A machinist with antislavery leanings, Paine had moved his family to Georgia in the early 1840s after accepting a position at an Upson County factory in the west central part of the state. Subsequently, he taught school prior to being confined more than five years in the state prison in Milledgeville for assisting a slave in his escape from bondage. He eventually returned northward after receiving a pardon from Georgia's governor George W. Towns and published an account of his experience with ample attention to slavery in the area of Georgia where he had lived. Unlike Captain Hall, Paine had the impression that Christmas holidays for enslaved people varied (from two to seven days). But he attributed that length disparity to "the disposition of their masters." When the preset length of Christmas expired on any given place, slaves had to hustle back to face a new year of work.[10]

Paine's impression, importantly, is reinforced by many enslavers' most intimate documents. These documents, their diaries, letters, and plantation journals, confirm that they (and occasionally their hired white overseers)—not enslaved workers—made the determinations about Christmas downtime for plantation laborers. Yules log simply played no role in antebellum southern whites' advance planning for Christmas or holiday rituals. I pored over seemingly endless numbers of documents of this sort and found no evidence that the white men and women running southern plantations had any intention of conceding time management over Christmas to their bondpeople, should a giant back-log prove especially stubborn.

And they should have, had that been the case. After all, just as with travelers' accounts, slaveholders' letters and journals sometimes provide meticulous detail about Christmas goings-on, such as when a South Carolina rice planter's wife noted in her diary in 1860 that their Christmas tree that year had miniature ships, chairs, tables, and omnibuses (horse-drawn public conveyances) for decorations. Members of slaveholding families frequently recorded in their Christmas season letters and diaries stocking food, buying presents, hanging stockings for Santa Claus's arrival, holding balls, throwing big dinners, joining fox hunts, entertaining neighbors, putting up relations, and going to church for special services. But they never, so far as I can tell, mentioned Yule logs at all, much less parsed their significance for their slaves' holidays.[11]

Conceding extra days off in December on the basis of unpredictable Yule logs, it must be emphasized, would have meant indirect extra costs to slaveowners, since there were always tasks like fixing fences that needed to be completed on slaveholding plantations and farms, even in early winter and even if all crops were harvested and marketed, which often was not the case—as Mississippi cotton planter William Ervin's plantation journal clearly shows. Though, for instance, he granted his slaves a holiday from Christmas Day through December 28 in 1839, two years later he tersely noted on December 24, "Picked cotton hoping to finish but failed." That Christmas, he gave his enslaved workforce a holiday of several days anyway, but during similar circumstances in 1843, he decided his crops took priority. So, he worked his slaves on Christmas Day ("picked cotton all hands") and afterward reimbursed them in cash for sacrificing their break. As historian Erin Dwyer explains, slaveholders "viewed enslaved contentment" in the form of Christmas releases from work as a "commodity" that should be curtailed or eliminated entirely if too much worker "output" was sacrificed by masters' concessions. Before assuming permissive enslavers casually allowed their workers to trick them out of more free Yuletide labor than they intended to concede by soaking logs in ponds and streams, we should pause. If slaveholders and overseers timed their laborers' Christmas breaks according to Yule logs, surely at least some of them would have said as much in their letters and journals.[12]

Surviving documents from slaveholders and their plantation managers lead to opposite conclusions, and this holds true not only for intimate sources like their letters and diaries but also for the manuals and newspaper and magazine articles that enslavers published concerning slave management. Though southern whites sometimes specified that their enslaved people got a holiday break of a week or more, they never attributed their own slaves' fortune to soaking trickeries. In explaining that time off, whatever the length, slaveholders repeatedly employed variants of the verb "give" more than any other verb, as in *I gave the Negroes a vacation of. . . .* So it was that planter Samuel Porcher Gaillard recorded in his Sumter County, South Carolina, "Orange Grove" plantation journal on December 28, 1849, much like Everard Baker who was quoted at this chapter's beginning, "Gave my negroes Christmas day & the two days following."[13]

Not all contemporary diaries and letters are that clear on the matter, but even ambiguous jottings contradict Yule log legends. Cotton planter Thomas B. Chaplin claimed ownership of several score of slaves and worked them on the lands of his Tombee Plantation on St. Helena Island off the South Carolina coast. Chaplin kept a journal containing his activities and thoughts during Christmastime. His entries clarify that he always kept control of decision-making regarding his slaves' labor when it came to holiday scheduling. He never mentions Yule logs burning in his mansion's fireplace, much less suggest that they had anything to do with holiday planning. Rather, Chaplin knew already, late on December 27, 1848, that the final "day of the holidays" for his slaves was about over. There was nothing contingent about its lapsing. There was no Yule log waiting to crack in two or burn out. Similarly, he could write confidently when making out his entry on December 27, 1850, two years later, that the "last day" of the holiday had drawn to its close. That year, on December 28, his workers began packing his "second bale of cotton, [but] did not finish it." Similar entries peppered his journal in other years.[14]

Slaveholder John B. Nevitt, whose 1826 to 1832 diary disclosed Christmas doings at his Clermont Plantation near Natchez, Mississippi, likewise revealed who was boss come holiday time. The day before Christmas in 1830, a Friday, Nevitt laconically reported, "Gave the negroes holyday until Tuesday next." Good to his word, he stayed up all night on December 27 while his enslaved people held their "Negro Ball," for which he had bought "sundry articles" earlier that same day. Then, he noted in his diary on December 28, "All hands went to work after sleeping until 8 o[']clock."[15] If Nevitt knew for certain on Friday, December 24, that a Yule log was bound to burn out on the night of the 27th, he would have possessed supernatural powers. Yule log lore, I would reemphasize, posits considerable variances as to just how long Christmas back-logs burned. If they all burned the same length of time, soaking them would have been irrelevant. And, of course, so would the length or timing of the soakings.

Consider the journal maintained for the Christmas season in 1847 by overseer Joshua N. Saunders for the middle Florida plantation, "El Destino." On December 24, Saunders noted, simply, "The negro holydays commenced," probably meaning the slaves' vacation from work started toward evening since the very same entry noted, "we cut up and salted 20 hogs this morning." Four days later, again without mentioning Yule logs, Saunders indicated that diverse labor tasks had been accomplished that day on the place. A Christmas holiday of some three-plus days hardly matches the supposed week or more specified in much southern Yule log lore, and although it is remotely possible that Christmas at El Destino included slaves soaking a Yule log that only lasted a disappointing three days, the weight of evidence speaks against that possibility. And even in the unlikely case that Yule logs truly determined enslaved peoples' vacation times, we can at the very least, if Saunders's remarks are indicative of anything, write off the possibility that they guaranteed long slave vacations along the lines vaunted in later lore.[16]

In most cases, masters and overseers predetermined well before Christmas Eve how long they intended to let their enslaved workforces off from labor over the holiday. That is the only rational conclusion to be drawn from the plantation rules dated 1857 that Mississippi planter J. W. Fowler drafted for the guidance of the overseers of his Coahoma County cotton estate. Fowler stipulated clearly that Christmas and the "two days following Christmas day" would be considered "holidays," when no "work of any sort or kind is to be permitted to be done by negroes," though they could "work for themselves" if they chose. His rules allowed no wiggle room for a carefully selected log to extend that time allotment. I insinuate the same from the 1854 Christmas season diary entries of a South Carolina plantation manager, who gave a detailed breakdown of how he divvied up holiday time for his field workers in a year that Christmas occurred on a Monday. After noting that his workers spent Saturday, December 23, cutting wood, raking, and other tasks, he left unsaid that his workers probably got the 24th off because it fell on a Sunday. Then he added, "Monday, Tuesday, & Wednesday, being Christmas all hands had holiday. Thursday, Friday & Saturday 28, 29 & 30th the hands were logging up & burning trees in 29 Acre [corn] field." No hint, here, either, that this master kept his eye on a Yule log when making his calendar calculations. And it is even more unlikely that Bertie County, North Carolina slaveholder Stephen A. Norfleet did so. He kept very thorough records of his daily plantation routines from 1856–1860 in his journal. Every year his hands worked hard on December 24—burning brush, "working in marsh," plowing up stubble, picking cotton, storing cotton bales and corn, ginning cotton, hauling fodder, ginning cotton, packing cotton, and the like. Every year Norfleet gave his enslaved people Christmas Day through December 28 off. Every year he had them back to work on December 29, except for 1860 when on December 28 his hands picked and ginned cotton and hauled lime for purposes of fertilizing his land. I have no idea what caused the slight date change in 1860 and whether it had anything to do with disputes over secession in North Carolina following Abraham Lincoln's election as president. But the near perfect rigidity of Norfleet's calendar all those years argues against Yule logs being a factor.[17]

Enslavers' correspondence about Christmas scheduling also suggests that in those instances when they truly made determinations on the fly about the duration of slave holidays, they did so according to the state of their crops, weather conditions, the health of their working force, the urgency of pending tasks, and other factors having nothing to do with fireplace back-logs. When the Black slave driver Henry on one of William S. Pettigrew's North Carolina plantations informed Pettigrew on December 19, 1857, that the hands had started gathering Pettigrew's corn crop and added that he hoped to "finish by the 25 of December if the weather will permit," he left unsaid what would happen to slaves' Christmases should the weather turn inclement but implied a relationship between weather conditions and enslaved peoples' holidays.[18] We are left to wonder, had Henry needed to pull the Pettigrew laborers off the crop between December 19 and December 25 because of bad weather, whether he would have asked the slaves to finish up the job on December 26 or 27 had conditions then improved.

The parameters set by plantation agricultural needs at Christmastime and their consequences for slaves were recorded by Louisiana sugar planter Francis DuBose Richardson during the 1846 holiday season, his family's first year of residence at Bayside Plantation on Bayou Teche. In a journal covering the holiday period, Richardson records that Christmas began at Bayside on December 24 and ended on December 31, when "All hands went to work." An entry for December 26 notes, "Gave black people a dinner," indicating not that Richardson's laborers got a rare evening meal the day after Christmas but rather that he splurged on a special holiday feast for them. Throughout this so-called Holliday period, however, he also regularly detached workers from their vacations to handle tasks he thought too essential to defer to December 31. So, on Sunday the 27th, he had men "engaged in hauling" sugar and molasses to his landing for shipment. Various slaves "worked to day," he noted on the 28th, and on December 29, he listed four workers as "retained to day doing jobs." On the 30th, three slaves were put to work. And it goes without saying that laboring in difficult assignments over Christmas was no more risk-free than at other times of the year. The day after Christmas in

1861, the first year of the Civil War, Richardson noted in his journal that one of his slaves had just "made a hair breadth escape from being ground up in the sugar mill" and did suffer his "toes mashed" in the incident. In all, Richardson seems to have given little regard to the preferences of his enslaved people in determining allocations of holiday leisure time.[19]

A late 1844 jotting in the journal of rice planter Charles Manigault regarding his "Gowrie" place on Argyle Island situated on the Savannah River in Georgia further confirms this point. In addition to specifying a short Christmas for his enslaved people, Manigault declared unambiguously that masters and overseers, not Black laborers, controlled such determinations. He wrote that his overseer "says *he gives* [italics mine] as Christmas Holidays 3 entire week days, half a pack of small Rice Extra, tobacco, & molasses & Pork 3 lbs. each." The overseer's decision, it can safely be assumed, correlated with factors unrelated to the kind, size, or condition of logs the bondpeople dragged to a fireplace, even assuming that Manigault wanted an unduly giant log to burn each Yuletide. Rather, decisions on Christmas's duration at Gowrie likely hinged on agricultural, weather, and disciplinary considerations. Had the harvesting of crops and all other essential work been completed by Christmas? Did the overseer wish to punish Manigault's workforce for misbehavior or work lapses by curtailing holiday privileges? When an overseer wrote Manigault one post-Christmas that "we finished threshing out the Crop on the last day of December," he certainly meant that there was labor being done at Gowrie sometime between Christmas and New Year's even if there had been a break for Black workers around December 25.[20]

What seeps through enslavers' documents about holiday scheduling is the boring mundaneness of their decision-making process. Yule log tales convey excitement, contingency, to the whole process of determining Christmas breaks for enslaved people. Will an enslaver's laborers pick the right log? Will they soak it long enough? What song lyrics will they sing as they carry their choice into the big house? Will the log's burning time exceed "massa's" expectations? But the actual evidence slaveholding southerners generated about their holiday decisions sports laconic comments like (in the words of a South Carolina planter) "28th Christmas over, commenced work." Put simply, there is no drama here![21]

***

A sampling of slaveholders' journal and diary entries, of course, no more captures the full diversity of Christmas experiences for several million southern slaves than do a couple of newspaper columns about Yule logs being soaked. But there are additional types of documents, like the nineteenth-century autobiographical accounts of former slaves, that also imply *by their omissions* that Yule logs had nothing to do with enslaved Christmas experiences. Many of these narratives, some by escaped fugitives, others by enslaved people who achieved their freedom by means other than running away, describe Christmastimes in bondage. As a corpus, moreover, they hold ample allusions to wood—a reflection of its importance in their daily lives and surroundings, including tending fires in their enslavers' kitchens and other rooms and maintaining open fires in their own quarters. One scholar investigating arson by slaves has discovered on the basis of a statistical breakdown of the 294 digitized slave narratives in the University of North Carolina's Documenting the American South Project that formerly enslaved Blacks were more far more likely to allude to *wood* in their memoirs even than to *cotton*.[22] But no nineteenth-century African American memoir, from my perusals, celebrated how enslaved people outfoxed their masters and mistresses by soaking Yule logs. Rather, nineteenth-century autobiographies, like writings that southern masters and overseers generated, indicate that slaveholders held the cards when it came to holiday timing.

William Craft, who one Christmas, accompanied by his wife, escaped from enslavement in South Carolina, recalled how the "best" slaveholders made it a custom to "give their favourite slaves" several holiday days off, a concession that ironically aided escapes from bondage. Frederick Douglass, rented out to labor all of 1833 for Maryland farm owner Edward Covey, explained in an autobiographical account published seven years following his bolt for freedom that Covey had provided enslaved workers on his Maryland place a six-day Christmas break other than for feeding and caring for livestock. This concession depended on *Covey's* calculations. Douglass specified that southern slaves received their vacations "by the grace of our masters." Masters chose to "give the slaves this time" not from unselfish concern for their welfare but because they thought they might risk insurrection if they canceled holiday privileges enslaved people were accustomed to receiving. Similarly, the Kentucky house slave Francis Fedric explained in a memoir published well after he fled bondage for Canada that come Christmas his master would grant his slaves "four or five days' holiday."[23]

Yet another perspective on the plantation master's absolute power over Christmas scheduling over Christmas scheduling comes from the famed narrative of Solomon Northup, a married free Black fiddler from Saratoga Springs in upstate New York who was kidnapped into slavery after being enticed to Washington, DC, in 1841 under the pretense that he would perform for a circus. Northup's story, the best remembered account of a free Black northerner abducted into southern enslavement by unscrupulous domestic slave traders before the Civil War, sold many copies after its publication in 1853 but is particularly well known because Black film director and producer Steve McQueen made it the basis for his 2013 release *12 Years a Slave* (after the title of Northup's published account). The movie garnered the Academy Award for Best Picture and is associated with one of modern America's most renowned Black scholars, Henry Louis Gates Jr., who served as a historical consultant for the production. Ultimately, as viewers of the film know, Northup was rescued from enslavement and reunited with his wife. But this occurred only after he passed twelve years of his life in bondage, mostly in Louisiana where his second "master," cotton planter Edwin Epps, sometimes hired him out during the fall and early winter to work on a sugar plantation where he labored cutting cane, sugar-making in a mill, and preparing fields for coming crop plantings. Northup included a vivid eight-page description of his Christmases on that sugar plantation. What he said should disabuse anyone of the illusion that enslaved people called the shots when it came to holiday vacation time, even though they enthusiastically capitalized on their break from work.

Had Yule log chicanery been part of Northup's story, he surely would have said so, given the detailed way he depicts the holiday scene in Louisiana's cane country. He tells us that the planters in the vicinity are in the habit of throwing an annual combined party at a single locale for all their slaves, generally between three and five hundred attendees in total, over Christmas. He explains how his fellow slaves dress up for the occasion, that their table is loaded with a variety of meat dishes (chicken, duck, turkey, ox) and desserts ("tarts, and every manner and description of pies, except mince"), and that a big dance follows upon the Christmas feast, at which the "genuine happiness" of the dancers is "rampant and unrestrained." He adds that for days after the big party, slaves receive passes to go wherever they want nearby, and that they are paid should they opt to remain and labor on the plantation during the interlude. He reports that they frequently get married at Christmastime. Yet, lest anyone reading this narrative simplistically conclude that enslaved people were contented with their situation in life because their holidays were so pleasant, he confides that these seemingly "happy looking mortals" were only the beneficiaries of a temporary reprieve from the misery of yearlong hardships. Usually, laborers on that sugar plantation live in "fear" and in subjection to "the lash." And avoiding any pretense that the Christmas privileges of enslaved Blacks were products of their own doing, Northup affirms who sets the rules not only where he labored but also in the neighborhood: "Epps allowed us three [days off]—others four, five and six days, according to the measure of their generosity." Slaveholder Edwin Epps and neighboring masters, not their coerced laborers, set and enforced the holiday time clock. Within Northup's eight pages on Christmastime, one searches in vain for mention of any log, much less a Yule fire.[24]

Another check on southern Yule log lore comes from the most important anthology of US fugitive narratives published before the Civil War. In 1855,

SOLOMON IN HIS PLANTATION SUIT.

Figure 6.1. Solomon Northup in his plantation suit. Frontispiece for the original 1853 edition of Northup's narrative.
Source: Courtesy of the New York Public Library.

an abolitionist public school principal and occasional journalist in Boston named Benjamin Drew, concerned that antislavery sentiment was waning in his city, traveled to Canada West (today's province of Ontario) to interview escaped refugee slaves living and working in Toronto, St. Catharine's, Chatham, and other locales close by. This trip resulted in Drew's *North-Side View of Slavery*, published later the same year by the firm that had published *Uncle Tom's Cabin*. For his anthology, Drew interviewed 128 Blacks formerly enslaved in the United States, virtually all, other than Harriet Tubman, inconspicuous figures unknown to public memory, and published the interviews supposedly verbatim as separate documents (though he apparently cleaned up hints of Black dialect when transcribing the interviews). None of these ex–southern slaves had anything nice to say about the Christmas holidays provided them by their masters and mistresses. Isaac Williams, however, did note that his last master whipped him for the final time after he was caught stealing corn so that he could make bread for Christmas. There is nothing about Yule logs in these accounts, but ample comment on masters' punitive uses of normal logs in regulating their lives. "Next morning, the master came for me, took me home, stripped me stark naked, made a paddle of thick oak board, lashed me across a pine log, secured my hands and feet, and whipped me with the paddle . . . till he broke the paddle," recalled ex–South Carolina slave Harry Thomas about his punishment for resisting his mistress's request that he scour some floors.[25]

Because antebellum Black fugitive autobiographers were preoccupied with convincing northern readers that southern slavery was abominable, their authors conceivably omitted details, including Yule log customs, they might otherwise have included had not the horrors of bondage and their own escapes been their driving concern. But autobiographies that ex-slaves published in the late nineteenth century, decades after Emancipation, remained mute about Yule logs and firm that slaveholders kept control over Christmas scheduling. "The hands were allowed four days off at Christmas," was the way Louis Hughes flatly put it when he wrote of his first Christmas at a Pontotoc County, Mississippi, cotton plantation in his 1896 autobiography. Shortly before Hughes's book appeared, George L. Knox, once enslaved in Kentucky, related in his memoir that in the part of the state where he was regularly hired out "it was the custom" to "give" slaves "the whole period between Christmas and New Year" to party and relax.[26] Enslaved people lacked agency regarding that tradition, regardless of the generosity of local norms in comparison to the three- or four-day Christmas break most southern enslaved plantation workers could expect.

William Wells Brown, born in Kentucky but enslaved for much of his youth in different capacities in and around St. Louis, recalled in *My Southern Home* (1880) how slaves used travel passes from their masters during their Christmas downtime on his owner's depleted tobacco farm north of the city to wander off to dances, cockfights, revival meetings, and other diversions. He reported, too, that bondpeople received clothing distributions over the holiday and that enslaved men took corn brooms, baskets, and other items they had previously made at night into St. Louis to sell and earn money. But when it came to the precise time allotments for these doings, Brown simply noted that each year the bondpeople got the same Christmas to New Year's off, which rules out significant variances according to Yule logs.[27]

And if we are going to credit those two interviews with ex-slaves during the Great Depression, mentioned several times in this book, indicating Yule log customs among people enslaved in the Old South, we should keep in view how lopsidedly these are offset by the number of FWP interviewees who discussed Christmas customs on plantations without a word about Yule logs. Pauline Grice sounded off about master control at holiday time just as had the nineteenth-century antebellum and postbellum Black autobiographers. She recalled to her Federal Writers' Project interviewer that in "de old days, if de niggers wants de party, massa am de big toad in de puddle. And Christmas, it am de day for de big time." Richmond, Virginia, native Horace Muse, hired out for farm labor before the Civil War, told a duo of Federal Writers' Project interviewers in 1937 that during those years of his hiring he was allowed to return to his home place "fer three or four days" at Christmas. Though Muse was fuzzy about the exact duration of his holidays, there is no suggesting that he and his peers got away with tricking his temporary enslaver (a "mean man" he called "Marser Riles") into extra time off. One can easily imagine that if Muse and his fellow slaves on the Riles place had outfoxed their abuser by soaking a gum log, he might have readily volunteered the anecdote for some mutual chuckling, since both of his interrogators were Black. Enslaved African Americans in the Old South, in other words, depended on their white masters' whims when it came to holiday celebrating, or so they said repeatedly.[28]

✳✳✳

When masters and mistresses granted their bondpeople more holiday time off than they (the slaveholders) preferred, it was not because enslaved people lucked out in their Yule log selection process or were well tutored in the techniques of soaking wood but, rather, for other reasons, including vocal pressure from their laborers. As one sugar planter complained in his diary in 1845, "getting tired of Hollidays, negros want too much." Although there was never a significant slave rebellion at Christmas in the South in the years before the Civil War, slaveholders felt more vulnerable to an uprising at Christmas than at most other times of the year, since they were so occupied with their own partying and failed to keep their usual close watch on their slaves' daily routines. Between the War of 1812 and the Civil War, mass panics about imagined Black uprisings at Christmas swept the South during several holiday seasons, with rumors running rampant that slaves intended to massacre whites, pillage, or set on fire white property, and commit acts of sexual violence against white women.[29]

As a result, it is hardly surprising that sometimes slaveholders discreetly capitulated to demands from their laborers for longer holidays, fearing that their workers would get restless or even violent if they failed to accede. This was especially true when masters tried to limit the number of Christmas days off in comparison to what they had permitted in prior years, or when their allotments of holiday time were stingier than those given by more liberal neighbors nearby. Informal channels of communication between enslaved peoples within given vicinities ensured that information got around. Historians allude to these information flows as the "slave grapevine." Enslaved persons ran errands from one place to another, married persons on nearby plantations and farms, and assembled beyond their own quarters for religious services or nighttime parties. They would find out and might become irritated if their peers on nearby estates got longer holidays. Such possibilities help explain why masters sometimes proved compliant when their bondpeople implored them for longer Christmas vacations.

No document better illustrates the kinds of leverage enslaved people sometimes commanded when negotiating with masters and overseers about Christmas vacation time than the speech of one of the delegates to the Kentucky Constitutional Convention of 1849, a body which met at the state capitol building in Frankfort and which included a very small minority of attendees seeking the emancipation of their state's slave population. According to press reporting, in the deliberations on April 25, delegate James M. Todd of Shelby County reflected that although he had been "nursed and suckled by a slave" as a babe, he had "never loved this institution of slavery." He believed, in fact, that it was a constant drain on progress in the state since coerced Black laborers were unproductive as well as insubordinate. To build his case, Todd explained that when trying to hire a slave servant, the potential hires were accustomed to making demands before acceding to work, and that these demands included "a week at Christmas" and all the hirer's old clothes before they wore out. Formerly, he explained, all white employers had to do was turn up at the slave trading block and make their hires. But times had changed. Todd's remarks said nothing about Yule logs. But they suggest that under certain conditions enslaved southern Blacks felt empowered enough to make Christmastime demands on whites. It is important to emphasize, however, that delegate Todd, who lived in northern Kentucky, was talking about a part of the state where freedom beckoned Blacks from across the Ohio River. In fact, in the same speech he complained that when "unruly" servants got flogged in Kentucky, they ran off. Most enslaved people did not have such geographies working for them as bargaining chips.[30]

One gets the sense of how neighborhood *expectations*, rather than Yule logs, governed Black laborers' Christmas breaks in the Old South by considering calculations at Senator John C. Calhoun's Fort Hill plantation in 1840. Over the holiday, Calhoun received a report from his son-in-law, Thomas G. Clemson, who was helping to manage the place during Calhoun's absence in Washington, DC. Clemson informed his father-in-law that he found it concerning that the place's overseer was overly generous in providing Calhoun's slaves with a holiday break of four days, but when he had raised his reservations with the overseer, the latter rebuffed him by noting that such holiday durations were "customary" and should not be tampered with. Perhaps the overseer meant neighborhood standards when talking about what was "customary." Perhaps he meant prior practices at Fort Hill. What he certainly did not imply was that the vagaries of Yule log flames governed his decision-making.[31]

More to the point is the diary of the owner of Oak Grove Plantation in Berkeley County, South Carolina. On December 27, 1829, the physician-planter John Peyre Thomas entered this crisp sentence: "Every one in this neighborhood commences work tomorrow, & so do I." Notice the arbitrariness of this declaration. Notice the synchronicity. Notice the all-but-stated insinuation of a pre-set collaborative determination of every slaveholder in his vicinity that Christmas vacations for enslaved people should end abruptly on December 28. Notice the entire exclusion of Blacks from the decision-making process, much less mention of Yule logs that of course, if we follow the legend, would have mitigated against work resumptions across the board on the same calendar date. And nothing changed over subsequent years. On Christmas Day in 1836, a Sunday, Thomas recorded, "Gave the Negroes . . . holy day until Tuesday night."[32] Christmas for enslaved men, women, and children could depend on fixed local standards.

And of course, the well-documented fact that many enslaved people over the holiday traveled "about" on their own (generally with written holiday travel passes from their masters) mitigates against Yule log lore. It should be immediately grasped that in those pre-telephone, pre-texting, and pre-internet days, such slaves would have regularly violated their permissions and returned to their home plantations too late (risking whippings and other punishments) if their off time depended on a single fireplace's back-log holding out. How would they know while "abroad" that those Yule logs had flamed out? There was no Pony Express or inter-plantation telegraph service at the ready to speed them that news! James Hammond, editor of the *Southern Times* in Columbia—the South Carolina capital—and master of the Silver Bluff plantation overlooking the Savannah River, put it this way on Christmas Day, 1831 (a Sunday), when explaining the blanket holiday travel rights of his scores of slaves: "Gave them . . . permission to go where they pleased during the holidays which last until Wednesday."[33] Hammond's scheduling failed to allow for contingencies at his fireplace.

✳✳✳

Perhaps in the end, given the paucity of evidence that enslaved people in North America extended their Christmas holidays by soaking Yule logs, we should wonder less whether there is any validity to a dubious legend than ponder the reasons for its durability over the last century and a half. What gives this tale, barely mentioned before the end of slavery in the country, so much staying power? Slaveholders omitted Yule logs from their pre–Civil War letters, diaries, journals, and published writings. Slaveholding family members described their many activities at Christmas without alluding to Yule logs. Not once until the twentieth century did formerly enslaved people broach in their memoirs the subject of their cunning with Yule logs. And although early and mid-nineteenth-century southern newspapers published all sorts of warnings about how Christmas might usher in a season of Black rebellions, none of these columns suggested that once Yule logs burned up all danger was over.

I suspect that Yule log–soaking legends enjoy their foothold in US popular culture primarily because of their colorful yet inoffensive character and perhaps, too, as a means of disengagement from the genuine, sickening power dynamics and abuses that governed enslaved peoples' lives in the US South before the Civil War. It is no wonder, as we have seen, that they surface from time to time at southern historic sites, given that tour guides and curators at such places have traditionally tended to avoid alienating their disproportionately white and middle-class paying visitors "with content that might challenge their views on race" (though programming is in the process of changing at many such locales). Stories of enslaved persons tricking their big house masters with soaked pieces of wood provide a kind of plantation "light" to persons seeking, at most, a superficial understanding of their nation's troubled record of racial oppression.[34] But there is more to ponder on this issue of reception.

For many African Americans, I suspect, the appeal of the legend depends on an *un*awareness that this story was first disseminated by a coterie of white southern women and men caught up in the glorification of the Old South and the Confederacy, an unawareness likely attributable to Black leader Booker T. Washington's appropriation of the tale in the early twentieth century. More importantly, it accords agency to enslaved people. Rather than being helpless when it came to the control that white masters, mistresses, and overseers daily imposed over their lives, enslaved Blacks purportedly seized command of their own destiny at Christmas by carefully selecting Yule logs and then cutting and preparing them for burning in ways that expanded their holiday privileges. Instead of passively accepting whatever their masters pronounced about how they should pass their holidays, enslaved Blacks utilized their intelligence and cunning to wrest away from their enslavers more days off than their masters and overseers wanted to grant. And it was all the better when the tales allowed Black log soakers the luxury of gloating smugly over their own sneakiness. They deserved that rare psychological energy boost, that special moment of having the sense that they had mastered their masters! Katie Bennett reflects such possibilities in *Soaking the Yule Log* by ruminating that the "very ingenuity and courage displayed with the Yule log helped them survive bondage and involuntary separations from their families." Suggesting that Yule log chicaneries helped offset decimations of Black nuclear families by the domestic slave trade is a comforting message.[35]

Additionally, the tale appeals for its humorous elements. Despite claims to the contrary by southern memoirists and fiction writers after the Civil War, the abuses of black bodies and minds by Old South enslavers continued over Christmas rather than ceased in deference to the holiday. In his New Year's Day entry for 1851, North Carolina plantation diarist William Valentine exposed such continuities, describing how he and his brother had been compelled just the day before to act against two slaves who had stolen a family hog and tried to sell it to a nearby poor white man, even though these same slaves had been "well treated, as well as we knew how." Since both slaves refused to implicate their peer workers in the plot and because the Valentine brothers were convinced that a widespread workforce conspiracy lay behind the scheme, "we tied them up and whipped them" in a futile effort to force a confession.[36] Such genuine documents are extremely disturbing. Not so, fictional Yule log–soaking tales. As embellishments of Christmas rituals at historic sites, and as filler matter in cookbooks, holiday encyclopedias, and the like, they wear well. They convey the impression that the end of the year was a safe and joyous period for masters and slaves alike. Why raise divisive issues about such periods of good will toward all?

Consider, in this regard, the *El Paso Herald*'s mellow reaction when LaSalle Pickett's *Yule Log* volume and her other tales about "Virginia life" first were published. The newspaper's reviewer lauded Pickett for her appealing "stories of the darky, his pathos and humor, his picturesque use of words, his faithfulness, courtesy and philosophy."[37] Most people think of humor and courtesy as positive character traits, but the underlying message is terrible, and not merely because of the *Herald* used the racial epithet "darkey," engaged in racial stereotyping, and implied that enslaved Blacks in the antebellum South accepted their fate as the unpaid laborers of white masters. Additionally, it portrays race relations in the South before the Civil War as markedly congenial, free of conflict, abuse, and resentment.

It is difficult, in all the renditions of Yule log plantation lore published in America between the 1870s and the civil rights movement of the 1960s, to uncover even faint hints that masters and mistresses were abusive or disdainful toward slaves at holiday time or, for that matter, throughout the year. Instead, Yule log tales cull up lovely visions of plantation holiday spaces where whites and Blacks coexisted harmoniously together, gave each other presents as tokens of their mutual affection, watched each other dance, and, yes, sometimes took bemusement in each other's quirks. And yet, one only need attempt the most cursory reading of texts from slave times to realize the insufficiency of such impressions. "You know this is Christmas dearest & how hard it is to get any thing done, each servant thinking they should have Holy day," remarked one plantation mistress to her daughter, clearly grudgingly, on Christmas Day 1856 about allowing her slaves to drop their usual work assignments. Josiah Henson, an escaped slave to Canada from the Upper South allowed, in his 1849 narrative, that he and his enslaved comrades greatly enjoyed the eggnog and extra meat that slaves got during their holiday vacation and the "fun" of what he called their "Christmas buffoonery." Henson made certain, however, to nudge his readers away from simplistic conclusions, pointing out that following Christmas his master compensated for the very "fun and freedom" he had just permitted. Once the holiday ended, Henson's enslaver "drove and cursed" his slaves "worse than ever."[38]

Yule log tales did differ, as we have seen, as to whether white masters and mistresses were flummoxed by their slaves' soaking the back logs or simply tolerated their laborers' trickery. In the very early Yule log report appearing in 1860 in the *Emporia* (KS) *News*, the slaves reveled in fooling their master. They "laugh in their dressed up sleeves to think the log will last long past New Years!" Years later, Innes Randolph's fictional Uncle Ned starts laughing so uncontrollably about putting a Yule log trick over on his master that he must consign himself to the back of Thornton Hall to avoid detection. There, he props himself up against a wall out of sight to ensure his master will never suspect his slaves are chortling at their owner's credulity. Conversely, many Yule log tales like Rebecca Cameron's "Christmas at Buchoi," in *Ladies' Home Journal*, give every impression that slaveholders were aware of and even encouraged Yule log soakings at Christmastime.[39]

Such differences, though, are immaterial. In all cases, masters come off looking good, even if gullible. In instances where slaveholders fail to detect their laborers' log tricks, they seem kindly, benign supervisors of laborers assigned reasonable yearlong workloads. They are so lackadaisical and forgiving—or dimwitted—about enforcing discipline among their workers, moreover, that they make no attempts even to detect malfeasance. And they are so unaccustomed to using corporal punishment as a means of preempting Black resistance that their behavior upends not only pre–Civil War abolitionist tracts and speechmaking about the physical abuse of slave bodies by slaveowners but also Thomas Jefferson's most famed censure of human bondage. Jefferson maintained in his *Notes on Virginia* (1785) that slave labor so empowered masters as to invite them into "the most unremitting despotism," while the workers found themselves reduced to "degrading submissions."[40] Jefferson's abusive masters are absented from Yule log–soaking stories. Rather, such tales' slaveholders are slow to anger and averse to laying on whips. To put it simply, many Yule log tales, by portraying unvigilant slaveholders, gave off the vibe that antebellum southern white men were instinctively laid-back, good guys, a message with undoubted appeal today to champions of the Lost Cause and preservers of Confederate memory. And it was certainly a soothing message for America's reading public in the late 1800s and early 1900s, when lynchings and race riots were at their height especially in the South but also in most other parts of the nation.

By the same token, Yule log iterations crediting masters with detecting but consciously overlooking the Yule log transgressions of their enslaved people, such as Harnett Kane's claim in his *Southern Christmas Book* that the master and his family "knew of the stratagem, and secretly chuckled over it," put masters in even better light. After all, such behavior implied the theme so common in proslavery, pre– and post–Civil War southern propaganda that slaveholders were never in it for the money, that they prioritized their caretaking responsibilities for their dependent enslaved laborers, that they were inordinately generous in countless ways toward their workers and never mistreated them without justifiable cause, and that they best exemplified these maxims of paternalistic oversight during the Christmas season.

The implied messaging threading through these fictions that all southern slaves enjoyed lengthy Christmas breaks because they cleverly soaked Yule logs misrepresents human bondage in the South by obscuring its traumas. It telescopes Christmastimes on southern slaveholdings into well-meaning games of wits between good-natured rivals, negating the involuntary nature and many traumas of human bondage. By insinuation, slaveholders who treated enslaved laborers gently when it came to Yule logs likely managed them humanely and with the lightest of discipline all year long. That Booker T. Washington and a handful of other African Americans in the twentieth century gave voice to such tales neither grounds them in historical reality nor justifies their repetition in print or at historic sites. Even if hard evidence one day surfaces that a few enslaved people before the Civil War really soaked Yule logs, it would not alter the fact that almost all did not.

✳✳✳

In a thoughtful three-page treatment of folklore's value in the front matter to his 1969 edition of three slave narratives, the historian Gilbert Osofsky counsels his readers that rather than surrender to the deficiency of traditional written records when it comes to unraveling the history of unlettered enslaved and working-class peoples, it becomes necessary to "turn to the oral record:—the songs, spirituals, and folk tales that were collected in the nineteenth century

150

and remain alive." While acknowledging the "innumerable difficulties" of employing oral sources and noting that specialists in folklore have been documenting those challenges for generations, Osofsky nonetheless maintains that such folklore holds great credibility given the consistency and durability of its themes. He insists on the necessity of turning to folklore when studying the stories of "people who left few written records about their feelings."[41]

On first glance, one might take my findings in this book as a refutation of Osofsky's endorsement of oral evidence when it comes to uncovering the history of Black Americans. After all, the lore about Yule log soakings in the Old South is all about Black people outsmarting the white enslavers who ruled them, and the finessing of powerful figures by weaker ones is one of the most documented themes in slave folklore. In African American folk stories, anthropomorphic animals like "Br-er Rabbit" and human tricksters like the generic slave "John" (thus, the "John" tales) explore their own needs, desires, and frustrations through their deceptions. And these tales in turn feature acts of thefts from masters (especially of food to compensate for inadequate provisions) just like Yule log stories. Soaking stories, stripped to their essence, amount after all to accounts of thefts of time and profits from enslavers—a particularly appropriate response to the yearlong, hour-by-hour appropriation of Black lives that masters and mistresses engaged in. As historian Sterling Stuckey sagely observed a long time ago, "there is little reason to doubt that most slaves considered it almost obligatory to steal from white people." Moreover, not only did Yule log tales correlate with the traditional Black folkloric emphases on theft but they also highlighted how such takings gave enslaved women and men a rare opportunity to laugh at their masters' shortcomings and ineffectiveness, a behavior that few slaves in real life dared to do casually when their owners were within hearing distance. Such mockery, however lighthearted, would have risked severe retaliatory punishment.[42]

Nevertheless, I would emphasize that my analysis, though discrediting Yule log–soaking legends, in no way refutes the legitimacy of Black folklore, folklore as genre, or oral testimony. Rather, I hope the takeaway is that Yule log stories were never firmly anchored in Black folklore in the first place, at least not before the twentieth century, and that though they may tell us something about racial understandings after Emancipation, they have little, perhaps nothing, to teach us about enslavement in North America. Historian John W. Roberts once observed that late nineteenth-century folklore collectors "constantly expressed amazement over the sheer number and the wide distribution and coherence of the black trickster tale repertoire."[43] In contrast, no folklore collector so far as I know during those same years expressed astonishment at the number of Black Americans relating Yule log–soaking tales. Expunging them from enslavement's history, therefore, does nothing to diminish the salience of tricksters in African American culture or the very real deceptions that enslaved people resorted to as means of resistance on a day-to-day basis throughout their years of labor. Enslaved people committed work slowdowns, sabotaged equipment, and undercut their masters' profit-making in countless ways, and did it frequently. What they did not do, so far as I can tell, is soak Yule logs to revenge their bondage. Or simply to gain a longer holiday.

I think we are best served by thinking of Yule log–soaking tales as white southern propaganda that belatedly and barely gained a foothold in African American culture rather than as genuine revelations of enslaved cultures. It took a group of late nineteenth-century and early twentieth-century white southern men and women—many of them descendants of Confederate soldiers and celebrators of the Confederate cause—to get these tales circulating in mainstream American culture in the first place through their poems, short stories, novels, *purportedly* nonfiction memoirs, and public speeches. And for that reason alone, scholars, popular writers, and museums and historic sites should consign these stories, however charming, into the dustbin of history. After all, until Booker T. Washington took up the legend in his effort to use historical memory as a tool for racial reconciliation at a time of escalating tensions between white and Black Americans, African American descendants of slaves knew better than to think that extracting extra-long Christmas vacations from recalcitrant masters was a simple matter of dunking a big log in water. Such tales might please people, but they also distract us from the very real horrors of enslavement in North America and the burdens of chattel slavery on America's historical conscience.

Coda

Samuel Agnew's Christmas Eve

Over the course of my research for this book, I ultimately despaired of ever finding hard evidence that white southerners burned special "Yule logs" for Christmas before the end of Black slavery in the United States or that enslaved people chose such logs, prepared them for the fire, and conveyed them ceremoniously amid chanting and singing to the "big house" on Christmas Eve. White southerners simply did not mention such things in their letters and diaries, nor did they express either suspicion or approval that their slaves had soaked such logs for lengthier vacations. They would have done so, I think, if Yule log ceremonies were as colorful as popular legend suggests and if the entire holiday calendar depended on the logs' flammability. After all, white southerners were hardly inhibited about other things they observed their enslaved field workers and house domestics doing over those same holidays, such as the Alabama cotton planter who told his diary on December 23, 1850, "X mas coming on my Negroes begged me to kill some hogs. I accordingly killed 25—although against my Judgment." Or—the Episcopalian minister who wrote to his wife from Wilmington, North Carolina, two days after Christmas in 1847 that John Cooners had been less conspicuous than during past holidays but that as he wrote he could just then hear one approaching with "his horn & singing."[1]

In rare instances when white southerners mentioned their fireplaces during Christmas week, they did so passingly, almost always in regard to the warmth fires provided at an often-inclement time of the year. I did, however, discover a single diary entry connecting, within a few sentences, enslaved people, "big house" fireplaces, and Christmas Eve. That entry, however, challenges conventional legends about Yule logs in the antebellum South in profound ways.

Samuel A. Agnew, a native of South Carolina, son of a slaveholder, and licensed minister of the Associate Reformed Presbyterian Church, maintained an unusually detailed and thoughtful diary in 1856 after accepting assignment to the small Shiloh Church congregation in Madison County in central Mississippi. And that diary meticulously reported Christmas season doings while he was boarding in the very comfortable big white home of one Thomas Simpson, a man credited with holding more than thirty slaves in both the 1850 and 1860 censuses who was wealthy enough to employ an overseer. Of particular interest to us, the diary gave special attention to a succession of events in the household and Simpson's neighborhood on Christmas Eve, 1856, the very time when, according to legend, Agnew should have caught sight of muscular Black workers shouldering a giant log to Simpson's fireplace.[2]

Christmas 1856 was an unusually fraught holiday through much of the South, because it arrived a month and a half after national elections in which for the first time in American history a major political party committed to slavery's containment and ultimate eradication—the Republican Party—fielded a presidential candidate. Although the party's candidate, the famed former US army explorer John C. Frémont, had lost by sixty electoral votes, the Republicans' solid showing and provocative rhetoric (its national platform dubbed slavery a "relic" of "barbarism") unleashed fears throughout the South about what lay ahead, perhaps as early as Christmastime. Might northern abolitionist provocateurs infiltrate the South and incite slave rebellion at a time when southern enslavers generally had their guard down as they became absorbed with their own gift exchanges, feasts, and dances?

The ensuing panic, arguably the most serious of many pre–Civil War Christmastime scares in the South over rumored mass slave uprisings, threatened Agnew, the Simpsons, and their immediate neighbors, and fortunately for us, Agnew's diary provides a nearly moment-by-moment account of what happened. He noted in his December 24 daytime entry that he had ridden into the nearby town of Camden to post a letter to his father, where he encountered "chat" and excitement over "full accounts" of recent "negro" insurrectionary efforts in Tennessee and Kentucky, and even locally. Further, he was informed that "the negroes in and around Camden" were expected to "rise" that very night. In fact, several slaves had already been hanged to discourage such resistance. For the time being, Agnew indicated an unconcern for his own safety, on the logic that because Blacks now realized whites were on to their plot, they would probably call everything off since they had forfeited the element of surprise. Still, he added, his landlord was playing things safe, ordering his slaves to remain on his place and not wander about as they customarily did over the holiday.

In his next entry, on December 26, Agnew described what had later transpired that same Christmas Eve, and what he wrote provides a stark counterpoint to the stereotypical impression conveyed in most articulations of southern Yule log legends that master–slave relations in the Old South were always congenial. In fact, Agnew's confidence in the stability of the slaveholders' régime was momentarily and easily shaken that night before Christmas.

Agnew relates that after retiring to bed at about 10 o'clock he overheard a couple of panicked men rush into the house exclaiming that the "'niggers'" were "playing thunder" (rebelling) nearby, news which made him hurriedly dress and rush downstairs, where the report became darker and more frightening. Not only had these men heard two guns fired in the direction of a nearby farm, but they also caught screams of women and children just prior to the shots ringing out. After explaining that a small group of pistol-bearing men including his host's son John had then set out from the Simpson place to investigate the matter, Agnew noted that he waited out those tense moments with Thomas Simpson and his wife, by a fire that was rapidly "built up." By that point, his confidence in the immunity of his hosts to racial upheaval had entirely shattered. Everyone's nerves, it seems, were on edge: "There couldn't a dog bark, a gun shoot, or a leaf scarcely rustle but we heard it, and our opinion was that the negroes on Lloyds place had risen on Acock the overseer and killed him and it might be this would be the next place they would attack." Eventually, fatigue got the best of Agnew, and he returned to his room but kept his clothes on while going back to bed, just in case of emergency.

That this taut situation resolved itself without bloodshed (the overheard gunfire, the investigators laughed on their return, had been purposely aimed to frighten but miss some Black children riding slaveholders' calves without permission) hardly mitigates Reverend Agnew's earlier plight that Christmas Eve, as he waited, likely shivering, by the growing Simpson family fire under the impression his life might be in imminent danger. There clearly was nothing special about the logs that fed that fire besides keeping everyone warm as they held vigil.[3]

Reverend Agnew's story can be read many ways. But it suggests that we should never lose sight of the lopsided power struggles that favored the Old South's masters and mistresses, if we ever wish to fully grasp the horrific plight of enslaved people in the United States. Yule log stories give the wholly erroneous impression that southern slaves enjoyed lengthy Christmas holidays courtesy of their Yule logs. They almost always imply that enslavement embodied harmonious relations bonding masters with their enslaved people, that white people and Black people regarded each other with deep mutual affection and delighted in laughing at each other's foibles. These are pleasing tales. But they are ahistorical and counterproductive to racial progress in America, including the nation's escalating debates over reparations for slavery and race discrimination. Nice stories about slave times do nothing to redress the racial oppression marking America's past. It is unfortunate that some American writers and historic sites perpetuate such mythologies, further embedding into our culture an apparently fictional tale popularized by proponents of the Confederacy and the South's Lost Cause.

Abbreviations

LC   Library of Congress, Washington, DC

NA   National Archives

Rawick, *American*   George P. Rawick, ed., *The American Slave: A*
   Slave   *Composite Autobiography*, 41 vols. in two series and
                two supplementary series (Westport, CT: Greenwood
                Press, 1972–1979)

SHC   Southern Historical Collection, Wilson Library,
                University of North Carolina at Chapel Hill

SRC   Sarah Rebecca Cameron Papers

Stampp, *Records*   Kenneth M. Stampp, ed., *Records of Ante-Bellum*
                Southern Plantations from the Revolution through
                the Civil War (microfilm, University Publications of
                America)

UKLSC   University of Kentucky Libraries Special Collections,
                Lexington

Notes

INTRODUCTION

1. Robert E. May, *Yuletide in Dixie: Slavery, Christmas, and Southern Memory* (Charlottesville: University of Virginia Press, 2019); Eugene D. Genovese, *Roll, Jordan, Roll: The World the Slaves Made* (1972; repr., New York: Vintage, 1974), 573; Steven Nissenbaum, *The Battle for Christmas* (New York: Alfred A. Knopf, 1996), 357n.

2. Jenny Proctor interview, Federal Writers' Project: Slave Narrative Project, vol. 16, Texas, pt. 3, Library of Congress, 208–17, esp. 220 (https://www.loc.gov/resource/mesn.163/?sp=214&st=image).

3. Tom Wilson interview, Rawick, *American Slave*, series 1, vol. 7, pt. 2, 166–67.

4. Elizabeth Silverthorne, *Christmas in Texas* (College Station: Texas A&M University Press, 1990), 51; Mary Daggett Lake, "Pioneer Christmas Customs of Tarrant County," in *Rainbow in the Morning*, ed. J. Frank Dobie (Hatboro: PA: Folklore Associates, 1965), 107–11, esp. 111; Monroe Dodd, *Christmastime in Kansas City: The Story of the Season* (Kansas City, MO: Kansas City Star Books, 2001), 16; James Benson Sellers, *Slavery in Alabama* (Tuscaloosa: University of Alabama Press, 1950), 123; Allen Cabaniss, "Christmas," in *The New Encyclopedia of Southern Culture*, ed. Charles Reagan Wilson (24 vols.; Chapel Hill: University of North Carolina Press, 2006–2013), vol. 4: *Myth, Manners, and Memory*, ed. Charles Reagan Wilson (Chapel Hill: University of North Carolina Press, 2006), 210–11. Cabaniss's essay reappears in vol. 16, *Sports and Recreation*, ed. Harvey H. Jackson III (2011), 271–72.

5. (Chicago) *Hardwood Record*, December 25, 1919, 67.

6. "D'Hart Has Tough Program at Duke," *Raleigh News and Observer*, August 17, 1930, Sports, pt. 2; *The Flower Grower* 18 (December 1931): 559.

7. Harnett T. Kane, *The Southern Christmas Book: The Full Story from Earliest Times to Present: People, Customs, Conviviality, Carols, Cooking* (New York: David McKay Company, 1958), 67–68.

8. Robert J. Myers with the editors of Hallmark Cards, *Celebrations: The Complete Book of American Holidays* (Garden City, NY: Doubleday, 1972), 317; Mary Gunderson, *Southern Plantation Cooking* (Mankato, MN: Capstone Press, 2000), 28; Tanya

Gulevich, *Encyclopedia of Christmas and New Year's Celebrations*, second edition (Detroit: Omnigraphics, 2003), 719.

9. Kathlyn Gay, *African-American Holidays, Festivals, and Celebrations . . .* (Detroit: Omnigraphics, 2007), 401–2; Ace Collins, *Stories Behind the Great Traditions of Christmas* (Grand Rapids, MI: Zondervan, 2003), 177; Carol Marsh, *The Amazing Book of Georgia Christmas Trivia* (Peachtree City, GA: Gallopade International, 2005), 18; *A Very Virginia Christmas: Stories and Traditions*, ed. and comp. Wilford Kale (Norfolk, VA: Parke Press, 2012); Emyl Jenkins, *Southern Christmas* (New York: Gramercy Books, 1992), 106.

10. Jerry Reunion, "A Southern Christmas," *North Carolina Roadways* 13 (November–December 1967), 47; Patty Carter Deveau, "Christmas on the Old Plantation," *Outdoors in Georgia* 8 (December 1978): 12–15; Nancy C. Hanks, "Spirit of Christmas Glows," *Journal of the U.S. Army Intelligence & Security Command* 2 (December 1979): 2.

11. "Historic site to offer glimpses of an 1830-style Christmas," *Asheville Citizen-Times*, November 30, 1999, section B, 1, 3; Sean Clancy, "Revelries of Christmas Past: Nineteenth-Century Arkansas Celebrations Involved a Lot of Alcohol and Fireworks," *Northwest Arkansas Democratic Gazette*, December 21, 2020 (https://www.nwaonline.com/news/2020/dec/21/revelries-of-christmas-past/); Wade Allen, "Get a Historical Perspective at these Two Holiday Events in Gaston County," *Gaston Gazette*, December 5, 2012 (https://www.gastongazette.com/story/news/2012/12/06/historical-holidays-events-show-how/34382307007/).

12. Suzanne R. Stone, "Redcliffe Relives Candlelit Past: Plantation Will Hold Holiday Tours," *Augusta* (GA) *Chronicle*, December 2, 2001, 1.

13. Suzanne R. Stone, "Redcliffe reflects on plantation holidays," *McClatchy-Tribune Business News*, December 21, 2008; "Redcliffe visitors learn about Christmastime for the slaves," *McClatchy-Tribune Business News*, December 20, 2009.

14. Dickson J. Preston, *Young Frederick Douglass: The Maryland Years* (Baltimore: Johns Hopkins University Press, 1980), 132; Frances T. Humphreville, *Harriet Tubman: Flame of Freedom* (Boston: Houghton Mifflin, 1991), 56–58; Deborah Hedstrom, *From Slavery to Freedom with Harriet Tubman* (Sisters, OR: Multnomah, 1997), 9–13, 18, 26.

15. Patricia C. McKissack and Frederick L. McKissack, *Christmas in the Big House, Christmas in the Quarters* (New York: Scholastic, 1994), 2. See also Vivian Yenika-Agbaw, "Taking Children's Literature Seriously: Reading for Pleasure and Social Change," *Language Arts* 74 (October 1997): 446–53, esp. 452.

16. Nissenbaum, *Battle for Christmas*, 357n; Rebecca Cameron, "Christmas on an Old Plantation," *Ladies' Home Journal* 9 (December 1891): 5–8; John Williamson Palmer, "Old Maryland Homes and Ways," *Century* 49 (December 1894): 244–60; Booker T. Washington, "Christmas Days in Old Virginia," in *The Booker T. Washington Papers*, 14 vols., ed. Louis R. Harlan (Urbana: University of Illinois Press, 1972–89), vol. 1: 394–97.

17. Ronald J. Grele, "Oral History as Evidence," in *History of Oral History: Foundations and Methodology*, eds. Thomas L. Charlton, Lois E. Myers, and Rebecca Sharpless (Lanham, MD: AltaMira Press, 2007), 33–91, esp. 74–75.

18. Claude H. Nolen's *African American Southerners in Slavery, Civil War and Reconstruction* (Jefferson, NC: McFarland, 2001), 31, 194n, cites Tom Wilson's FWP interview. Encyclopedia and historical dictionary entries perpetuating these legends lack documentation, as most such reference works do not require their articles to be documented. See, for example, "Holiday Celebrations" in *Encyclopedia of the Antebellum South*, eds. James M. Volo and Dorothy Deneen Volo (Westport, CT: Greenwood Press, 2000), 130–31.

19. Barbara Brackman, *Facts and Fabrications: Unraveling the History of Quilts & Slavery* (Lafayette, CA: C&T Publishing, 2006), 6–9; Hoag Levins, "New Jersey's Underground Railroad Myth-Buster," HistoricCamdenCounty.com, June 4, 2001 (http://historiccamdencounty.com/ccnews11.shtml); Jacqueline L. Tobin and Raymond G. Dobard, *Hidden in Plain View: A Secret Story of Quilts and the Underground Railroad* (New York: Doubleday, 1999). The black spots and troop movements are mentioned in Gladys-Marie Fry, *Stitched from the Soul: Slave Quilts from the Antebellum South* (1990; repr. with new preface, Chapel Hill: University of North Carolina Press, 2002), 65. Fry's footnote for this information only cited a source in which an ex-slave in the 1930s discussed slave superstitions about quilting on Fridays and said nothing about quilts as maps. Fry, *Stitched*, 93n.

20. René Ostberg, "urban legend," *Encyclopedia Britannica*, January 16, 2024 (https://www.britannica.com/topic/urban-legend).

21. Robert S. Starobin, *Industrial Slavery in the Old South* (New York: Oxford University Press, 1970), 3–34.

22. Catherine Clinton, *Tara Revisited: Women, War, and the Plantation Legend* (New York: Abbeville Press, 1995), 191.

23. Clinton, *Tara Revisited*, 191.

CHAPTER 1

1. Drew Gilpin Faust, *A Sacred Circle: The Dilemma of the Intellectual in the Old South, 1840–1860* (Philadelphia: University of Pennsylvania Press, 1977), 27–30 (quote on 27), 90, 164n23; Bruce Collins, *White Society in the Antebellum South* (New York: Longman, 1985), 70–71; John McCardell, *The Idea of a Southern Nation: Southern Nationalists and Southern Nationalism, 1830–1860* (New York: W. W. Norton, 1979), 146–60 ("animal" quote on 151); William W. Freehling, *The Road to Disunion*, vol. 1: *Secessionists at Bay, 1776–1854* (New York: Oxford University Press, 1990), 236–45 ("cardboard" on 244).

2. William Gilmore Simms, *Castle Dismal; or, The Bachelor's Christmas. A Domestic Legend* (New York: Burgess, Stringer, 1844), 32; Simms, "Maize in Milk; A Christmas Story of the South," in Simms, *Marie De Berniere: A Tale of the Crescent City, Etc. Etc. Etc.* (Philadelphia, PA: Lippincott, Grambo, 1853), 320–422, esp. 321–23, 340–63 (quotes on 362–63). Simms originally published this story serially in *Godey's Magazine* in 1847.

3. *Oxford English Dictionary* (Purdue University Library online collections), s.v. "yule-log."

4. Henry Bourne, *Antiquities Vulgares; or, The Antiquities of the Common People* (Newcastle, UK: J. White, 1725), 126–35 (quotes on 129 and 126).

5. Robert Herrick, "Ceremonies for Christmas," quoted in Walter W. Schmauch, *Christmas Literature through the Centuries* (Chicago: Walter M. Hill, 1938), 111.

6. Nathan B. Warren, *The Holidays: Christmas, Easter, and Whitsuntide: Their Social Festivities, Customs, and* Carols (New York: Hurd and Houghton, 1868), 10; Ace Collins, *Stories Behind the Great Traditions of Christmas* (Grand Rapids, MI: Zondervan, 2003), 173; William D. Crump, *The Christmas Encyclopedia* (Jefferson, NC: McFarland, 2001), 254–55.

7. Barbara Hallman Kissinger, *Christmas Past* (Gretna: Pelican, 2005), 30–33; Tom Flynn, *The Trouble with Christmas* (Buffalo, NY: Prometheus Books, 1993), 38–39; Eve Blantyre Simpson, *Folk Lore in Lowland Scotland* (London: J. M. Dent, 1908). Some authorities point out similarities between descriptions of Yggrasils and ash trees.

8. (Washington, DC) *Daily National Intelligencer*, December 25, 1858, 3; Tanya Gulevich, *Encyclopedia of Christmas & New Year's Celebrations*, second edition (Detroit, MI: Omnigraphics, 2003), 850 ("little can be determined").

9. "The Demon of the Pocumptuck; Or the Warrior of the Wampanoags," *Manchester* (NH) *Union Democrat*, August 30, 1859, 1; (n.a.), *History of Queens County, New York . . .* (New York: W. W. Munsell, 1882), 27; Maud Wilder Goodwin, *The Colonial Cavalier; or, Southern Life before the Revolution* (Boston: Little, Brown, 1895), 154. See also Edward Eggleston, "Social Life in the Colonies," *Century Illustrated Magazine* 30 (July 1885): 387–407, esp. 399; Collins, *Stories*, 176.

10. John E. Baur, *Christmas on the American Frontier, 1800–1900* (Caldwell, ID: Caxton Printers, 1961), 23; "Observance of Christmas Was Once Forbidden in Colonial New England" (published in scores of American newspapers between December 6 and 27, 1962, in some cases under the title "Christmas Observance Once Illegal").

11. Smellycat Productions LLC, "Bacon's Castle Christmas," posted December 18, 2013, Vimeo video, 04:22 (https://vimeo.com/82210061); Michael Philip Manheim, "Savannah Shares Its Christmas," *Baltimore Sun*, December 23, 1990, section K, 1, 5; Official Guides of Savannah LLC, "Colonial Christmas at Wormsloe," posted December 2022 (https://savguides.com/lobby-list-events/2022/12/10/colonial-christmas-at-wormsloe); Georgia Department of Natural Resources, "Wormsloe Historic Site" (https://explore.gastateparks.org/events?p=7).

12. [Nathan Boughton Warren], *Recollections of Revolutionary Times: Or, Round About the Yule-Log, by a Church-Warden* (Boston: F. H. Gilson, 1895), 7–9.

13. *Autobiography and Letters of Orville Dewey*, ed. Mary E. Dewey (Boston: Roberts Brothers, 1883), 11, 23 (quote).

14. (Washington, DC) *Daily National Journal*, December 24, 1824, 2; "Our Christmas Party," *Worchester* (MA) *Weekly Spy*, December 29, 1858, 3.

15. "A Christmas Greeting," *Boston Bee*, December 25, 1848, 2; "Christmas," *Belfast* (ME) *Republican Journal*, December 21, 1849.

16. Hester Dorsey Richardson, *Side-Lights on Maryland History*, vol. 1 (Baltimore: Williams and Wilkins, 1913), 26; Maud Wilder Goodwin, *The Colonial Cavalier; or Southern Life Before the Revolution* (New York: Lovell, Coryell, 1894), 154.

17. Chronicling America: Historic American Newspapers, Library of Congress, search on January 1, 2023 (https://chroniclingamerica.loc.gov/).

18. John D. Rockefeller Library, "The Yule Log Ceremony," December 2, 2021 (https://www.colonialwilliamsburg.org/learn/living-history/the-yule-log-ceremony/); Carl Childs, Colonial Williamsburg Foundation, email to Robert E. May, April 24, 2023.

19. Jerry M. Rose and Barbara W. Brown, *Tapestry: A Living History of the Black Family in Southeastern Connecticut* (New London, CT: New London County Historical Society, 1979), 10–11, 135n36; Daniel L. Phillips, *Griswold—Being a History of the Town of Griswold, Connecticut, From the Earliest Times to the Entrance of our Country Into the World War in 1917* (New Haven, CT: Tuttle, Morehouse & Taylor, 1929), 171; Debbie Loser, president, Griswold Historical Society, email to Robert E. May, February 7, 2023; Tom Schuch, email to Robert E. May, February 7, 2023; Pat Schaefer, New London County Historical Society, email to Robert E. May, February 13, 2023. President Loser's message mentions not only that the Griswold Historical Society Museum lacks documents confirming the Phillips story but also that town historian Mary Rose Deveau "knew of no letters or documents" about Yule logs.

20. John Davis, *Travels of Four Years and a Half in the United States of America; During 1798, 1799, 1800, 1801, and 1802* (London: T. Ostell, 1803), 62–65 (quotes on 65).

CHAPTER 2

1. James A. Rawley, *Race and Politics: "Bleeding Kansas" and the Coming of the Civil War* (New York: J. B. Lippincott, 1969), 111–12.

2. "Pictures of Southern Life," *Emporia* (KS) *News*, March 10, 1860, 2; "All Sorts of Paragraphs," *Janesville* (WI) *Daily Gazette*, April 21, 1860, 6; Henry C. Whitney, *Lincoln the Citizen* (New York: Current Literature Publishing, 1907), 265; Teri D. Barnett, newspaper librarian, Abraham Lincoln Presidential Library and Museum, Springfield, email to Robert E. May, March 25, 2024.

3. Curtis J. Evans, *The Conquest of Labor: Daniel Pratt and Southern Industrialization* (Baton Rouge: Louisiana State University Press, 2001), 11–19, 31–42, 53, 83, 123–25; "Cotton Gin Manufactory, Prattville, Ala." (advertisement), *Tuscaloosa* (AL) *Independent Monitor*, May 25, 1854, 4; "Prattville Still Improving," *Prattville* (AL) *Southern Statesman*, June 23, 1860, 2; "Rail Road Meeting," *Prattville* (AL) *Southern Statesman*, April 14, 1860, 2; Fred Bateman and Thomas Weiss, *A Deplorable Scarcity: The Failure of Industrialization in the Slave Economy* (Chapel Hill: University of North Carolina Press, 1981), 12, 186; "Daniel Pratt to N. J. Fogarty and others," quoted in *Autauga* (AL) *Citizen*, February 23, 1860, 2.

4. Evans, *Conquest of Labor*, 54, 80–83; "Pictures of Southern Life."

5. *Elkton* (MD) *Cecil Whig*, December 25, 1847, 2.

6. Gilbert Osofsky's introduction to Osofsky, ed., *Puttin' On Ole Massa: The Slave Narratives of Henry Bibb, William Wells Brown and Solomon Northup* (New York: Harper & Row, 1969), 9–44, esp. 10–14; John W. Blassingame, "Using the Testimony of Ex-Slaves: Approaches and Problems," in *The Slave's Narrative*, eds. Charles T. Davis and Henry Louis Gates Jr. (New York: Oxford University Press, 1985), 78–97, esp. 79–82.

7. "North American Slave Narratives, Documenting the American South," University of North Carolina at Chapel Hill (https://docsouth.unc.edu/neh/chronautobio .html).

8. William W. Winn, *The Magic and Mystery of Westville* (Lumpkin, GA: Westville Historic Handicrafts, 1999), 1; "Westville, Georgia, Grows and Prospers in Mode of the 1850s," *History News* 27 (November 1972): 256–57; Bob Harrell, "Westville Once Knew Christmas as Settlement Day," *Atlanta Journal and Constitution*, December 23, 1984, section B, 2; *Columbus* (GA) *Ledger-Enquirer*, December 6, 2006, "Northland Neighbors" section, 19.

9. Judith Gray, reference specialist, American Folklife Center, Library of Congress, email to Robert E. May, February 8, 2024; Sallie Long emails to Robert E. May, February 27, March 13, 2024. It should be noted that Legacy Project nominations required congressional sponsors, not endorsements by professional historians. Georgia US senator Paul Coverdell sponsored the Westville project.

10. *Fredericksburg News* quoted in *Alexandria Gazette*, December 25, 1855, 2; "Christmas," *Charleston Daily Courier*, December 25, 1857, 2; *Ravenna* (OH) *Portage County Democrat*, December 20, 1854, 3.

11. "Editorial Greetings for the New Year," *Richmond* (VA) *Southern Literary Messenger* 14 (January 1848): 1–2; "Christmas," *New Orleans Daily Picayune*, December 25, 1844, 2; "Christmas!" *Richmond Whig and Public Advertiser*, December 26, 1856, 3.

12. Charles J. Peterson, "Christmas and Its Customs," *Winchester* (TN) *Home Journal*, December 16, 1858, 1.

13. "Christmas," *Eufaula* (AL) *Express*, December 23, 1858, 2.

14. Brenda Chambers McKean, *Blood and War: North Carolinians in the War Between the States*, vol. 2 (Bloomington, IN: Xlibris, 2011), 1109; Pauline Grice narrative in *Slave Narratives: A Folk History of Slavery in the United States from Interviews with Former Slaves*. Typewritten records prepared by the Federal Writers' Project, 1936–1938, assembled by the Library of Congress Works Progress Administration for the District of Columbia, sponsored by the Library of Congress, vol. 16: *Texas Narratives*, pt. 2 (Washington 1941), 98–102 (quote on 100) https://www .gutenberg.org/files/30967/30967-h/30967-h.htm.

15. Albert Pike, "Christmas," *Mechanicstown* (MD) *Cacoctin Clarion*, January 13, 1872, 1; Lillian (Pike) Roome, comp., *Gen. Albert Pike's Poems* (Little Rock, AR: Fred. W. Allsopp, 1900), 199; "Christmas in Olden Time," *Charleston Daily Courier*, December 25, 1858, 2; "The Yule-Feast," *Charleston Daily Courier*, December 24, 1859, 2.

16. Sam W. Haynes, *Unfinished Revolution: The Early American Republic in a British World* (Charlottesville: University of Virginia Press, 2010), 54; John Brand,

Observations on Popular Antiquities: Chiefly Illustrating the Origin of Our Vulgary Customes, Ceremonies, and Superstitions (London: Charles Knight, 1841), 255; Yule E'en, "Songs and Ballads By a Backwoodsman," *Anglo-American Magazine* 1 (July–December 1852): 544; *Pictorial Calendar of the Seasons, Exhibiting the Pleasures, Pursuits, and Characteristics of Country Life for Every Month in the Year* (London: Henry G. Bohn, 1854), 562, 563.

17. "Christmas," *Lancaster* (PA) *Intelligencer*, December 26, 1848, 2; "The Festival of the Yuletide," *New York Herald*, December 25, 1859, 1; "The Festival of Christmas," *Pittsfield* (MA) *Berkshire County Eagle*, December 19, 1861, 1; "Christmas Eve!" *Leavenworth* (KS) *Daily Commercial*, December 25, 1869, 4.

18. *Kalispel Inter Lake*, December 21, 1894, 3.

19. William C. Richards, *Harry's Vacation; or, Philosophy at Home* (New York: Evans and Dickerson, 1854), 146–54 (gravity lesson on 48–50).

20. "William Carey Richards," in biographical appendix in *The Complete Works of Thomas Holley Chivers*, vol. 1, eds. Emma Lester Chase and Lois Ferry Parks (Providence, RI: Brown University Press, 1957), 303; "Richards, William Carey," in *Lamb's Biographical Dictionary of the United States*, vol. 6 (Boston: Federal Book Company, 1903), 467; Bertram Holland Flanders, *Early Georgia Magazines* (Athens: University of Georgia Press, 1944), 68–69; Edward L. Tucker, "Two Young Brothers and Their *Orion*," *Southern Literary Journal* 11 (Fall 1978): 64–80; Ernest Hynds, *Antebellum Athens and Clarke County, Georgia* (Athens: University of Georgia Press, 1974), 98–99; John David Wade, *Augustus Baldwin Longstreet: A Study of the Development of Culture in the South* (New York: Macmillan Company, 1924), 208–11.

21. "New-York Correspondence," *Charleston* (SC) *Daily Courier*, December 13, 1854, 1; "A Great Book for the Holidays," *New-York Daily Tribune*, December 15, 1854, 1; "Metropolitan Correspondence," *Raleigh* (NC) *Southern Weekly Post*, November 25, 1854, 2; "New and Desirable Books," *Richmond Enquirer*, January 4, 1855, 3; "New Books for the Young," *Wilmington* (NC) *Daily Herald*, January 13, 1855, 2; "A Capital Book for the Home-Circle," *Raleigh* (NC) *American Signal*, July 12, 1856, 1.

22. Emma D. E. N. Southworth, "Hickory Hall: Or the Outcast," *Washington* (DC) *National Era*, November 28, 1850, 1 ("white-headed negro" and "blazing hickory fire"), November 14, 1850 ("eldest son"), 1, December 5, 1850, 1. Southworth's story was first released in book form by Philadelphia publisher T. B. Peterson in 1861. Virginian Lizzie Petit Cutler's antebellum novel *Household Mysteries: A Romance of Southern Life* (New York: D. Appleton, 1856), 21, mentions a Yule log burning at an aristocratic Virginia household with no mention of it having anything to do with enslaved people. Joy Jordan-Lake notes *Household Mysteries*'s erasure of enslaved life in *Whitewashing Uncle Tom's Cabin: Nineteenth-Century Women Novelists Respond to Stowe* (Nashville, TN: Vanderbilt University Press, 2005), 31.

23. "Stray Leaves from the Diary of a Country Lady," (Augusta, GA) *Southern Field and Fireside*, June 25, 1859, 35.

24. "The Yule Clog," *Freedom's Journal*, November 21, 1828, 275.

CHAPTER 3

1. Argo, "Yule Log," *Ottawa* (KS) *Journal*, December 26, 1872, 2. Unfortunately, the pseudonymous "Argo" who wrote the piece failed to divulge where in Kentucky these enslaved people lived or the identity of their bamboozled owner.

2. John David Smith, *An Old Creed for the New South: Proslavery Ideology and Historiography, 1865–1918* (1985; repr., Carbondale: Southern Illinois University Press, 2008), 4–7; Jeffrey Robert Young, "Proslavery Ideology," in *The Oxford Handbook of Slavery in the Americas*, eds. Robert L. Paquette and Mark M. Smith (2010; New York: Oxford University Press, 2016), 399–423, esp. 409–13; "The Holidays," *Oakland* (MD) *The Republican*, December 15, 1892, 5.

3. David W. Blight, *Race and Reunion: The Civil War in American Memory* (Cambridge, MA: Harvard University Press, 2001), 216–31 (quotes on 216).

4. Innes Randolph, "The Back-Log; Or, Uncle Ned's Little Game," *Baltimore Gazette*, December 26, 1877, as reprinted in the *Easton* (MD) *Star*, January 8, 1878, 1.

5. Thomas Tusser, "The fermers dailie diet," in Tusser, *Five Hundred Pointes of Good Husbandrie* (1557; repr. London: Turner and Co., 1878), 27–28; Thomas Miller, "Christmas Comes but Once a Year," in *Christmas with the Poets*, ed. Henry Vizetelly (London: David Bogue, 1851), 159–63; George Wither, "Christmas," in *The Poets of the Elizabethan Age: A Selection of Their Most Celebrated Songs and Sonnets* (New York: Bunce and Huntington, 1866), 71–75; slave pass quoted in Sally E. Hadden, *Slave Patrols: Law and Violence in Virginia* (Cambridge, MA: Harvard University Press, 2001), 112–13; A. S. W. Rosenbach, "The Earliest Christmas Books," *Ladies' Home Journal* 44 (December 1927): 14. See "No Paper To-morrow," *Richmond Enquirer*, December 26, 1859, 2, for an example of the phrase's antebellum pervasiveness in Virginia.

6. "Susan Peyton Armistead Randolph," Find a Grave, database and images, memorial ID 121876990 (https://www.findagrave.com/memorial/121876990/susan-peyton-randolph); Eighth US Census, 1860, Schedule 1 (Population), District of Columbia, NA (Ancestry.com); Susan Peyton Randolph obituary in *New Orleans Daily Picayune*, November 3, 1884, 4.

7. "Congressional Directory of the Thirtieth Congress, Second Session" (Washington, DC), *Daily National Whig*, January 29, 1849, 3; (Washington, DC) *Evening Star*, February 22, 1856, 2; "Criminal Court," *Washington* (DC) *Union*, February 21, 1858, 3.

8. *Register of Hobart Free College, at Geneva, NY, for the Academical Year, 1855–1856* (Geneva, NY: S. H. Parker, 1856), unpaged; Students Records, vol. 1, Records of the Faculty of Geneva College from September 1839, Hobart and William Smith Library, Geneva, NY; *General Catalogue of Officers, Graduates and Students, 1825–1897* (Geneva, NY: W. F. Humphrey, 1897), 207, 231; K. Huntress Baldwin, "James Innes Randolph Jr.," in *Southern Writers: A New Biographical Dictionary*, eds. Joseph M. Flora and Amber Vogel (Baton Rouge: Louisiana State University Press, 2006), 331–32.

9. W. G. Bender to J. I. Randolph, First Lieutenant Engineers, October 28, 1862, *Official Records of the Union and Confederate Navies in the War of the Rebellion*,

series 1, vol. 8 (Washington, DC: Government Printing Office, 1899), 187–88; Robert E. L. Krick, *Staff Officers in Gray: A Biographical Register of the Staff Officers in the Army of Northern Virginia* (Chapel Hill: University of North Carolina Press, 2003), 249; Clara Egli LeGear, comp., *The Hotchkiss Map Collection: A List of Manuscript Maps, Many of the Civil War Period . . .* (Washington, DC: Library of Congress, 1951), 12; Baldwin, "Randolph."

10. Thomas C. De Leon, *Four Years in Rebel Capitals: An Inside View of Life in the Southern Confederacy . . .* (Mobile: Gossip Printing, 1892), 390–11; advertisement for "O, I'm a Good Old Rebel," under "New Music" in *Richmond* (VA) *Times*, January 8, 1867, 2; "O, I'm a Good old Rebel," reprinted in *Richmond* (VA) *Planet*, June 7, 1890, 2; "Democratic Campaign Song," *Delaware* (OH) *Gazette*, May 24, 1867, 2; Horatio C. King, "Innes Randolph, Poet," *Brooklyn Daily Eagle*, July 18, 1895, 6. For an excellent analysis of the song's conflicted history and reception, see Joseph M. Thompson, "The 'Good Old Rebel' at the Heart of the Radical Right," *Southern Cultures* 26 (Winter 2020): 124–39.

11. "Mount Vernon," *New Orleans Times-Democrat*, July 9, 1883, 8.

12. *Harrisonburg* (VA) *Old Commonwealth*, January 3, 1878; *Easton* (MD) *Star*, January 8, 1878, 1; *Westminster* (MD) *Democratic Advocate*, December 21, 1878, 4, December 24, 1887, 6; "Mount Vernon," *New Orleans Times-Democrat*, July 9, 1883, 8; Mary French Caldwell, "Yuletide Brings Old Customs to Life," in *Selections for Reading and Oratory*, ed. John G. James (New York: A. S. Barnes, 1879), 322–25; *One Hundred Choice Selections, No. 18. A Rare Collection of Oratory, Sentiment, Eloquence and Humor for Public Readings, Winter Gatherings, Social Entertainments, Elocution Exercises, Temperance Societies, Exhibitions, Lyceums, & C.* (Chicago: Garrett, 1890), 58–60; "Holiday Closing," *Fort Scott* (KS) *Daily Monitor*, December 20, 1889, 5; "32 Years Ago," *Butte* (MT) *Miner*, January 24, 1925, 4; *Richmond* (VA) *News Leader*, December 25, 1936, 4; Mary French Caldwell, "Yuletide Brings Old Customs to Life," *Nashville Banner*, December 18, 1937, Features, 3. Other reprintings include the *Richmond* (VA) *Evening Journal*, December 24, 1913, 10.

13. John William Tebbel and Mary Ellen Zuckerman, *The Magazine in America, 1741–1990* (New York: Oxford University Press, 1991), 142.

14. "The Holly Back-Log," *Youth's Companion*, December 22, 1887, 575. Cuttlefish are marine invertebrates related to squid.

15. David Goldfield, *Still Fighting the Civil War: The American South and Southern History* (Baton Rouge: Louisiana State University Press, 2002), 20.

16. Frank Luther Mott, *A History of American Magazines, 1865–1885* (1938; repr. Cambridge, MA: Harvard University Press, 1970), 6; Amanda Hinnant and Berkley Hudson, "The Magazine Revolution, 1880–1920," in *The Oxford History of Popular Print Culture*, ed. Christine Bold, vol. 6 (New York: Oxford University Press, 2012), 112; T. C. Evans to Perry Mason & Co., November 16, 1886, in *Evans Advertising Hand Book*, sixteenth edition (Boston: T. C. Evans, 1887), 6; "The Youth's Companion," *Boston Evening Transcript*, December 10, 1886, 1; *Bel Air* (MD) *Aegis and Intelligencer*, November 12, 1886, 3.

17. "The Holly Back-Log," *Anthony* (KS) *Harper County Enterprise*, December 23, 1887, 1; "The Holly Back-Log," *Spring Lake* (KS) *Artois Hornet*, December 30, 1887, 2; "The Holly Back Log," *Buffalo Enquirer*, December 21, 1900, 3; "The Holly Back-Log," *Seneca* (NE) *Tribune*, December 26, 1918, 1.

18. Emma L. Powers, "Cynthia Beverley Tucker Washington Coleman," in *Dictionary of Virginia Biography*, Library of Virginia, published in 2006 (https://www.lva.virginia.gov/public/dvb/bio.asp?b=Coleman_Cynthia_B_T); Eighth US Census, 1860, Schedule 2, Slave Inhabitants, James City County, VA, NA (Ancestry.com). Coleman's father served with the Third Virginia Cavalry. See "Search For Soldiers," *The Civil War*, National Park Service (https://www.nps.gov/civilwar/search-soldiers.htm#sort=score+desc&q=Charles+Coleman+Virginia+Third+Cavalry). Coleman's parents were Cynthia Beverly Tucker and George Washington Coleman.

19. C. W. Coleman, "A Virginia Plantation," *The Chautauquan* 9 (April 1889): 412–14; "A Virginia Plantation," *The Congregationalist,* March 28, 1889, 9; *N. W. Ayer & Son's American Newspaper Annual* (Philadelphia: N. W. Ayer & Son, 1889), 450.

20. Anya Jabour, *Scarlett's Sisters: Young Women in the Old South* (Chapel Hill: University of North Carolina Press, 2007), 239–49.

21. W. Fitzhugh Brundage, *The Southern Past: A Clash of Race and Memory* (Cambridge, MA: Harvard University Press, 2005), 15, 22; Caroline E. Janney, *Remembering the Civil War: Reunion and the Limits of Reconciliation* (Chapel Hill: University of North Carolina Press, 2013), 92–93, 234 ("tenaciously"); Janney, *"Burying the Dead but Not the Past": Ladies' Memorial Associations and the Lost Cause* (Chapel Hill: University of North Carolina Press, 2008), 2–3, 8; Anne E. Marshall, *Creating a Confederate Kentucky: The Lost Cause and Civil War Memory in a Border State* (Chapel Hill: University of North Carolina Press, 2010), 84–85; Paul D. Escott, *Uncommonly Savage: Civil War and Remembrance in Spain and the United States* (Gainesville: University Press of Florida, 2014), 83–84.

22. Janney, "Remembering the Civil War," 242; James M. McPherson, "Long-Legged Yankee Lies: The Southern Textbook Crusade," in *The Memory of the Civil War in American Culture*, eds. Alice Fahs and Joan Waugh (Chapel Hill: University of North Carolina Press, 2004), 64–78.

23. Third US Census, 1810, Brunswick County, NC, NA (Ancestry.com); Will of Alfred Moore Sr., July 25, 1810, Wills, vol. A–B. 1868–1924, Superior Court, Brunswick County, NC (Ancestry.com); Allen Alexander and Pauline O. Lloyd, *History of the Town of Hillsborough, 1754–1991* (Hillsborough, NC: privately published, 1966?), 225; James M. Clifton, "Moore, Alfred," in Dictionary of North Carolina Biography, ed. William S. Powell, posted January 1, 1991 (https://www.ncpedia.org/biography/moore-alfred); "Married," *Raleigh* (NC) *Standard*, December 25, 1837, 3; "Memorable Moores," *Raleigh* (NC) *News and Observer*, December 31, 1887, 2; "Buchoi Plantation," *Plantations*, Genealogy Trails History Group (https://genealogytrails.com/ncar/newhanover/plantations.html); James Iredell Waddell Family Papers, PC. 87, State Archives of North Carolina, NC, SHC (https://axaem.archives.ncdcr.gov/findingaids/PC_87_James_Iredell_Waddell_Fam_.html).

24. Fourth US Census, 1820, Brunswick County, NC, NA (Ancestry.com).

25. Alfred Moore Jr. Will, January 6, 1837, Wills, Orange County, Probate Court (Ancestry.com); "Trust Sale," *Hillsborough Recorder*, February 22, 1844, 3; William Alexander Graham to Susan Washington Graham, February 17, 1837, in *The Papers of William Alexander Graham*, vol. 1 (Raleigh, NC: State Department of Archives and History, 1957), 484–85; "Married," *North Carolina Standard*, December 25, 1837, 3.

26. Anne Cameron Will and Codicil, May 24, 31, 1856, North Carolina Wills, 1665–1998, Orange County, North Carolina County Court of Pleas and Quarter Sessions (Ancestry.com); Anne Call Cameron and others bill of complaint against Alexander M. Kirkland and his wife Anna, filed in Equity, Orange County, March Term, 1838, and Decree of the Court, September Term, 1838, in North Carolina Wills and Probate Records, 1665–1998 (Ancestry.com); Bill of Sale of slave "John" to John Berry of Orange County, November 27, 1841, Mary E. Strayhorn Berry Papers, SHC; "Trust Sale," *Hillsborough Recorder*, February 22, 1844, 3; Seventh US Census, 1850, Schedule 2, Slave Inhabitants, Orange County, NC, NA (Ancestry.com); Eighth US Census, 1860, Schedule 2, Slave Inhabitants, Hillsboro, Orange County, NC, NA (Ancestry.com).

27. Anna Cameron Diary (misidentified as Emma Cameron's diary), November 22, 1863, SRC, series 4, vol. 2, SHC.

28. "Orange Light Artillery," *Fayetteville* (NC) *Observer*, March 13, 1862, 3; Kent McCoury, "Alfred Moore Waddell, 1834–1912," North Carolina History Project (https://northcarolinahistory.org/encyclopedia/alfred-moore-waddell-1834-1912/); James Iredell Waddell Family Papers, PC. 87, State Archives of North Carolina, NC (https://axaem.archives.ncdcr.gov/findingaids/PC_87_James_Iredell_Waddell_Fam _.html); Spencer C. Tucker, *A Short History of the Civil War at Sea* (Wilmington, DE: Scholarly Resources, 2002), 133–35.

29. Anna Alexander Cameron Diary, January 29, 1864, SRC, SHC, series 4, vol. 2; "Soldier Life in the Army of Northern Virginia," *Southern World* 2 (May 15, 1883): 222; Anna Alexander Cameron to Alfred Moore Waddell, November 5, 1887, quoted in James J. Broomall, *Personal Confederacies: War and Peace in the American South, 1840–1890* (PhD diss., University of Florida, 2011), 279; Rebecca Cameron to Alfred M. Waddell, October 26, 1898, Alfred M. Waddell Papers, SHC; *Raleigh News and Observer*, February 10, 1903, 6; Anna Alexander Cameron to Mrs. A. L. Dowdell, August 1902, in *Montgomery* (AL) *Advertiser*, August 24, 1902, 12.

30. Anna Alexander Cameron, "Christmas on the Old Plantation," *The Home Maker* 3 (December 1889); "Christmas on the Old Plantation," *Montpelier Vermont Watchman*, December 25, 1889, 6.

31. *Augusta Chronicle*, December 27, 1890, 4.

32. Rebecca Cameron, "Christmas on an Old Plantation," *Ladies' Home Journal* 9 (December 1891): 5.

33. "Card," *Hillsborough Recorder*, June 10, 1863, 3. William Cameron had resumed his medical practice in Hillsborough in June 1863 following his Confederate service. The 1870 and 1880 US censuses both place all three Cameron sisters in their father's household. The 1880 census lists the former slave child "Evalina" as still with the family as a domestic servant named Evelina Nelson, aged eighteen.

34. Rebecca Cameron to "Charlie," June 22, 1861, Rebecca Cameron to "My *own dear sweet* Auntie!," July 24, 1861, SRC, SHC (https://dc.lib.unc.edu/utils/ajaxhelper /?CISOROOT=04021&CISOPTR=536&action=2&DMSCALE=51.387461459404 &DMWIDTH=1946&DMHEIGHT=3190). This Cameron sister's given name was Sarah according to her gravestone (https://cemeterycensus.com/nc/orng/cempic.htm ?cem=066&pic=066-210.jpg&wrd=Cameron,_Sarah_Rebecca), but she signed her letters and authored publications using her middle name Rebecca or, in the case of letters, sometimes variants like "R. S. C." and "Beck."

35. Janney, *Remembering the Civil War*, 136.

36. "The Shotwell Monument," *Windsor* (NC) *Public Ledger*, March 14, 1888, 2; J. G. De Roulhac Hamilton, "The Prison Experiences of Randolph Shotwell," *North Carolina Historical Review* 2 (April 1925): 147–61; Jeffry D. Wert, "Shotwell, Randolph Abbott," NCPEDIA, January 1,1994 (https://www.ncpedia.org/biography /shotwell-randolph); "The Great Event," *Raleigh* (NC) *Daily Press*, May 22, 1894, 1; *Minutes of the Twelfth Annual Convention of the United Daughters of the Confederacy, North Carolina Division* (Newton, NC: Enterprise, 1907), 187.

37. Rebecca Cameron to Alfred M. Waddell, October 26, 1898, Alfred M. Waddell Papers.

38. Rebecca Cameron to Evans & Cogswell, August 17, 1867, Rebecca Cameron to "My dear Mr. Hayne," February 27, 1868, Edward W. Bok to Rebecca Cameron, November 7, 1890, SRC; Rebecca Cameron, "Christmas on an Old Plantation," 5.

39. Walter H. Conser Jr., *A Coat of Many Colors: Religion and Society along the Cape Fear River of North Carolina* (Lexington: University Press of Kentucky, 2006), 128–29.

40. *Boston Patriot & Mercantile Advertiser*, April 11, 1825, 2; "Buchoi Plantation," *Wilmington* (NC) *Advertiser*, November 16, 1838, 3; S. H. Waddell [Susan Henrietta Moore Waddell?] to "My own dear sister" [Emma Clair Moore Cameron?], from Wilmington, March 23, 1868, SRC.

41. "Memorable Moores;" "James Iredell Waddell Family Papers"; "Notice of Sale of Buchoi Plantation," *Wilmington* (NC) *Chronicle*, June 1, 1842, 1; J. Christy Judah, *The Two Faces of Dixie: Politicians, Plantations and Slaves* (Wilmington, NC: Coastal Books, 2009), 63.

42. Rebecca Cameron, "Christmas on an Old Plantation," *Gettysburg Compiler*, December 15, 1891, 1; Rebecca Cameron, "Christmas on the Buchoi Plantation," *Raleigh* (NC) *News and Observer*, December 22, 1895, 2; Rebecca Cameron, "Christmas at Buchoi, A North Carolina Rice Plantation," *The North Carolina Booklet* 13 (July 1913): 3–10; Genevieve Tapscott Gill, "Christmas on a Southern Plantation Before the War," *Little Rock Arkansas Gazette*, December 24, 1916, section 2, 7.

43. Bill York, *John Fox, Jr.: Appalachian Author* (Jefferson, NC: McFarland, 2003), 58–70, 156–57; Warren I. Titus, *John Fox Jr.* (New York: Twayne, 1971), 17–18, 51; Harriet R. Holman, "John Fox Jr.: Appraisal and Self-Appraisal," *Southern Literary Journal* (Spring 1971): 18–38.

44. Harper and Brothers to John Fox Jr., October 12, 17, 1898, John Fox Jr., Duncan Tavern Papers, box 1, folder 1, UKLSC; John Fox Jr. to his mother, undated, Fox Family Papers, box 5, folder 5, UKLSC.

45. John J. Crittenden, for example, was a US senator from Kentucky before the Civil War.

46. John Fox Jr., *Crittenden: A Kentucky Story of Love and War* (New York: Charles Scribner's Sons, 1900).

47. Titus, *John Fox Jr.*, 54 ("sentimental rubbish" and "complete failure"); York, *John Fox Jr.*, 168.

48. Frederick Remington to John Fox Jr., November [no exact date] 1900, typed letterbook copy in Fox Family Papers, box 5, folder 5, UKLSC; Gretchen Murphy, *Shadowing the White Man's Burden: US Imperialism and the Problem of the Color Line* (New York: New York University Press, 2010), 92.

49. Fox, *Crittenden*, 243–56.

50. John Fox Jr. "Personal Sketch," in Holman, "John Fox Jr.," 25–38, esp. 25; John Fox Jr., "Br'er Coon in Old Kentucky," *Century Magazine* 55 (February 1898): 594–601, esp. 595; John W. Fox Sr. to James W. Fox, November 19, 1899, Fox Family Papers, box 5, folder 5, UKLSC; "The Sam Davis Monument," *Confederate Veteran* 5 (December 1897): 626.

51. Edmund Wilson, *Patriotic Gore: Studies in the Literature of the American Civil War* (1962; repr., New York: Oxford University Press, 1966), 605–6; Edward L. Ayers, *The Promise of the New South: Life after Reconstruction* (1992; repr., New York: Oxford University Press, 1993), 32.

52. James W. Fox to John W. Fox Jr., November 19, 1900, Fox Family Papers, box 5, folder 5, UKLSC; Mary Brabson Littleton, *Confederate Veteran* 14 (April 1906): 162–63.

53. Glenn O. Carey review of *John Fox and Tom Page As They Were: Letters, an Address, and an Essay*, ed. Harriet R. Holman (Miami, FL: Field Research Projects [1970?], *South Atlantic Bulletin* 37 (November 1972): 90–93; "The Quiet of Lent," *Illustrated Buffalo Express*, March 21, 1897, 7; "John Fox's New War Novel Well Under Way," *Louisville Courier-Journal*, December 25, 1898, S3, 8; report from Washington Bureau, *Chicago Tribune*, January 8, 1899 in *Chicago Tribune*, January 8, 1899, 7; John Fox Sr. to James W. Fox, May 23, 1999, Fox Family Papers, box 5, folder 5, UKLSC; John Fox Jr. to "Dear Major," July 26, 1899, John Fox Jr. Papers, Albert and Shirley Small Special Collections Library, University of Virginia, Charlottesville.

54. *Lexington* (KY) *Morning Herald*, November 11, 1905, 5; *New York Times*, February 16, 1901; *New-York Daily Tribune*, February 16, 1901, 8; *Boston Evening Transcript*, December 21, 1910, 10; (Honolulu) *Pacific Commercial Advertiser*, April 18, 1901, 13; "Crittenden," *San Francisco Call*, January 24, 1904, 2–3 (fourth installment with Yule log scene); "Royalty Report August First 1901," Fox Family Papers, box 5, folder 5, UKLSC.

55. "Current Literature," *Buffalo Courier*, November 25, 1900, 27; "Books and Bookmakers," *Kansas City Times*, December 3, 1900, 8; "John Fox's Story of the Cuban War," *Brooklyn Daily Eagle*, December 8, 1900, 3.

56. Virginia Simkins, "Christmas Theme of Many Stories, Poetry, Songs," *Lumberton* (NC) *The Robesonian*, December 24, 1953, 2.

57. O. B. H., "Yuletide in Dixie," *Urbana* (IL) *Daily Courier*, December 24, 1924, 1.

58. "200 Gather at Madison Rally," *Greensboro* (NC) *Record*, November 28, 1934, 2; Alberta Miller death certificate, October 2, 1948, North Carolina Death Certificates, 1909–1976, Microfilm Series 123, North Carolina State Archives, Raleigh, Ancestry.com; "Death of a Good Man," *Union* (SC) *Times*, January 8, 1915, 1; Eighth US Census, 1860, Schedule 2, Slave Inhabitants, Chester County, SC, NA (Ancestry. com).

CHAPTER 4

1. Durwood Ball, *Army Regulars on the Western Frontier, 1848–1861* (Norman: University of Oklahoma Press, 2001), 139–49.

2. William Faulkner, *Intruder in the Dust* (1948; repr. New York: Vintage, 1972), 194–95.

3. *Suffolk Nansemond Historical Society* (newsletter) 19 (November 2010): 2, 4; Eighth US Census, 1860, Schedule 2, Slave Inhabitants, Nansemond County, VA, NA (Ancestry.com); Leslie J. Gordon, *General George E. Pickett in Life and Legend* (Chapel Hill: University of North Carolina Press, 1998), 35, 49–53, 75, 77, 106, 121–23, 156–63, 196n; "Lynchburg Female College Commencement," *Lynchburg Daily Virginian*, June 23, 1860, 3; Thomas A. Desjardin, *These Honored Dead: How the Story of Gettysburg Shaped American Memory* (Cambridge: MA: Da Capo Press, 2003), 121–25; LaSalle Corbell Pickett, "Yule Log," in Pickett, *Yule Log* (Washington: The Neale Co, 1910), 47 ("diagonally opposite"); *Charlestown* (WV) *Spirit of Jefferson*, August 30, 1887, 1.

4. LaSalle Corbell Pickett File, file no. 23, US Department of the Interior, National Archives at St. Louis, National Personnel Records Center ("knightly" in George C. Cabell to L. Q. C. Lamar, June 29, 1885); Caroline E. Janney, "'One of the Best Loved, North and South': The Appropriation of National Reconciliation by LaSalle Corbell Pickett," *Virginia Magazine of History and Biography* 116, no. 4 (2008): 370–406, esp. 374–75, 383; "Mrs. Pickett has Painful Accident," *Richmond* (VA) *Times-Dispatch*, May 16, 1904, 9; *Savannah Morning News*, November 20, 1904, 29. Pickett apparently returned to her Pension Office clerkship at some later point, as she earned pay from it again prior to August 1, 1912, and was not dropped from the rolls until 1913. See assistant secretary, Department of the Interior, to Mrs. LaSalle DeC. Pickett, August 25, 1913, Pickett File.

5. Richard F. Selcer, *Civil War America, 1850 to 1875* (New York: Facts on File, 2006), 424.

6. "The Gettysburg Reunion," *Norfolk* (VA) *Landmark*, July 2, 1887, 3; "On the Battlefield," *Atlanta Constitution*, July 5, 1887, 1; "Mrs. Pickett at Gettysburg," *Carlisle* (PA) *Daily Evening Sentinel*, July 23, 1887, 2.

7. "The Reinternment," *Richmond* (VA) *Dispatch*, May 30, 1893, 1; "Protest from Mrs. Pickett," *New York Times*, July 20, 1899, 6; Sarah E. Gardner, *Blood and Irony: Southern White Women's Narratives of the Civil War, 1861–1937* (Chapel

Hill: University of North Carolina Press, 2004), 136–37. Gardner emphasizes that Pickett steered the discussion away from slavery as a key to the war's causation, emphasizing that "blameless" southerners waged war to uphold principles of states' rights established in the US Constitution.

8. "Mrs. Pickett's Speech," *Baxter Springs News*, August 31, 1905, 8; Janney, "Appropriation," 394; "Lecture by Mrs. Pickett," *Nashville Banner*, August 3, 1907, 4; advertisement for "Twin City Chautauqua" in *Champaign* (IL) *Daily News*, August 8, 1907, 2.

9. *Macon* (MO) *Times-Democrat*, August 12, 1909, 5; "Washington Widows," *Helena* (MO) *Independent*, June 22, 1890, pt. 2, 1; *Washington* (DC) *Evening Star*, May 9, 1906, 7; Janney, "Appropriation," 371; LaSalle Corbell Pickett to Mrs. Frank G. Odenheimer, November 12, 1912, *Minutes of the Nineteenth Annual Gathering of the United Daughters of the Confederacy, Held in Washington, DC, November 13–16, 1912* (Nashville, TN: United Daughters of the Confederacy, 1913), 419.

10. LaSalle Corbell Pickett, *Pickett and His Men* (Atlanta: Foote & Davis, 1899); LaSalle Corbell Pickett, *The Heart of a Soldier: As Revealed in the Intimate Letters of Genl. George E. Pickett, C. S. A.* (New York: S. Moyle, 1913); LaSalle Corbell Pickett, *What Happened to Me* (New York: Brentano's, 1917); Janney, "Appropriation," 396.

11. Gary W. Gallagher, "A Widow and Her Soldier: LaSalle Corbell Pickett as Author of the George E. Pickett Letters," *Virginia Magazine of History and Biography* 94 (July 1986): 329–44. A second, slightly changed edition of the Pickett letters appeared under a different title in 1928. Arthur Crew Inman, ed., *Soldier of the South: General Pickett's War Letters to His Wife* (Boston: Houghton Mifflin, 1928).

12. "Lincoln, Prohibition's Morning Star," *Chicago National Prohibitionist*, April 16, 1908, 10; Janney, "Appropriation," 381–82; Gerald Prokopowicz, *Did Lincoln Own Slaves? And Other Frequently Asked Questions about Abraham Lincoln* (2008; repr., New York: Vintage, 2009), 132.

13. Robert Penn Warren, *The Legacy of the Civil War: Meditations on the Centennial* (New York: Random House, 1961), 5.

14. "Southern Literature," *Lexington* (KY) *Sunday Leader*, May 26, 1901, section 2, 8.

15. Paula T. Connolly, *Slavery in American Children's Literature, 1790–2010* (Iowa City: University of Iowa Press, 2013), 59–60, 85–87; Catherine Clinton, *Tara Revisited: Women, War, and the Plantation Legend* (New York: Abbeville Press, 1995), 202; Albert Tricomi, "Dialect and Identity in Harriet Jacobs's Autobiography and Other Slave Narratives," *Callaloo* 29 (Spring 2006): 619–33, esp. 619; Ben Rialton, *Contesting the Past, Reconstructing the Nation: American Literature and Culture in the Gilded Age, 1876–1893* (Tuscaloosa: University of Alabama Press, 2007), 26–27. Such authorial contortions were hardly exclusive to southerners. George Armstrong Custer's Michigander wife "Libby" (Elizabeth), in her published memoir about post–Civil War army life (*Tenting on the Plains; or, General Custer in Kansas and Texas*) reduced the speech of a once-enslaved African American cook with her and her husband to dialect while admitting the woman had never talked like a field hand and had lived in the North so long that her accent had all but disappeared.

Cecily N. Zander, "One Widow's Wars: The Civil War, Reconstruction, and the West in Elizabeth Custer's Memoirs," in *Civil War Witnesses and Their Books: New Perspectives on Iconic Works*, eds. Gary W. Gallagher and Stephen Cushman (Baton Rouge: Louisiana State University Press, 2021), 229–60.

16. Pickett, *Yule Log*, 9–19 (quote on 11). The volume *Yule Log* was second in a four-volume set published by Neale in 1900–1901 titled "In de Miz Series."

17. "Southern Literature," *Lexington* (KY) *Sunday Leader*, May 26, 1901, section 2, 8; *El Paso Herald*, June 27, 1901, 7; "Summer Reading," *Butte* (MT) *Miner*, May 13, 1901, 4 (Harris quote).

18. La Salle Corbell Pickett, "An Old-Time Virginia Christmas," *Harper's Bazar* 41 (January 1907): 48–54. The spelling of the magazine's title changed to today's *Harper's Bazaar* with the November 1929 issue. Pickett's given name here is as printed.

19. "The Origin of the Yule Log: As Told by La Salle Corbell Pickett (Courtesy of Pictorial Review, December 1913)," in *Bowling Green* (OH) *Sentinel Review*, November 22, 1913. I have identified a reprinting of this story in the November 30, 1913, issue of the *Washington* (DC) *Herald* and in fifteen additional US newspapers in December 1914. There were undoubtedly others.

20. Pickett, *What Happened to Me*, 64–78, esp. 64–69, 76.

21. S. A. Kenner, "A Tale of Reconstruction Days," *Western Monthly* 11 (December 1909): 45–50, esp. 46; "Scipio Africanus Kenner" (https://greatbasinmuseum.com /index.php/articles/13-great-basin-historical-society-comments-by-j-owen-neilsen); J. Walter McSpadden, *Indiana: A Romantic Story for Young People* (New York: J. H. Sears, 1926), 12–13. For insight into McSpadden's white southern perspectives, see his *Storm Center: A Novel about Andy Johnson* (1947) and his preface as editor of the index volume of the multivolume set *The South in the Building of the Nation* (vol. 13).

22. Mrs. Hugh Miller, "Reminiscences of Argyle, the Home of William R. and Margaret Campbell" (paper to Washington County Historical Association, March 3, 1913), in *Memoirs of Henry Tillinghast, Papers of the Washington County Historical Society, 1910–1915* (Jackson: Mississippi Department of Archives and History, 1954), 166–70; "Mrs. Hugh Miller [Louise Campbell Miller], of Pioneer Local Family Dies," *Greenville* (MS) *Delta Democrat-Times*, July 12, 1965, 2; Genevieve Tapscott Gill, "Christmas on a Southern Plantation before the War," (Little Rock) *Arkansas Gazette*, December 24, 1916, section 2, 7; Walter E. Campbell, "The Yule Log," *Greensboro Daily News*, December 25, 1938, section B, 5; Mary Alice Blackmore, "Christmas in the Old South," *Kenansville* (NC) *Duplin Times*, December 23, 1949, 1 and 10. Louise Miller's physician husband, Hugh Robert Miller, died in 1945.

23. Nell Battle Lewis, "The Yule Log in the Old South," *Raleigh News and Observer*, December 25, 1955, section 4, 2. Campbell's article was reprinted in the same newspaper's December 20, 1942 issue, section 2, 5.

24. Quimby Melton, "Good Evening," *Griffin Daily News*, December 22, 1971, 1. According to an article in another Georgia paper, consisting of a reprinting of Melton's column preceded by a brief introduction, Melton first published his version of the Yule log legend in the *Daily News* in December 1958. See Vincent Jones, "The

Last Straw," *Jackson* (GA) *Progress-Argus*, December 11, 1958, 2. The story also appeared in the *Atlanta Journal and Constitution* (Leo Aikman, "Christmas Lasted 'til Backlog Burned in Plantation Times," December 24, 1967, 19). LeGrand checks out as a servant on the college campus. See George Burk Johnston, *Thomas Chalmers McCorvey: Teacher, Poet, Historian* (Blacksburg, VA: White Rhinoceros Press, 1985), 60.

25. John Walker Davis, "An Air of Defiance: Georgia's State Flag Change of 1956," *Georgia Historical Quarterly* 82 (Summer 1998): 305–30, esp. 318, 318n41; Ada Ramp Walden, "Noted Speakers to Feature UDC Memorial Observance," *Atlanta Constitution*, April 19, 1931, section M, 8; "Spirit of Reconstruction Days Needed in Georgia, says Melton," October 28, 1931, 6 ("deluded negroes," "staggering," "greatest organization," "War Between the States"); "Melton Hails Confederate Womanhood," *Newnan* (GA) *Herald*, April 30, 1937, 1 ("equalled"); *Atlanta Constitution*, April 21, 1940, section C, 9; Mary Denmark, "State UDC Convention In Albany," *Atlanta Constitution*, October 18, 1955, 23.

26. Janice Holt Giles, *The Kinta Years: An Oklahoma Childhood* (Boston: Houghton Mifflin, 1973), 17–18. Tate's article seems to have been published earlier in a pre-Christmas 1911 issue of the (Covington, LA) *St. Tammany Farmer*, but I have been unable to identify the exact issue.

27. J. H. K. Shannahan Jr., "Romantic Old Wye House," March 10, 1907, 13; "John H. K. Shannahan," *Confederate Veteran* 24 (September 1916): 414; "Organized in Maryland," *Confederate Veteran* 25 (March 1917): 130. In 1913 the senior Shannahan helped raise funds for a monument to Confederate soldiers from Talbot County, Maryland. Susan Cooke Soderberg, *"Lest We Forget": A Guide to Civil War Monuments in Maryland* (Shippensburg, PA: White Mane Publishing), 115.

28. J. M. Tate, "Covington Years Ago" (Greensburg, LA) *St. Helena Echo*, January 5, 1912, 1; "John McNeill Tate," *St. Helena* (LA) *Echo*, February 21, 1936, 3; "John Milton Tate I (1903–1985)," WikiTree, profile last modified May 26, 2024 (https://www.wikitree.com/wiki/Tate-3149); *Confederate Veteran* 38 (October 1930): 370.

29. Miller, "Reminiscences of Argyle,"167; "Mrs. Hugh Miller of Pioneer Local Family Dies"; US, Confederate Soldiers Compiled Service Records, 1861–1865 (https://www.ancestry.com/discoveryui-content/view/12790:5256?tid=&pid=&queryId=c868a642-38e1-43da-87d9-0f9b2e8f9e05&_phsrc=WsY454&_phstart=successSource); Andrew Johnson pardon of William R. Campbell, October 5, 1865 (https://www.ancestry.com/discoveryui-content/view/12790:5256?tid=&pid=&queryId=c868a642-38e1-43da-87d9-0f9b2e8f9e05&_phsrc=WsY454&_phstart=successSource); "Mount Olive Chapter, UDC Holds Meeting," *Jackson Daily Clarion*, October 14, 1930, 6; "Mississippi Division UDC President is Feted in Mount Olive," *Jackson* (MS) *Daily Clarion*, April 28, 1940, Society Section, 9; "Mount Olive UDC Chapter to Honor Outstanding Senior," *Jackson* (MS) *Clarion-Ledger*, February 28, 1947, 9; *Minutes of the Fifty-Ninth Annual Convention of the United Daughters of the Confederacy, Held at Biloxi, Mississippi, November 9–13, 1952* (Raleigh, NC: Edwards & Broughton, 1953), 344.

30. *Warsaw* (NC) *Duplin Times*, November 4, 1949, 9; "After 50 Years as Magistrate, He's Retiring," *Raleigh News and Observer*, November 5, 1950, section 4, 3; "Mary Alice Blackmore," *Raleigh News and* Observer, May 22, 1998, section B, 6.

31. Giles, *Kinta Years*, 228–40 (quotes on 229, 240); Company Muster Roll, 19 (Dawson's) Arkansas, copy provided by Arkansas State Archives, Little Rock. Janice Holt was the daughter of schoolteachers and married Henry Giles in 1945. According to the muster roll, James Knox Polk Holt's service with the nineteenth expired on June 11, 1862, but indications suggest the nineteenth became depleted in manpower and was folded into a different Arkansas regiment, probably the sixth, with Holt continuing to soldier.

32. Miller, "Reminiscences of Argyle," 168.

33. "UDC Officers Installed," *Richmond* (VA) *News Leader*, September 12, 1950, 32; "'Christmas Customs Peculiar to the Southern States, Particularly those of the Past' Presented at UDC Meeting," *Front Royal* (VA) *Warren Sentinel*, December 14, 1950, 8.

34. Nancy St. Clair, "Century-Old Christmases are Reviewed," *Richmond* (VA) *News Leader*, December 18, 1957, 30; "Lee Chapter UDC Forms Auxiliary," *Richmond Times-Dispatch*, October 24, 1951, 20; "Lee Chapter, UDC, Announces Year's Programs," *Richmond* (VA) *Times-Dispatch*, September 29, 1952, 23; *Minutes of the Sixty-First Annual Convention of the United Daughters of the Confederacy, Virginia Division, Incorporated, Held at Danville, Virginia, October 2–4, 1956* (Bassett, VA: Basset Publishing, 1956), 121–22; "UDC District Conference Held Here," (Williamsburg) *Virginia Gazette*, May 12, 1950, 6; "Confederate Daughters Assemble (Williamsburg) *Virginia Gazette*, May 8, 1959, 8; "Subject for UDC Chapter Meeting," *Kilmarnock* (VA) *Rappahannock Record*, December 21, 1972, 3; "Bessie Clentonia *Booth* Croswell" (https://www.findagrave.com/memorial/86953900/bessie-clentonia-croswell).

35. Charles O. Bell, "Gardening," *Greensboro* (NC) *Daily News*, December 18, 1971, 16; "Confederate Books Given for Students," October 29, 1952, 34.

CHAPTER 5

1. Aisha R. Knight, "'To have the benefit of some special machinery': African American Book Publishing and Bookselling, 1900–1920," in *The Oxford History of Popular Print Culture*, vol. 6: *US Popular Print Culture 1860–1920*, ed. Christine Bold (New York: Oxford University Press, 2012), 437–56; Patrick S. Washburn, *The African American Newspaper: Voice of Freedom* (Evanston: Northwestern University Press, 2006), 23, 48–49.

2. Bettye Collier-Thomas, comp. and ed., *A Treasury of African American Christmas Stories*, 2 vols. (New York: Henry Holt & Co., 1997, 1999). Some Black newspapers established during the period had short print runs.

3. Winona Butler, "Old Time Customs," *Afro-American Sentinel*, December 18, 1897. The piece did *not* originate in the *Sentinel* and appeared in many other midwestern and plains state newspapers.

4. E. Davis, "Customs and Legends of the Yule Tide" (Howard University) *University Journal* 4 (December 21, 1900): 1.

5. *Southern Workman and Hampton School Record* 26 (February 1897): 28; John David Smith, "Southern Workman," in *Encyclopedia of African American History 1896 to the Present*, ed. Paul Finkelman, vol. 4 (New York: Oxford University Press), 365–66.

6. "Yule Log," *Monroe* (LA) *News-Star*, December 18, 2004, section D, 1.

7. See #TeamEBONY, "Rethinking Booker T. Washington," *Ebony*, January 18, 2012 (https://www.ebony.com/rethinking-booker-t-washington/); Rebecca Carroll, ed., *Uncle Tom or New Negro? African Americans Reflect on Booker T. Washington and Up from Slavery 100 Years Later* (New York: Broadway Books, 2006); John Flynn, "Booker T. Washington: Uncle Tom or Wooden Horse," *Journal of Negro History* 54 (July 1969): 262–74.

8. Louis R. Harlan, *Booker T. Washington: The Making of a Black Leader, 1850–1901* (New York: Oxford University Press, 1972), 3–156.

9. Harlan, *Washington: The Making of a Black Leader*, 157–324 ("sorcery" on 157, "catapulted" on 204; "death to the Afro-American" on 225–26); Susan D. Carle, *Defining the Struggle: National Organizing for Racial Justice* (New York: Oxford University Press, 2013), 96–114.

10. Booker T. Washington, Atlanta Exposition Address, September 18, 1895 (https://www.nps.gov/bowa/learn/historyculture/atlanta1-1.htm).

11. Booker T. Washington, *Up from Slavery: An Autobiography* (New York: Doubleday, Page & Company, 1901), 133.

12. "The Modern Library/100 Best Nonfiction," The Greatest Books, (https://thegreatestbooks.org/lists/15); Chicago Public Library, Charlemae Hill Rollins Papers (https://www.chipublib.org/fa-charlemae-hill-rollins-papers/); Charlemae Hill Rollins, comp., *Christmas Gif': An Anthology of Christmas Poems, Songs, and Stories Written By and About African Americans* (orig. pub. 1963; New York: Morrow Junior Books, 1993); Jay Parini, ed., *The Norton Book of American Autobiography*, with preface by Gore Vidal (New York: W. W. Norton, 1999); John Edgar Wideman, ed., *My Soul Has Grown Deep: Classics of Early African-American Literature* (New York: Ballantine Books, 2001); Joanne Martell, *American Christmases: Firsthand Accounts of Holiday Happenings from Early Days to Modern Times* (Winston-Salem, NC: John F. Blair, 2005); "Christmas and Africans in America—The Other Story," *Dilemma X*, December 24, 2013 (https://dilemma-x.net/2013/12/24/christmas-and-africans-in-america-the-other-story/). *Up from Slavery*'s serialization appeared in *The Outlook* from November 3, 1900, to February 23, 1901.

13. John David Smith, *An Old Creed for the New South: Proslavery Ideology and Historiography, 1865–1918* (1985; repr. Carbondale: Southern Illinois University Press, 2008), 201, 204–6.

14. Ronald LaMarr Sharps, *Black Folklorists in Pursuit of Equality: African American Identity and Cultural Politics, 1893–1943* (Lanham, MD: Lexington Books, 2023), 2, 13, 16, 27–64 ("tributes" on 51).

15. Booker T. Washington, "Negro Public Schools in the Gulf States," *Southern Workman* 29 (February 1900): 73–75; Nathalie Lord, "Booker Washington's School

Days at Hampton," *Southern Workman* 31 (May 1902): 255–59; "The South and the Negro: Extracts from Address by Booker T. Washington, LLD, at Hampton's Anniversary, May Second and Third, 1905," *Southern Workman* 34 (July 1905): 400–404.

16. "Clubs and Clubmen," *Philadelphia Inquirer*, April 29, 1906; *Richmond Times Dispatch*, April 22, 1906, 6; "Society in Richmond," *Washington Post*, April 8, 1906, section 2, 7. Rosa Lee married Richard Armstrong, the nephew of the Hampton Institute's founder and Washington's benefactor, General Samuel C. Armstrong. The couple would never have any children. William Usher Parsons, comp., *Quindecennial Records of the Class of 1895 Sheffield Scientific School of Yale University* (New Haven, CT: Yale University Press, 1912), 8.

17. Booker T. Washington, "Christmas Days in Old Virginia," *Suburban Life* 5 (December 1907): 336–37.

18. *Tuskegee Student*, 19 (December 21, 1907): 1; *Presbyterian Banner*, December 19, 1907, 12; "Christmas Days in Old Virginia," Booker T. Washington National Monument, Virginia, National Park Service (https://www.nps.gov/bowa/learn/ historyculture/full-text-christmas.htm; https://smithmountainlake.com/news/local/ booker-t-washington-national-monument-to-host-christmas-tours/article_70d1a49a -6a8e-11ed-b15c-93f2e65469c4.html); Wilford Kale, comp. and ed., *A Very Virginia Christmas* (Norfolk, VA: Parke Press, 2012), 17–21; *Richmond Times-Dispatch*, November 26, 2009, section J, 15; "Travel Tips," *Hampton-Newport News* (VA) *Daily Press*, December 2, 2001, section K, 7; "Christmas Celebrated at Booker T. Washington National Monument," *Lynchburg* (VA) *News & Advance*, December 19, 2002, Commercial Report Section, 7; "Happenings," *Lynchburg* (VA) *News & Advance*, November 22, 2007, SD, 3; Denise Membreno, "Reenactors Bring History to Life at an Old Virginia Christmas," Laker Weekly, December 10, 2019, last updated December 4, 2020 (https://smithmountainlake.com/news/local/reenactors -bring-history-to-life-at-an-old-virginia-christmas/article_6073c129-5af4-598d-bf0a -512a375b8c6e.html); "Old Virginia Christmas Returns," *Laker Weekly*, November 23, 2021 (https://smithmountainlake.com/news/local/old-virginia-christmas -returns/article_9fbeb17a-4c9f-11ec-b8e8-5b035519dacb.html; https://www.nps.gov/ planyourvisit/event-details.htm?id=620112EC-9FFA-AE1B-8FC82617BEBB52B9).

19. Washington, "Christmas Days," 337; Harlan, "Making of a Black Leader," 20.

20. H. Wallace Thurman, "Christmas: Its Origin and Significance," *The Messenger* 7 (December 1925): 397; Effie Lee Newsome, "The Little Page: Christmas and New Year Greeting for CRISIS Children," *The Crisis* 33 (January 1927): 144–45.

21. Jenny Proctor interview, Federal Writers' Project: Slave Narrative Project, vol. 16, Texas, pt. 3, Lewis-Ryles, 213 (https://www.loc.gov/resource/mesn.163/?sp=214 &st=image); Tom Wilson interview, Rawick, *American Slave*, series 1, vol. 7, pt. 2, 167; Jennifer Ritterhouse, *Growing Up Jim Crow: How Black and White Southern Children Learned Race* (Chapel Hill: University of North Carolina Press, 2006), 49, 245n22; Bertram Wilbur Doyle, *The Etiquette of Race Relations in the South: A Study in Social Control* (Chicago: University of Chicago Press, 1937), 21, 195n23.

22. Ellen Tarry, *The Third Door: The Autobiography of an American Negro Woman* (New York: David McKay, 1955), 64 ("good friend"), 77, 78 ("walking many weary miles"), 79 ("reread"), 80 ("Mr. Hoover"), 292.

23. Tarry, *Third Door*, 163–64.

24. Katie Brown Bennett, *Soaking the Yule Log: Biographical Sketches of the Brown, Cheshier, Sain, and Allied Families, 1749–1995* (Decorah, IA: Anundsen Publishing, 1995), 79, 93, 107–8 (quote on 108).

25. *Soaking the Yule Log* apparently sold out its print run quickly and was neither reprinted nor rereleased by a mainstream publisher. When I checked WorldCat on September 14, 2023, only sixty-five libraries had copies. And that same day, there was only a single rating for it on "Goodreads."

26. "Before the Dream; Pauline Myers, Foot Soldier in a Long-Ago March for Civil Rights," *Washington Post*, August 26, 1993; John H. Bracey Jr. and August Meier, *A Guide to the Microfilm Edition of The Papers of A. Philip Randolph* (Bethesda, MD: University Publications of America, 1990), ix.

27. Beulah D. Carter to Esther Allen, December 6, 1960, Carter to Maggie Bailey Pugh, [n.d., but clearly December 1964 as it refers to a Sunday, December 6, program], both in NACWC correspondence on DC, 1958–1961, folder 001556-003-0578, Records of the National Association of Colored Women's Clubs, 1895–1992, pt. 2, President's Office Files, 1958–1968, ProQuest History Vault; "Natl. Clubwomen's Yule Log Ceremony," *Philadelphia Tribune*, December 29, 1964, 9; "Yuletide Tea," *Pittsburgh Courier*, December 16, 1967, 11.

28. "Before the Dream."

29. "Legend of the Yule Log," *Baltimore Afro-American*, December 17, 1949, 14.

30. Mary McLeod Bethune, "Christmas in Florida," *Pittsburgh Courier*, January 15, 1938, 14.

31. Sarah Sabalos, "Old South Traditions More Social," *Columbia* (SC) *State*, December 24, 2005, section B, 6; "Meet Anita Singleton Prather" (https://www.gullahkinfolktravelingtheater.org/aunt-pearlie-sue); Judy A. Strausbaugh, "Another Side of Christmas from Bethel," *Lancaster* (PA) *Sunday News*, November 27, 2005, section G, 5; Bethel African Methodist Episcopal Church, Lancaster Pennsylvania, homepage (https://bethelamelancaster.com/our-local-church-history).

32. Atlanta History Center, "Historic Holiday Traditions," November 21, 2019 (https://www.atlantahistorycenter.com/blog/historic-holiday-traditions/); Atlanta History Center, "Historic Holidays" (https://www.atlantahistorycenter.com/tag/historic-holidays/).

CONCLUSION

1. Everard Green Baker Diary, December 25, 28, 1852, Everard Green Baker Papers, SHC, Stampp, *Records*, series J, pt. 6, reel 16; "Everard Green Baker Papers" finding aid, SHC (https://finding-aids.lib.unc.edu/00041/). The plantation was most likely in Panola County.

2. Jane Evans Elliot Diary, December 25, 1858, SHC; "George D. Elliot," in *History of North Carolina*, vol. 5 (Chicago: Lewis Publishing, 1919), 271.

3. William Ethelbert Ervin Journal (Lowndes County, MS), December 26, 1842, SHC.

4. Unidentified judge's letter, undated, to James Kirke Paulding, in *Slavery in the United States* (New York: Harper & Brothers, 1836), 194; Joe Shapiro, "White Slaves in the Late-Eighteenth and Nineteenth-Century American Literary Imagination," in *The Oxford Companion to Slavery in American Literature*, ed. Ezra Tawil (New York: Cambridge University Press, 2016), 55–69, esp. 61.

5. J. G. Randall and David Donald, *The Civil War and Reconstruction* (second edition, revised; Lexington, MA: D. C. Heath, 1969), 68.

6. "The Yule Log," *Zebulon* (NC) *Record*, December 24, 1937, 7; "Yule Log," *Monroe* (LA) *News-Star*, December 18, 2004, section D, 1.

7. Eugene D. Genovese, *Roll, Jordan, Roll: The World the Slaves Made* (1972; repr. New York: Vintage, 1974), 573; Katie Brown Bennett, *Soaking the Yule Log: Biographical Sketches of the Brown, Cheshier, Sain and Allied Families, 1749–1995* (Decorah, IA: Anundsen Publishing, 1995), 79.

8. Magin McKenna, "Christmas Unwrapped," December 18, 2004, SD, 1; Naomi Lede, "The Great Traditions of Christmas," *Huntsville* (TX) *Item*, December 23, 2005 (https://www.itemonline.com/naomi-lede-the-great-traditions-of-christmas/article_127bd7e3-857f-588b-9b53-e00a2e3339d0.html); Christopher Crittenden, "For Holidays," *Greensboro Record*, December 17, 1964, SD, 8.

9. Rogene A. Scott to Hannah Scott Warren (from Cheneyville, Rapides Parish, LA), December 26, 1859, Scott Family Papers, SHC.

10. Basil Hall, *Travels in North America, in the Years 1827 and 1828*, 3 vols. (Edinburgh: Cadell, 1829), 3: 214–47, esp. 218, 224; Lewis W. Payne, *Six Years in a Georgia Prison: Narrative of Lewis W. Paine . . .* (New York: privately published, 1851), "disposition of their masters" on 185.

11. Margaret Ann ("Meta") Morris Grimball Diary, December 15, 1860, SHC.

12. William Ethelbert Ervin Journal, December 24–29, 1841, December 25–31, 1843; Erin Austin Dwyer, *Mastering Emotions: Feelings, Power, and Slavery in the United States* (Philadelphia: University of Pennsylvania Press, 2021), 87.

13. Samuel Porcher Gaillard Plantation Journal, December 28, 1849, South Caroliniana Library, University of South Carolina, Columbia, Stampp, *Records*, series A, pt. 2, reel 1.

14. William D. Valentine Diary, December 27, 1838, SHC; Thomas B. Chaplin Journal, December 27, 1848, December 27, 1850, *Tombee, Portrait of a Cotton Planter*, ed. Theodore Rosengarten (New York: William Morrow, 1986), 448, 515.

15. John B. Nevitt "Record Book," December 24, 27, 28, 1830, SHC, Stampp, *Records*, series J, pt. 6.

16. Journal of Joshua N. Saunders, December 24–28, 1847, in *Florida Plantation Records from the Papers of George Noble Jones*, eds. Ulrich Bonnell Phillips and James David Glunt (St. Louis: Missouri Historical Society, 1927), 326–27 (quote on 326).

17. J. W. Fowler, "Rules for Plantation Management . . . ," in *Plantation and Frontier Documents: 1649–1863, Illustrative of Industrial History in the Colonial & Ante-Bellum South*, ed. Ulrich B. Phillips (Cleveland: Arthur H. Clark, 1909), 112–22, esp. 117; Ben Sparkman Plantation Journal, "Memorandum of Planting for

1854" and Stephen A. Norfleet variously titled plantation journals 1856–1860, Norfleet Family Papers, all at SHC.

18. Henry to William S. Pettigrew, December 19, 1857, Pettigrew Family Papers, SHC. Black drivers were specially selected men in a slave workforce entrusted with supervisory responsibilities over their enslaved peers in the field and who usually received special privileges in return when their performances were satisfactory to their masters.

19. Francis DuBose Richardson, Bayside Plantation Journal, vol. I, Bayside Plantation Records, 1846–1866, SHC (https://finding-aids.lib.unc.edu/00053/#folder_1#1).

20. Charles Manigault Plantation Journal (December 1844), James Haynes to Charles Manigault, January 6, 1847, both quoted in *Life and Labor on Argyle Island: Letters and Documents of a Savannah River Rice Plantation, 1833–1867*, ed. James M. Clifton (Savannah, GA: Beehive Press, 1978), 21, 46.

21. John W. Leak, "Notes on farming, Chesterfield District," December 28, 1843, Leak and Wall Family Papers, SHC.

22. Daniel Immerwahr, "Burning Down the House: Slavery and Arson in America," *Journal of American History* 110 (December 2023): 449–73, esp. 451–55 and 452n9.

23. William Craft, *Running a Thousand Miles for Freedom; Or, the Escape of William and Ellen Craft from Slavery* (London: William Tweedie, 1860), 31; Frederick Douglass, *Narrative of the Life of Frederick Douglass, An American Slave. Written by Himself* (Boston: Anti-Slavery Office, 1845), 68–77 (quotes on 74 and 75); Francis Fedric, *Slave Life in Virginia and Kentucky: A Narrative*, ed. C. L. Innes (Baton Rouge: Louisiana State University Press, 2010), ix, 29.

24. *Twelve Years A Slave: Narrative of Solomon Northup, A Citizen of New-York, Kidnapped in Washington City in 1842 . . .* (Auburn, NY: Derby and Miller, 1841), 213–21 ("measure of their generosity" on 213).

25. Benjamin Drew, *A North–Side View of Slavery: The Refugee, or, Narratives of Fugitive Slaves in Canada . . .* (Boston: John R. Jewett, 1855), esp. 38, 140–41, 187, 284, 301 (quote), 382, and introduction to 1969 edition of the same book by Tilden G. Edelstein, in Benjamin Drew, *The Refugee . . .*, ed. Tilden G. Edelstein (Reading, MA: Addison-Wesley, 1969), ix–xxii.

26. Louis Hughes, *Thirty Years a Slave, From Bondage to Freedom . . .* (1896; repr., Milwaukee: South Side Printing, 1897), 15; *Slave and Freeman: The Autobiography of George L. Knox*, ed. Willard B. Gatewood Jr. (Lexington: University Press of Kentucky, 1979), 44. Historian David Thomas Bailey documented the thematic consistencies between pre– and post–Civil War slave autobiographies in "A Divided Prism: Two Sources of Black Testimony on Slavery," *Journal of Southern History* 46 (August 1980), 381–404, esp. 402.

27. William Wells Brown, *My Southern Home; or, The South and Its People* (1880; repr. New York: Negro Universities Press, 1969), 91–97.

28. Pauline Grice narrative in *Slave Narratives: A Folk History of Slavery in the United States from Interviews with Former Slaves. Typewritten Records Prepared by the Federal Writers' Project, 1936–1938 . . .*, vol. 16: *Texas Narratives*, pt. 2, 98–102 (quote on 100); Horace Muse narrative in *Weevils in the Wheat: Interviews with Virginia Ex-Slaves*, compil. and eds. Charles L. Perdue Jr., Thomas E. Barden,

and Robert K. Phillips (1976; repr. Bloomington: Indiana University Press, 1980), 215–17, 356.

29. Robert E. May, *Yuletide in Dixie: Slavery, Christmas, and Southern Memory* (Charlottesville: University of Virginia Press, 2019), 119–55.

30. "Convention of the Friends of Emancipation in Kentucky," April 25, 1849, transcription in *Frankfort Kentucky Commonwealth*, reprinted in (Washington, DC) *National Era*, May 10, 1849, 2–3; Harold D. Tallant, *Evil Necessity: Slavery and Political Culture in Antebellum Kentucky* (Lexington: University Press of Kentucky, 2003), 133–63.

31. Thomas G. Clemson to John C. Calhoun, December 27, 1840, in *The Papers of John C. Calhoun*, ed. Clyde N. Wilson (Columbia: University of South Carolina Press, 1981), vol. 15: 404–5.

32. John Thomas Diary, December 27, 1829, December 25, 1836, South Caroliniana Library, University of South Carolina, Stampp, *Records*, series A, pt. 2, reel 5.

33. James Henry Hammond Diary, December 25, 1831, South Caroliniana Library, University of South Carolina, Stampp, *Records*, series A, pt. 1, reel 1.

34. Ella Howard, "Slavery in the Big Easy: Digital Interventions in the Tourist Landscape of New Orleans," in *Public Memory, Race, and Heritage Tourism of Early America*, eds. Cathy Rex and Shevaun E. Watson (New York: Routledge, 2022), 86–103, esp. 87.

35. Bennett, *Soaking the Yule Log*, 93.

36. William Valentine Diary, December 31, 1851.

37. "Stories of the Negro," *El Paso Herald*, July 27, 1901, 7.

38. Anna Matilda King to "My own . . . child," December 25, 1856, William Audley Couper Papers, SHC; *An Autobiography of the Rev. Josiah Henson (Mrs. Harriet Beecher Stowe's "Uncle Tom"). From 1789–1877*, ed. John Lobb (London: Christian Age, 1878), 13–25, esp. 15, 24–25.

39. "Pictures of Southern Life," *Emporia* (KS) *News*, March 10, 1860, 2; Innes Randolph, "The Back-Log; or, Uncle Ned's Little Game," *Baltimore Gazette*, December 26, 1877, as reprinted in the *Easton* (MD) *Star*, January 8, 1878, 1.

40. Thomas Jefferson, *Notes on the State of Virginia* (1785), in *The Portable Thomas Jefferson*, ed. Merrill D. Peterson (New York: Penguin Books, 1975), 214.

41. Gilbert Osofsky, "A Note on the Usefulness of Folklore," in *Puttin' On Ole Massa: The Slave Narratives of Henry Bibb, William Wells Brown, and Solomon Northup*, ed. Osofsky (New York: Harper & Row, 1969), 45–48.

42. Lawrence W. Levine, *Black Culture and Black Consciousness: Afro-American Folk Thought from Slavery to Freedom* (New York: Oxford University Press, 1977), 80–135; Sterling Stuckey, "Through the Prism of Folklore: The Black Ethos in Slavery," *Massachusetts Review* 9 (Summer 1968): 417–37 (quote on 431n42).

43. John W. Roberts, *From Trickster to Badman: The Black Folk Hero in Slavery and Freedom* (1989; repr. Philadelphia: University of Pennsylvania Press, 1990), 17.

CODA

1. Philip Henry Pitts Diary, vol. 1, December 23, 1850, SHC; Moses Ashley Curtis to Mary Curtis, December 27, 1847, SHC. Curtis was a Massachusetts native but had been holding teaching and ministerial positions in North Carolina and South Carolina since the mid-1830s.

2. Samuel A. Agnew Diary, November 19–December 21, 1856, SHC; Seventh US Census, 1850, Slave and Free Inhabitant Schedules, Madison County, MS, NA (Ancestry.com); Manuscript Census Returns, Eighth US Census, 1860, Free Inhabitants, Madison County, MS, NA (Ancestry.com); Stephen V. Ash, *A Year in the South: 1865* (2002; repr., New York: Perennial, 2002), 14.

3. Agnew Diary, December 24, 26, 1856.

Acknowledgments

Throughout my career, I've always been humbled and thrilled by the willingness of fellow historians to give of their valuable time in reading and critiquing my work, suggesting new sources to consult, detecting errors of fact and flaws in style, guiding me toward the best way of making my case, and simply encouraging me to persist during moments of self-doubt and disappointment. This time around is no exception. I want to thank, especially, the following scholars, who have read either parts or the entirety of this book in manuscript, and/or provided me with invaluable leads and or suggestions: John David Smith, Charles H. Stone Distinguished Professor of American History, University of North Carolina at Charlotte; Gary W. Gallagher, John L. Nau III Professor in the History of the American Civil War, University of Virginia; Raymond Krohn, Department of History, Boise State University; Eleanora A. Reber, professor, Anthropology Department, University of North Carolina, Wilmington; Richard Selcer, author.

This book, however, could not have been written without a far larger and more varied cast of supporters than any of my prior works given how much of it required my tracking down the life stories of mostly very obscure southern white writers from the late nineteenth and early twentieth centuries. This support network included especially the staffs of state historical societies and archives, university and collegiate archives and libraries, and a miscellany of local historical institutions and public libraries. Most especially I owe a debt of gratitude to the following people at these institutions: Judith Gray, reference specialist, American Folklife Center, Library of Congress; Stephanie Haught Wade, executive director, and Star Mitchell, former education director, both at Historic Arkansas Museum, Little Rock; Heather Reinold, archivist, and Lauren Jarvis, archival manager, public services, both at Arkansas State Archives; Carolyn Wilson, Special Collections Research Center and Jessica Ramey, instruction and research librarian, both at William & Mary; Teri D. Barnett, Abraham Lincoln Presidential Library and Museum, Springfield, Illinois; Robert Grady, Union County

Museum, Union, South Carolina; Linda Barrett, Fort Worth History Center manager/city archivist, Fort Worth Public Library; Ann Boutwell, historian, Autauga County, Alabama, Heritage Association; Deborah Loser, president of the Griswold, Connecticut, Historical Society; Pat Schaefer, New London County, Connecticut, Historical Society; Tom Schuch, Niantic, Connecticut; Matthew E. Guillen, reference coordinator, Virginia Museum of History and Culture, Virginia Historical Society, Richmond; Regina Rush, reference librarian, Albert and Shirley Small Special Collections Library, University of Virginia; Teresa Roane, archivist, United Daughters of the Confederacy, Richmond, Virginia; Sallie Long, ex-president, Stewart County, Georgia, Historical Commission; Dianne Ballman, information technology coordinator, Central Rappahannock Heritage Center, Fredericksburg, Virginia; Priscilla Nowell, historian, Washington County, Mississippi; Clinton Begley, historian, Mississippi Department of Archives and History, Jackson; Carl Childs, executive director of research and education, Colonial Williamsburg Foundation; Sarah Coblentz, research services archivist, Special Collections Research Center, University of Kentucky Libraries; Lindsey Milam, director, Autauga-Prattville Public Library, Prattville, Alabama; T. J. Blakeman, president, Board of Trustees, Champaign County, Illinois, History Museum, Champaign. Additionally, this book depended significantly on the interlibrary loan service of the Timberland Regional Library in Olympia, Washington.

Charles (Chuck) Elston, my "buddy" in graduate school at the University of Wisconsin and former director of Special Collections and University Archives, Marquette University, provided incisive advice about this book's themes and organization. Liz (Elizabeth) Berry Schatzlein, one of my very bright undergraduate students at Purdue and the former news anchor at WANE-TV, Fort Wayne, was one of the manuscript's first readers, and her reactions helped guide me as I finished the book. My children Heather (H) and Beth and my sons-in-law Kelly Walker and Dennis Smith all assisted in different ways. My closest friend, my devoted wife (and sometime coauthor), Jill, lent me her steadfast support and critical eye throughout this project. She has always been my most vigorous and sometimes searing stylistic critic, and if this book manages to keep you turning pages, it is largely due to her constantly prodding me to do better and rewrite.

Finally, I could not be more appreciative of the University of Virginia Press, which published my earlier work on the enslaved Christmas experience, *Yuletide in Dixie: Slavery, Christmas, and Southern Memory*. This book expands on a discussion of Yule logs on pages 41 to 44 of the former work and provides further perspectives on issues of historical memory related to slavery in the South raised in *Yuletide in Dixie*.

Index

abolitionists, 30, 39, 141, 148, 154
African Americans: institutions of
   higher education, 108–9, 108–12;
   literacy rates, 107; lynchings of,
   125, 149; periodicals and press,
   39–40, 107–8, 122, 126; population
   figures, 30; in Spanish-American
   War, 70–71; in Wilmington (NC)
   public life, 57. *See also* slaves; Yule
   log legends (American), and African
   American culture
Agnew, Samuel A., 153–56
Alabama, 33–34, 153; Yule log customs
   in, 2, 3, 27–29, 99–100. *See also*
   Tarry, Ellen; Washington, Booker T.
ale, and English Yule log traditions,
   36–38
Arkansas, 34, 103, 176n32; and Yule log
   customs, 6, 66, 99
Atlanta History Center, 127, 131
Aurora (IL) *Beacon*, 27–30

"The Back Log; or, Uncle Ned's Little
   Game." *See* Randolph, James Innes
Bacon's Castle (VA), 21
Baker, Everard Green, 129, 135, 180n1
Bennett, Katie Brown, 124–25, 131, 147
Bethel African Methodist Episcopal
   Church (Lancaster, PA), 127

Bethune, Mary McLeod, 126
Blackmore, Mary Alice, 99, 102
bladders (hog), and southern Christmas
   customs, 33–34
Blight, David, 42
Bok, Edward W., 61
Booker T. Washington National
   Monument, 121
Bourne, Henry, 18, 19
Brown, William Wells, 142
Buchoi Plantation, 53–55, 62, 64–65

Cabaniss, Allen, 3
Calhoun, John C., 144–45
Cameron, Anna Alexander (daughter
   of William and Emma Clair Moore
   Cameron), 53–59, 64–66
Cameron, Emma (daughter of William
   and Emma Clair Moore Cameron),
   59, 60
Cameron, Emma Clair Moore, 54–56
Cameron, Sarah Rebecca (daughter of
   William and Emma Clair Moore
   Cameron), 9, 56, 59–66, 122, 148,
   170n34
Cameron, William, 54–56, 169n33
Campbell, Walter E., 99
Cavalier myth, 17, 23

187